WICK OLD BRIDGE

1648 and 2nd September 1651 The

The Civil War in Worcestershire, 1642—1646;

and

The Scotch Invasion

of 1651.

by

J.W. Willis Bund

Alan Sutton
1979

ISBN 0 904387 32 1

First published 1905

Reprinted from a copy kindly
lent by Worcestershire County Library

Printed in Great Britain by
Redwood Burn Limited
Trowbridge & Esher

3538

PREFACE.

In the Autumn of 1904 the Worcestershire County Council organised courses of lectures for teachers in the elementary schools, and did me the honour to ask me to give one of the courses. The subject I selected was the Civil War in the County, and this for two reasons. First, that there should be some connected account of the part the County played in the great struggle; none existed, and ideas as to the fighting were disconnected and vague. Secondly, I hoped that if once an interest could be excited in the subject that some of the legends of the war that still remain might be preserved. After all, 250 years is not so very long. I knew, when a boy, an old lady who told me that her nurse's father, as a young man, was on duty on Worcester Bridge at the battle. Mr. Burton, in his History of Bewdley, tells of an old inhabitant who had been informed by his grandfather that he had heard the sound of the guns at the battle. There are numbers of legends as to where Charles I. slept when in the County, and some few as to where Cromwell stayed; but all are stated to relate to the Battle of Worcester. Possibly most of them have a foundation of truth, and they are at least worth preserving.

I cannot lay claim to any original research, or to having done anything to throw light on some of the dark places of the County history. I have failed to get any clear account of several of the less known incidents of the Civil War, such as Lord Willoughby's fight before

Edgehill with Rupert's cavalry ; Wilmot's attempted relief of Dudley ; Fox's carrying off Sir Thomas Lyttelton ; the fight at Corse Lawn ; the Clubmen ; the plots in 1647 and 1648. These are only some of the points on which further information is wanted.

Except that certain additions (mainly extracts from different authorities) have been made, the lectures are printed substantially as they were given. Various points which deserve to be treated at length are consequently very briefly noticed.

The book is only a concise summary, not a history, of the Civil War in the County. On one point I have ventured to depart from the generally received opinion, and to put forward my own views,—the campaign of 1651. I do not believe that Cromwell ever intended to finish the battle in the way it was finished, but when the chance came to him he took advantage of it.

I have to thank various persons for help. Mr. Duckworth, of the Worcester Victoria Institute, for the old plan of Worcester as it stood fortified; Rev. J. R. Burton, for view of Bewdley Old Bridge; Mr. Wm. North, Tewkesbury, for permission to reproduce Old Bridge at Upton-on-Severn; and Mr. Mason, of the County Education Office, for arranging the lectures.

J. W. B.

Shirehall,
    Worcester,
        31st August, 1905.

CONTENTS.

CONTENTS.

CHAPTER I.

1642.

Worcestershire is one of the smaller English Counties. Its greatest length is but 43 miles, its width 34, and its area 738. Yet in this confined space more fighting went on during the great Civil War than in most other Counties. Within it the first and the last Battles were fought. Worcester was both the first and the last city to realise all that a military occupation meant. In every year of the war there was more or less fighting within it. Dudley and Evesham were besieged, Ripple and Camp Hill, Redmarley, and Hawkesley, all saw fighting, and fighting that was no child's play. Through Worcestershire Charles I. retreated after the siege of Gloucester was raised. Through Worcestershire Charles I. advanced to meet his fate at Naseby. The County was also the scene of Charles' two greatest tactical exploits—his campaign of June, 1644, and his relief of Hereford in 1645. Into Worcestershire Rupert led the Royalist Cavalry for their first fight. Out of Worcestershire Astley manœuvred, and manœuvred in vain with the last handful of Royalist troops which were slaughtered on the Cotswold Hills. At Worcester itself that mercy was vouchsafed, "the dimensions of which," so Cromwell wrote, "were above his thoughts." *

Why was Worcestershire the scene of so much fighting? A glance at the map of England gives the answer. Charles had to rely upon Wales for men and money. Worcestershire was on the direct route between Wales and London, or, rather, between Wales and Oxford, the Royalist head-quarters. Throughout the war Charles was in the utmost need of supplies such as the County was able to furnish. The Court of the Welsh Marches, a local jurisdiction which gave the Crown very large and very arbitrary powers over both individuals and property, included Worcestershire in its area, although the County again and again tried to get free from it.† Worcestershire was a valuable recruiting ground. For many years, as appears from the minutes of the Privy Council as to recruiting and from entries in the Worcestershire Sessions Records‡ as to maimed soldiers, men were habitually drawn from Worcestershire for service in Ireland. If, as seems

---

* Whitelock, 483.   † Sessions Records I., p. ccxxiv.   ‡ Ib., 44, 68, 105.

not unlikely, Sir Charles Wilmot was a Worcestershire man, the County had in him a leader who did not shrink from any service, however desperate or "forlorn," against Irish rebels or Spanish troops. Ireland, from the constant fighting that went on there, was a most valuable training ground for soldiers, both officers and men. It is very difficult to say to what extent the men raised in Worcestershire for service in the Civil War had been trained there, yet there can be but little doubt that not a few in the Royalist ranks, both officers and men, had received their "baptism of fire" in Ireland.

It was necessary for the Royalists to keep open their communications with Wales, it being the place on which they relied for support. Nothing can shew more clearly that they did not rely in vain than a letter, written years after the war by the then Marquis of Worcester to Charles II. "How came," he writes, "His Majesty's army to be considerable before Edgehill fight but by the men I brought;"* and he goes on to state that Sir John Byron's Regiment, the first regiment raised for the King, was only mustered by means of a sum of £5000 paid for the purpose by his father (the Earl of Worcester), who, he says, "spent in the whole for King and country £918,000," which, if money is be taken as at five times its present value, the rate usually stated, amounts to about £4,000,000; an almost incredible sum for a subject of that day to provide, when American and African millionaires did not exist. It was not only money that the Earl of Worcester sent the King; on several occasions he furnished such numerous reinforcements as to amount almost to an army. He wholly provided the force that Waller, whether by tactics or by treachery, defeated before Gloucester in 1643.

Men and money came to the Royalists from Wales in more or less constant supplies. They had to come through Worcestershire, so the County had to be garrisoned for the King. Whoever held Worcestershire had practically the command of the Severn, which was a point of the greatest moment to the Royalists. In addition there were other reasons which added to the importance of the County. It could supply, and was one of the few places that could do so, various military stores of which the King was in dire need. As he had failed to secure the arsenals of Portsmouth and Hull, he did not possess any supply of swords, pikes, guns, shot; all these Worcestershire could and did provide. From Stourbridge came shot, from Dudley cannon. The numberless small forges which then existed on every brook in the north of the County turned out successive supplies of sword blades and pike heads. It is said that among the many causes of anger Charles had

---

* Hist. MSS. Com. xii. rep., app. 9, p. 60.

against Birmingham was that one of the best sword makers of the day, a man named Porter, who lived and made his blades in Worcestershire, but sold them in Birmingham, refused at any price to supply swords for "the man of blood," or any of his adherents.

As a set off to this sword maker, the Royalists had among their adherents Colonel Dud Dudley, who had invented a means of smelting iron by the use of coal, and who claimed he could turn out "all sorts of bar iron fit for making of muskets, carbines, and iron for great bolts,"* both more cheaply, more speedily, and more excellent than could be done in any other way. His method was now employed on the King's behalf. The two following receipts will shew how Worcestershire was engaged in providing for the King in the early days of the war :—

" Ultimo die Decembris, 1642.

" Received the day and year above written, of Sir William Russell, Baronett, " High Sheriff for the County of Worcester, the sum of five pounds, towards ' the casting of shot for His Majesty's service. I say received   £5.

" per me, William Duddeley."

" Die quart' Jan., 1643.

" Received the day and year above written, of Sir William Russell, Baronett, " High Sheriffe for the County of Worcester, the sum of seven pounds, towards " the casting of ordinance for His Majesty's service in the said County. I say " received   7li.

" per me, Bryan Newton."

There are other similar receipts among the Russell Papers, one on the 8th February, 1643, for casting ordinance ; one on the 10th February, 1643, for casting iron ordinance, all of which prove what a valuable source of supply Worcestershire was to the Royalists. Besides cannon, shot, swords, and pikes the County provided other supplies. Droitwich gave an unfailing store of salt ; the Worcestershire Forests a constant store of charcoal, pike handles and palisades. In fact all that the Royalists were most in need of, the County could and did supply.

If Worcestershire was important as a source of supply, it was equally important as a line of communication. It is difficult for us to realise what a centre Worcester then was. No one, for instance, would think that Worcester had any connection with Ireland, yet the following passage in a letter from Lord Ormonde's man of business in London to him in Ireland would show it was. The letter is dated the 5th October, 1641.†

" The clothes are not yet done. I shall have them this night or to-morrow, " being the 5th of this instant October, which if I do I shall have fit opportunity " to send them by waggon to Worcester, which I conceive now to be the readiest " passage for them."

---

* Metallum Martis, p. 10.   † Hist. MSS., Ormonde Papers, NS. I. 45.

Possibly Worcester being a point from which Bristol or a northern port might be reached, made it a spot where the traveller could decide on the route to follow.

Some six roads met at Worcester which, to apply to them a term of to-day, carried " through " as opposed to local traffic.   These roads are :—

(1.)   The Oxford and London Road.   This entered the County near Honeybourne, passed through Bretforton, over the Avon at Offenham at Twyford Bridge, where Offenham Boat is now, then through Norton, Wyre, Pinvin, White Ladies' Aston, Spetchley, Red Hill, to Worcester.   This is and was the direct road from Worcester to Oxford, and by it all convoys of supplies and all detachments of recruits would have to pass.

(2.)   At Worcester this road divided, one branch to the right is the road to the north, spoken of, near Birmingham, as the " Bristol Road."   It crossed Barbourne Bridge and went to Droitwich, Bromsgrove, over the Lickey to Northfield, and passed out of the County into Warwickshire at Bourn Brook.

(3.)   Another branch, also going to the north, after crossing Barbourne Bridge, went to the left through Ombersley and Hartlebury; here it again branches off the road to the right, going through the parishes of Chaddesley Corbett and Belbroughton, past Hagley and Pedmore to Stourbridge into Staffordshire.   This is the road by which Charles II. went after the Battle of Worcester.   The road to the right at Hartlebury passed through Kidderminster, and so on to Bridgnorth.

(4.)   The road crossing the Severn at Worcester, and going by Kenswick, Martley, crossing the Teme at Ham Bridge, through Clifton-on-Teme to Tenbury, and then into Shropshire.   On this road is the Tenbury Bridge over the Teme. When this was damaged in 1615, the town of Tenbury asked the Sessions to help to repair it, as it was " the great thoroughfare from most places in Wales to the City of London."*

(5)   The road from Worcester crossing the Severn, proceeding by Cotheridge, Broadwas, across the Teme at Knightsford Bridge, and so on to Bromyard, thence to Hereford and Wales.   Along this road the troops sent with Lord Stamford to occupy Hereford in 1642 returned,† and Charles I. marched along it to relieve Hereford in 1645.

(6)   The road from Worcester going south along the east bank of the river (the Bath) road, passing through Kempsey, Severn Stoke, to Tewkesbury and Gloucester.   It was along this road Waller advanced to attack Worcester in 1643.

There were other important roads, but they were more of

---

* Sessions Records, March, 1615, p. 212.   † Archæologia, xxxv., 332.

WORCESTERSHIRE 164..

Showing the Main Roads,
Garrisons, and
Sites of the Battles.

Shipston on Stour.
Stratford on Avon
Bidford
Honeybourne
Campden
Broadway
To Oxford
Alcester
Evesham
Birmingham.
Edgbaston
Camp Hill.
Kings Norton.
Fankley.
Hawkesley
Dudley.
Stourbridge
Bromsgrove
INKBERROW
No. 2.
Droitwich
No. 1. London & Oxford
R. Avon
Kidderminster
Hartlebury
Worcester
Pershore
O Strensham
Ripple
TEWKESBURY
To Bridgnorth
No. 3.
Bewdley
R. Severn
No. 6.
Powick
Teme Lane
No. 4.
No. 5.
Madresfield
Upton on Severn
Redmarley
Corse Lawn.
Tenbury
BROMYARD
Ledbury

local importance, or else served as alternative routes. Thus the road on the west bank of the Severn, through Powick and Hanley Castle to Upton, by which Fiennes' cavalry retreated after Powick, and by which Fleetwood advanced at the Battle of Worcester. The road leading out of the Oxford Road at Spetchley, and going by Upton Snodsbury to Inkberrow and Alcester, the road by which Fiennes advanced to attack Worcester in September, 1642. As all these roads converged at Worcester, and as they were practically the only modes of communication with other parts of England and Wales, the importance of Worcester as a centre is obvious.

This must not be considered as in any way a list of either the main or the important roads of the County. There were others, such as the road from Droitwich to Feckenham, through the Old Feckenham Forest, along which the Scots marched on their way to Hereford in 1645; and the old Roman Road, the " Icknild Street," called locally the " Buckle Street," along the upper end of which Rupert marched when he fought at Camp Hill ; but these did not directly converge on Worcester.

Along all these roads during the nine years of the war troops were being constantly marched and convoys sent. Heavy waggons, drawn by teams of oxen, following one after the other could not have been good for the roads, not even if, possibly, they were in a fair state of repair at the beginning of the war, or, at least, in sufficient repair to be passable by the ordinary waggons with comparative ease; they could not have long continued even in this state. The system then in force of compelling the owners and occupiers of land to send their men and teams to do so many days' work on the roads in each year was not an ideal one, and if it was effective in times of peace when there was only ordinary traffic, which is very doubtful, it must have completely broken down with the extraordinary traffic of the war. There are, however, two facts that lead to the conclusion that the roads were to a great extent if not impassable, yet extremely difficult to travel. It appears from the Sessions Records that the bridges on the roads were always breaking down and becoming " difficult of passage." Thus on the most important road—the London Road—there is a bridge still standing at Wyre, one of the few that retain a trace of once having had an image of a saint as part of its structure, possibly because it was a bridge the Bishop of Worcester was liable to repair. However the bishops of those days discharged their other duties, they neglected that of repairing bridges, for the Bishop was not infrequently indicted for neglecting to repair this bridge. A little further on towards Oxford the road crossed the Avon by a bridge, known as " Twyford Bridge."

The liability to repair this bridge rested on the inhabitants of Offenham. They were on several occasions indicted for non-repair of this bridge.

If this important road was in such a state, it is not wonderful to find that in more remote parts of the County landowners and parishes were constantly being "presented" for their neglect in keeping the bridges in good repair. Matters must have got worse and worse during the war, as breaking down bridges was a frequent part of the military operations. For instance, it is said that in Charles' march from Broadway to Bewdley in 1644, the damage done to the County from breaking down bridges amounted to £10,000, which seems to be a prodigious sum, taking money at its present value. The bridge at Bewdley, in 1662, caused the inhabitants to petition Sessions to repair the bridge, an arch of which was broken down in the course of the Civil Wars. The cost of repair was much beyond what the borough was of itself able to bear. The bridge at Upton-on-Severn, although a charitable inhabitant of Upton named Hall left an annual sum which still goes to its repair, never got over the damage it received during the Civil War, in spite of two centuries' patching, until it was removed in 1853 and replaced by the present iron erection.

But the bridges were not the only part of the roads that were out of repair. The presentments sent in annually by the constables of each parish in the County had to state the condition of the roads in the parish. Unfortunately, only a portion of these have survived, but from those that have we are able to form some idea of the state of the roads. The usual thing stated is not that the roads were in good repair. They could not bring themselves to swear that, but "our roads are well repaired for the time of year," or " our roads are in sufficient repair." Notwithstanding these statements the fact remains that no less than 24 of the parishes in the County were in 1636, just before the outbreak of the Civil War, indicted for their roads being out of repair.* Bad as the main roads were, the bye-roads were worse. Probably in Worcestershire they were especially so, for the simple reason that in some parts they had never been made. Two large districts of the County, the area of Malvern Chase, that is, speaking broadly, all the County west of the Severn and south of the Teme, and the area of the Forest of Feckenham, that is, again speaking broadly, the area north of the road from Worcester to Spetchley, Upton Snodsbury and Inkberrow, and south of the line of hills from Redditch, Alvechurch and The Lickey, there were no roads, merely forest tracks. Charles, in the early part of his reign, had been much pressed for money,

---

* Sessions Records, 1633, p. 525.

and had sold his forestal rights in various districts, including Malvern Chase and Feckenham. Some clearing had been done, and tracks had been made across the forest without let or hindrance, but roads in the strict sense there were none. A presentment to the Sessions in 1635 brings this out quite clearly.*

"The roads in the enclosed Forest of Feckenham," it says, "are in great "decay, and very dangerous for the King's Majesty's liege people and cattle to "pass over, and we desire that there may be a course taken in this Court that "the occupier of the said late enclosed land may make good the same as we "think it fit."

The best idea of the state of the roads is given in the following letter from the Vicar of Alvechurch to Sessions :—†

"The Parish of Alvechurch has many roadways and thoroughfares for "travellers, both on horseback and for carriages by wains and carts, and other "common highways to divers market towns through sundry parts of the said "parish, but all so ill and negligently repaired that divers enormities redound "therefrom, not only to many of the parishioners themselves, but also to many "others travelling by those ways. In particular myself, in the harvest time, "riding about my lawful and necessary occasion of tythes, have been twice fast "set in the mire in common roads and market ways not without danger. By "occasion of these ill-repaired highways I am forced to sell much of my tythes "under value. Much of this ill-repair is caused by some who staunch up "water in ditches, turning them out of their course to water and overflow the "adjoining grounds, and in some of the roads, formerly used for passage on "horseback and loaded waggons and cattle, cannot be used for passage on "horseback without danger of getting fast and miring."

How far this description of the Alvechurch roads applied to the whole County it is impossible to say. What can be said is that the Sessions Records shew complaints from all parts of the County, and not merely from one district, and not alone from those parts that were at one time included in the meetes and bounds of the ancient forests.

Along these roads, across these bridges, wagons drawn mainly by oxen had to haul the supplies for the troops. What the state of the roads was after being cut up by one or two wagons or marched along by one or two cavalry regiments can better be imagined than described, especially when it is borne in mind the quantity of baggage the armies of that time took with them. For instance, in May, 1644, when Charles marched from Oxford to Bewdley, the ladies and their belongings who came with his army are said to have required thirty carriages for their transport.

It might be thought from this account of the roads that rapid marches were out of the question, but this was by no means the case. Rupert, in September, 1642, with only cavalry and without baggage it is true, marched 16 miles from Bewdley to Worcester, fought a battle, and marched to Tenbury, 20 miles, within 24 hours from his start. Very rapid marches were made by

---

* Sessions Records, 1635, p. 599.   † Sessions Records, 1633, p. 528

the King's army to get between the Earl of Essex and London as he was retiring there after raising the siege of Gloucester. It is no uncommon thing to hear of troops marching 16 to 20 miles in a night, as was the case of Fiennes and his men marching from Alcester to Worcester one night in September, 1642. If delayed with baggage, and obliged to keep to the roads, progress was slow, as in the case of Byron's march from Oxford to Worcester in September, 1642, when with a heavy convoy he could not do more than 10 miles a day, taking six days to do the 60 odd miles.

Rapid progress was only made when the men were not obliged to keep to the roads. There were no fences, but the roads crossed the large open fields, so that anyone could do that which it is said he was legally entitled to do, quit the road when "foundrous," and go over the adjoining land. This right was largely made use of, and it must have rendered a column on the march particularly liable to be attacked, broken up and scattered. This accounts for what is so often stated in the narratives of the war, how a troop of cavalry swooped down on a column or convoy on the march, and routed, if it did not destroy it. Hedges were only found round the small enclosures and gardens near the villages, the rest of the County was open, or, as it was called, "champaign" country.

To horsemen not encumbered with baggage there was another way by which they could get over the country rapidly. Crossing from place to place, usually by the shortest route, were bridle ways or pack ways, along which men led long strings of horses or mules laden with merchandise. Many of these have been shut up of recent years, but some still remain. Along these pack ways cavalry would move rapidly and without difficulty. But these roads, though well adapted for rapid movement of horses, were wholly unfit for the passage of guns, wagons, or baggage. Outside the villages the land lay open and unfenced. The properties of different owners were separated by grass "baulks" or ridges. It was an easy matter to wander about the open country and get lost. In one instance some troops from Worcester did this, and thereby caused the Royalists to be defeated at Redmarley. The numerous Enclosures Acts passed in the 18th and first part of the 19th century, up to about 1825, shew that enclosed land in Worcestershire was the exception. Large arable fields, where each landowner had a small patch or patches, " so many selions of arable land in a certain common field," large grass meadows or Hams, some of which remain to this day, on which all the village cattle fed, and where certain individuals had a right to mow so many perches. Such was the County where it was not wooded. No country could be better suited for the movements of cavalry, and the fighting during the Civil War was far more that of cavalry than of infantry. In the cavalry encounters, as a rule, the casualties were not very heavy, but where the country was enclosed and cavalry could not be used, as was sometimes the case, as, for instance, at the Battle of Worcester, when the infantry came, as they called it, to "thrust of pike," then the casualties were often very numerous and the battle undecided.

Another point in considering the fighting in Worcestershire must be remembered, the part played by the rivers. The Severn runs north and south, dividing the County into two unequal parts. Roughly, the Avon runs east to west, and forms the southern frontier of the County. These two rivers give a strategic importance to certain places. At the date of the Civil War there were only three bridges across the Severn. This made each of these bridges an important post—Bewdley, Worcester, and Upton. Bewdley was partly a garrison, and its importance was due to its bridge. It seems to have had walls, as the gates are mentioned, one of which remained up till some time last century. Its bridge led to the Scots occupying it in 1645. Worcester was a garrison, which acted as a *tête du pont* to the bridge, and during both the Civil Wars was usually in Royalist hands. Upton, the only bridge between Worcester and Gloucester, was the cause of much fighting, and probably led to more contests for its possession than almost any other place. On the Avon the bridges that were the scenes of the fighting were the Twyford Bridge and the Borough Bridge at Evesham, the bridge at Pershore, which Charles broke down, losing some 80 men in doing it, and the bridge at Tewkesbury, which was the reason, or rather one of the reasons, for the importance of that place, and why it changed owners so often. Curiously enough, there is hardly any mention made of Eckington Bridge, possibly because it was not in a state to permit of its being used for the passage of troops or baggage. With the exception of Powick, not much is heard of the Teme bridges, but Bransford was broken down once, certainly at the Battle of Worcester, and probably oftener, while Knightsford Bridge, the next up the river, was also broken down more than once. There are no records that the other Teme bridges were broken down, but most likely they were from time to time.

Having given some account of the country, the towns must be considered. At the outbreak of the war there were only two walled towns in the County, Worcester and Bewdley. The towns of Evesham, Pershore, Bromsgrove, Droitwich, Kidderminster, Stourbridge, and Upton-on-Severn were open towns, or, to speak more accurately, large villages, which could be rushed at any time by either side, and which were hardly capable of defence. At a later date Bewdley and Evesham were fortified, and Evesham stood a siege. No attempt was made to garrison Pershore, Bromsgrove, Droitwich, or Upton. Kidderminster and Stourbridge were frequently occupied by troops, often by those of the Parliament ; in fact, of all the places in the County Kidderminster and Stourbridge leant most to the Parliament.

With Worcester it was different. Worcester was a regularly fortified, walled town, with a ditch, but the ditch did not go all the way round. The wall had been allowed to fall into decay, and stood in urgent need of repair. The city had seven gates—The Foregate, the north ; St. Martin's, the east ; Friar's, also on the east ; Sidbury, the south gate, with Frog Gate also on that side, below the Castle ; on the west, next the river, the Priory Gate, guarding the Priory Ferry, the only one of the gates that still remains, and the Bridge or Water Gate at the river end of Newport Street. The gates were all standing, and although rotten and in bad repair were closed at night, a fact which made the city imagine itself to be, if not safe from attack, at least safe from surprise. As they played so very important a part in the subsequent fighting, it will be well to give a brief account of the defences of Worcester at that time.

Beginning at the north-west corner of the wall adjoining the river at the bottom of Newport Street, where the Bridge Gate stood, opening out on to the bridge, the wall ran along the river bank for a short distance so as to include St. Clement's Church, which then stood in the north-western angle of the wall. The walls then ran along the south side of the Butts —here traces of it can still be seen (1904). Continuing along the south side of Shaw Street, by the side of the Berkeley Hospital, it included that institution in the city. It crossed over Foregate Street just where the new Hop Market Hotel stands. Here, at the corner of the street between the Berkeley Hospital and the Hop Market Hotel, the gate—the north, or Foregate—stood. The wall then continued along the south side of Sansome Street. This used, until comparatively recent times, to be called the " Town Ditch," but the inhabitants, not liking " Town Ditch " as an address, induced the city authorities to change it to the present unmeaning appellation of Sansome Street. On reaching Lowesmoor it crossed over on the top of the hill by the Old Police Station, along Watercourse Alley, which runs out of Lowesmoor at the bottom of the hill, indicating the site of the Town Ditch, which appears to have started near this point and gone regularly round the wall till the river was reached. The wall ran parallel to Watercourse Alley across Silver Street. Here at the corner by the Corn Market, but where a street leads off to

who had been Sheriff of Staffordshire, as military governor, and he held it until its surrender in 1646.

The other place of strength in the County during the war was Hartlebury Castle, which was garrisoned for the King. When it first was garrisoned does not appear, but in 1644 Captain Sandys was appointed Governor, and he considerably strengthened the place, compelling the people round to come in and work at the defences. In the Bewdley accounts there is an entry :—

"Pd. for wine for Mr. Turton, to get off our men from going to work at "the Castle."

Hartlebury was held for the King till 1646, when it surrendered on terms. It was, however, re-garrisoned during the second Civil War for the Parliament.

Strensham, Sir William Russell's house, was fortified towards the close of the war. Hawkesley, the home of the Middlemores in King's Norton Parish, a family who were strong Catholics and Royalists, was taken from them by the Parliament troops, occupied and fortified as a Parliamentary garrison, and held till the summer of 1645, when it was besieged and taken by Rupert on the Naseby march. Madresfield, the home of the Lygons, was occupied as a Royalist garrison, and held by the Royalists till July, 1646, when it was surrendered to the Parliament, it is said, by agreement.

Connected with Worcestershire, but not actually in it, were other fortified houses, such as Edgbaston Hall, which "Tinker" Fox fortified and made his head-quarters, and which the Royalists attacked but failed to take in 1644. Stourton Castle, near Stourbridge, which was garrisoned by Fox from Edgbaston, but was taken and dismantled by the Royalists in 1644. Campden, in Gloucestershire, on the road from Worcester to Oxford, which became a very important post for the King. Stoke, between Campden and Evesham, which was a subordinate Royalist post. Sudeley Castle, near Winchcombe, which was of importance with regard to Tewkesbury and the lower Avon. Tewkesbury itself, though never really a garrison, became a place of much importance, being taken and re-taken by the Royalists and Parliamentarians something like ten times during the period when Massey was Governor of Gloucester.

It was fortunate for the County that it did not possess more of these fortified houses, or "garrisons" as they were called, than those mentioned. It was thought that the Parliament might have made one at Frankley, the home of the Lytteltons, as in 1645, on the Naseby march, Rupert, after having taking Hawkesley, burned down Frankley to prevent it being made a Parliamentary garrison. The fortified houses became one of the great curses of the County, reproducing, in modern form,

the old castles of the days of Stephen. They were a favourite
method of Rupert's by which he secured his hold on a district.
In each of them a number of armed men were quartered, who
could be sent wherever wanted in the district, and who, in the
intervals during which they were not wanted, gave themselves
up to plundering their neighbours, nominally those on the
opposite side, practically those, on whichever side, who had
anything that could be plundered. So the garrisons became,
whatever they might be called, little better than a series of
dens of robbers.

Some of them had been formed by the owners for their
protection ; some had been formed against the will of the
owners by the party that was predominant in the district,
and which the owners had to maintain, whether they liked it
or not. Some on the main roads were formed as posts to keep
open the lines of communication. In some cases a strong
Parliamentary landowner was compelled to keep a Royalist
garrison, so as to prevent his rendering help to the other side.
In such a case the landowner and his tenants felt the weight
of the Governor's hand. In many of the garrisons the men
lived at practically free quarters, and, having no sympathy with
the owner or the neighbours, cared not what suffering was
inflicted, or outrage committed. Most likely the accounts
that have come down to us of the barbarities of the soldiers in
these garrisons are gross exaggerations, but after making every
allowance there can be no doubt that the dwellers in the
garrisons were no respecters of property or life. It does not
really appear that one side was worse than the other, only they
did their barbarities in different ways. The Royalists justified
what they did as part of the recognised law of war ; the
Parliamentarians justified what they did as part of the Divine
law as revealed by Moses.

Some account is necessary of the soldiers and their arms in
order to understand the different movements of the armies.
The cavalry consisted of cuirassiers, dragoons, and horse. The
cuirassiers were mostly gentlemen who provided their own
arms and equipments. They were dressed most gorgeously.
Feathers in their helmets, gold and silver trimmings,
silver-mounted swords and pistols ; in fact, the typical
Cavalier of the time, as depicted in picture and in poetry.
They formed the men that Rupert led in his most reckless
charges and in his most desperate fights, but their numbers
were few compared with those of the other cavalry They
wore armour—a back and front piece—which had at one time
been made of leather, hence their name, but afterwards, and at
this time, usually made of iron. Under this armour they wore
buff leather coats, thick enough to turn a sword cut or a spent
bullet. They were armed with swords and pistols. If

Royalists, they usually wore over their armour a silk scarf, some of one colour, some of another. If Parliamentarians, they wore orange scarves, the colours of Lord Essex, and Parliament ordered that "anyone setting up any other colour than orange were to be held malignants and ill-affected to the Parliament's cause."[*] It will be remembered that at Edgehill, when Sir Faithful Fortescue's troop went over to the King, as a sign of their desertion they tore off their orange scarves. Probably the most celebrated of the cuirassiers among the Royalists were Rupert's so-called "Show Troop," among the Parliamentarians "Haselrigge's Lobsters."

Dragoons wore buff leather coats, iron caps or helmets, iron front and back pieces. They were armed with carbines, muskets, and swords. They were not strictly horse soldiers, but foot soldiers, who used a horse only in order to arrive with more speed at the place where military service was to be performed.[†]

The ordinary horse were wore buff coats and iron helmets, and were armed with swords for fighting on horseback, and muskets, which could be used either on horseback or on foot.

It is this use of the musket, by foot or by horse as required by circumstances, that explains what is at first sight so opposed to our ideas as incongruous, the attacks on towns by troops of horse. Whenever they found it necessary they dismounted and fought on foot, like other infantry; the great advantage they possessed being that, as mounted men, they were able to move about much more rapidly than if on foot, and in much of the Civil War fighting quickness of movement was all important.

Of foot soldiers there were two kinds—musketeers and pikemen. Musketeers had rather a difficult task, as they were much hampered by their weapons. Their muskets, or to speak more accurately, their matchlocks, had not reached the stage of flint and steel, but were fired by a piece of rope soaked in saltpetre, which on being lighted smouldered, and on being applied to the touch-hole discharged the piece. The musket was larger, heavier, and more powerful than the old arquebuss, being some four feet in length, was, on account of its weight, provided with a long rest, forked in the upper part, and furnished with a spike or stick to attach it to the ground.

In addition to his musket and its rest a musketeer had to carry a bullet bag—12 bullets weighed a pound—a flask of powder for loading, priming, a number of pieces of spare rope for firing, and a bandolier with from twelve to twenty charges of powder for his musket. It will be seen that the musket was not a very easy weapon to manage, and the loading and discharging took

---

* Whitlock, p. 59.   † Nugent's "Hampden," p. 282.

some time, and while these operations were going on the musketeer was comparatively powerless. It is for this reason that we so often hear of cavalry, with little or no loss, riding down infantry. When dismounted, dragoons usually fought as musketeers.

The pikemen were armed either with a full pike, a cumbrous weapon, some 12 or 16 feet long, an ash pole with a sharpened steel head; or a half-pike, a much more handy weapon, some six to eight feet long. The pike had to do all the bayonet has to do now, and was the mode of fighting used when men came to close quarters, to " push of pike." It was with the pike that all the really hard infantry fighting, the storming, the hand to hand struggles, were done. Pikemen had iron caps and corselets. One of Clarendon's complaints at the outbreak of the war was that the Royalist pikemen had no corselets, the musketeers no swords.

The artillery appear to have been very cumbrous and not very effective, except for siege works. They had cannon, the heaviest of which would throw about a 34lb. shot; culverins, throwing shot from 2lb. to 15lb.; falcons, throwing shot of 1lb.; falconets, of ½lb.; drakes, with a still smaller ball. In some accounts, as in those of Charles II's. Scotch army that fought at Worcester, leather guns are spoken of, which shew that the gunpowder of the time was of no great strength.

One other weapon—a survival from an older age—is also mentioned, bows and arrows. In the Commissions of Array they had always been specified. It was still the duty of the parish to provide butts for the practice of archery, and of the parish constable to see that archery was practised. In 1627 an information was laid against

" certain persons in Worcestershire who, being lawfully summoned by the
" constables to show themselves furnished with bows and arrows, made default
" in doing so."*

The list includes six persons at St. John-in-Bedwardine, three at Overwick, five at Powick, three at Broadwas, and three at Claines. Essex† is said to have held very strong views in favour of the revival of archery, and in 1643 issued an order to raise a company. Charles I., in 1633, issued an order for the use of the bow and pike, giving notice that in former times bows and arrows had been found serviceable weapons for war, whereby great and victorious conquests had been gotten. By sundry statutes the use had been enjoyned, which statutes were still in force. The King expected his servants to conform thereunto, and directed Mead, an ancient archer, to instruct the trained bands therein.‡

---

* Sessions Records, 1627, p. 429.   † Rushworth, V., 370.   ‡ Rushworth, II, 243.

In 1644, at the surrender of Essex's army at Liskeard, among the list of arms surrendered were a waggon load of arrows. At the siege of Gloucester, in 1643, bows and arrows were used for shooting letters into the town. In 1642 a company of pikemen with bows and arrows were formed in Herefordshire. At Devizes, Sir Jacob Astley was nearly shot by an arrow, it going between his legs. At Chester the suburbs were set on fire by arrows fired from the city.

In one thing the troops in the Civil War differed greatly from the troops of to-day—they had no regular uniform. We are apt to think that the Royalists wore red and the Parliament blue, and this is often stated to be so, but "blue coats" and "red coats" were found in both armies, as there were no distinctive colours to distinguish each party. The Parliament troops often wore the orange scarf of Essex, but this was the only general distinctive colour. Regiments either adopted their own colours or those of their colonels, and were often described and spoken of by the colour of their coats. Thus Hampden's men wore grey, and were called "Hampden's Grey Coats." A regiment raised by Lord Grey, the son of the Earl of Stamford, wore blue, and were called "Grey's Blue Coats." Newcastle's northern levies were called "Newcastle's White Coats."

One great difficulty both sides experienced was the question of how to pay their men. There is some evidence as to the rates of pay the troops were promised. What they did receive was a different matter, as on both sides there was always a difficulty about money. From some papers and accounts as to the pay of the troops forming the Worcester garrison,* it would appear that 100 horse cost £52 10s. od. a week, or 10s. 6d. a day each.

From the 4th December, 1642, to the 29th April, 1643, the first item is " entertainment (that is board and lodging) of 150 men at 13s. a man." The whole sum spent during the period is £1282 4s. 6d., but that includes other items besides pay, and the exact number of the men is not given.

The officers entitled to allowances appear to have been :— Captain, lieutenant, cornet, quartermaster, serjeant, drummer, and farrier. A week's pay of 51 men "unhorsed" was £15 6s. od., while a week's pay of 53 men "horsed" was £27 16s. od.

A receipt, dated the 6th February, 1649, given by Thomas Maylard, makes the pay of a company less than 10s. 6d. a day, that is assuming a company to have been 100 men, but there is nothing to show of what number the company consisted.

---

* Russell MSS., in the possession of the Worcestershire Historical Society.

" Received of Sir William Russell, Baronet, Governor of Worcester and
" Tewkesbury, the sum of £20 for payment of his own company of dragoons
" here at Tewkesbury."

On the Parliament side the nominal rates of pay were a
little higher than on the Royalist. A regiment of foot
consisted of 1000 men, divided into ten companies of 100 each,
and the pay per day was :—Officers, £19 14s. 0d.; soldiers,
£33 6s. 8d.; or £53 0s. 8d. a day.* The officers in the
Parliament Regiment were:—

		£	s.	d.	
Colonel ...	... ...	2	5	0	per day.
Lieutenant-Colonel	... ...	1	10	0	,,
Major ...	... ...	1	4	0	,,
7 Captains	... ...	5	5	0	,,
10 Lieutenants ...	... ...	2	0	0	,,
10 Ensigns	... ...	1	10	0	,,
20 Serjeants	... ...	1	11	6	,,
1 Drum Major ...	... ...	0	1	6	,,
20 Drums	... ...	1	0	0	,,
10 Gentlemen ...	... ...	0	10	0	,,
30 Corporals ...	... ...	1	10	0	,,
Chaplain and Man	... ...	0	8	8	,,
Chirurgion and 2 Mates	... ...	0	9	0	,,
Marshal and his Man ...	... ...	0	4	8	,,
Quartermaster and Man	... ...	0	4	8	,,
All Officers, per diem	... ...	19	14	0	
1000 Soldiers, per diem	... ...	33	6	8	

The Regiment complete, per diem ... £53 0 8

Roughly, the pay of a cavalry soldier on the Royalist side
was nominally 12s. a week.† It appears that under Fairfax the
nominal pay of a cavalry soldier on the Parliament side was
14s. It is very probable that the rate of pay varied under
different generals; it is more than likely that neither Royalist
nor Parliamentarian received his full pay with any regularity,
but had to make it out as best he could, often by plunder.

If, as it seems was the fact, the Parliament troops were
better paid than the Royalist, this may have been one of
the causes which, as the war went on, operated to enable the
Parliament to recruit with more facility than the King, and
obviated the still greater difficulty of keeping and retaining the
troops that had been recruited. If this is so it would tend to
confirm the statement which is often made, that when
Parliament formed their new modelled army in 1645 many of
the men who enlisted in it were deserters from, or persons
who had served in, the Royalist ranks. Added to this the
fact that while both armies plundered freely, it was, to all
appearances, more likely after the new modelled army was
formed that the Parliament troops would have a greater chance

---

* Birch's Memoirs, p. 67.   † Webb's Civil War in Herefordshire, I., 358.

of plunder than the Royalist, operated as an inducement to the soldiers of fortune to join the Parliament army.

Before describing the fighting a word should be said about the men who fought.

One striking thing about the Worcestershire fighting in the Civil War is that on neither side had any of the great generals much to do with it. Most of the fighting was done by men who were in the second rank. It is true that Rupert on several occasions took part in military operations in the County; that Maurice was for a time Military Governor of the County, or, to speak more accurately, the County was within his military command. But the active operations of Maurice were confined to those against Massey, when Waller came to his relief, in 1643, and which, so far as Maurice was concerned, ended in his victory at Ripple. Maurice, though here later, did not take much part in the fighting. Charles himself was present on several occasions ; Wilmot made a brave, but unsuccessful, attempt to raise the siege of Dudley Castle; Sir Jacob Astley fought a great fight on the Cotswold Hills, near Stow-on-the-Wold. But, with these exceptions, the absence of the great Royalist generals from the Worcestershire fighting is very marked.

It is the same on the Parliament side. Essex, it is true, was present in and commanded in the County before the Battle of Edgehill, and again after the relief of Gloucester. Waller on two occasions, in 1643, when at Gloucester he commanded against Maurice and tried to take Worcester, and in 1644, when he followed the King from Oxford to Bewdley, took part in the fighting; but neither Fairfax or Skippon, Lambert or Middleton, Harrison or Ludlow, nor Cromwell himself appeared in the County during the first Civil War. The fighting was confined on both sides to men in the second rank. The general impression that the local noblemen and gentry were almost all united in defending the County against the King's enemies was not really the case. With one or two exceptions the Worcestershire landowners took very little part in the fighting. Sir William Russell, of Strensham, Sir Thomas Lyttelton, of Frankley, and Colonel Sandys, of Ombersley, are the most notable exceptions. One looks, and looks in vain, for the names of any of the great Worcestershire families taking part in the struggle. The Lord Coventry of the time was abroad during most of the war. Sir John Pakington gave a general support to the King, but did not take much personal part. Sherrington Talbot, of Salwarpe, was active among the Commissioners of Array, but as a rule one looks in vain for the local gentlemen acting as Royalist leaders as we find them in other counties.

If the Royalist landowners did not take an active part

neither did those of the Parliament, with one or two exceptions. The Wildes, of Droitwich, were active as administrators,
but not as soldiers. The Rouses, at Rous Lench, the
Lechmeres, at the Rhydd, were strong Parliamentarians, and
did not hesitate to act up to their convictions when necessary,
but they did very little fighting.

Most of the Royalists who fought belong not to Worcestershire, but to general history. We all know and have all made
up our minds as to Charles and Rupert. A word should be said
as to some of the others.

First of Maurice, who was for a long time the nominal
head of the Royalists in the County. He was the younger
son of Charles' sister, who had married the Prince Palatine,
the Palsgrave, as he was usually called. Born in 1620, he
came with his brother Rupert to England in 1642. Without
military experience, with an over-weening sense of his own
importance, with nothing to recommend him but personal
courage, he considered he was able to conduct a campaign. At
first he served under his brother Rupert; he was present and
wounded at Powick, was at Edgehill, and at the storming of
Cirencester in 1643. Later in that year, to check Waller's
operations in Worcestershire and Gloucestershire, the King
determined to make a separate command, to include these
counties, and on the 2nd March, 1643, gave this to his nephew
Maurice. Soon after he took over the duties. On the 9th
April he was at Tewkesbury, where, it is said, he and Lord
Gerrard received the sacrament. On the 14th April he got
£200 out of Sir William Russell, the Governor of Worcester,
as appears by his receipt.*

"Received of Sir William Russell, Governor of Worcester, the sum of two
"hundred pounds.   200li.   o   o
"April 14th, 1643.   Maurice."

Maurice defeated Waller at Ripple, his greatest military
performance in these parts. Soon after he was recalled to
Oxford. He was present at the Battle of Lansdowne, the rout
of Roundway Down, and the capture of Bristol. A command
was given him in the west, but he was not successful. He
failed to take Plymouth, probably from illness ; he besieged
but was unable to take either Taunton or Bridgewater. In
1644 he was appointed Major-General of the Counties of
Worcester, Salop, Hereford, and Monmouth. Between this
and July, 1646, when he left England, he spent much of his
time at Worcester, residing there on several occasions for
considerable periods. On Charles coming to Worcester,
in 1645, from Oxford, Maurice joined him, being present
at the capture of Leicester and the defeat at Naseby. On

---

* MS. Russell Papers.   W. H. S.

Charles returning through Worcestershire on his way to Wales, Maurice went back to Worcester to hold it against the Scots, who were then advancing to attack it. When they passed on to Hereford without attacking Worcester, he joined the King at Bromyard on the 15th September, but returned to Worcester soon after. On the 28th September he again met the King at Chirk, but soon after returned to Worcester, where he remained for some time. He was there with Rupert on the 13th November. It is not quite clear when he finally left Worcester. He and Rupert were at Oxford during the siege of 1646, and were present at its surrender on the 20th June. Maurice finally left England on the 8th July, 1646.

Other Royalists who should be mentioned are Sir Thomas Lyttelton, who was Governor of Bewdley, Sir William Russell, Colonel Sandys, and Sir Gilbert Gerrard (who were all Governors of Worcester), Vavassour, and Mynne (who commanded in the south of the County against Waller and Massey), and Washington, who was the Royalist Governor of Evesham and Worcester. Of these only Lyttelton, Russell, and Sandys were really Worcestershire men.

Sir William Russell, of Strensham, was the head of the family of Russell, who had long been owners of Strensham. In his house, and under his eye, the great Worcestershire poet of the Civil War, Butler, the author of " Hudibras," was brought up as clerk to Sir William Russell. That worthy baronet might have sat for the portrait of " Sir Knight." It is quite probable that many of the characters in that poem are drawn from local celebrities. Russell was Sheriff of the County in 1642, and one of the Commissioners of Array. He was one of the first of the gentry in Worcestershire who began to raise men for the King. When Colonel Essex left Worcester at the end of 1642, and it was taken for the King, Russell was appointed Governor, and he held that office for some time. He was in the city when it surrendered in 1646; the Parliament insisting that Russell should be excepted from all benefit of the surrender. He was subsequently fined for his malignancy, but survived the Restoration.

Sir Thomas Lyttelton, of Frankley (1596-1650), was in the north of the County what Russell was in the south. He had sat in several of the early Parliaments of Charles, and was member for Worcester City in the short Parliament of 1640, in which year he was also Sheriff for the County. When Charles erected his standard at Nottingham, Lyttleton offered to raise a regiment of foot and a troop of horse for the King. He was summoned to Shrewsbury by the King to consult on the state of Worcestershire, and was appointed colonel of the horse and foot raised in the County, and afterwards Governor of Bewdley.

While at Bewdley he resided in the Palace of Ticknell. In May, 1644, Tinker Fox one night possessed himself of Bewdley and carried off Sir Thomas Lyttelton as prisoner. So important was his capture considered that he was taken from Fox and sent to the Tower, and although soon after liberated on bail, by order of Essex, he was again arrested and sent back to the Tower. Subsequently released, he was made to pay £4000 for his malignancy. He died in 1650.

Samuel Sandys, of Ombersley, was a grandson of the Archbishop of York who had at one time been Bishop of Worcester. Round Ombersley he exercised considerable influence, which he used to its utmost on the Royalist side. He was very active in raising men for the King. Early in the war he was appointed Governor of Evesham. Afterwards he took a leading part in the defence of Worcester, of which place he acted at times as Governor. He so acted in 1643, when Waller attacked the city, and in revenge for his defeat the Parliament troops attacked and plundered Sandys' property at Ombersley.

Sir Gilbert Gerrard is one of those men of whom it is most difficult to give an accurate account. As there were no less than seven Colonel Gerrards in the Royalist army, and at least three had the name of Gilbert, it is very hard to avoid confusion. This one acted as Governor of Worcester from 1644 until his death in 1645. He is, perhaps, best known from the fact that he was one of the active adversaries of "Tinker Fox." Gerrard was able to take Stourton Castle, a garrison near Stourbridge established by Fox, but was repulsed in his attack on Fox's head-quarters at Edgbaston. He also tried, but without success, to raise the siege of Dudley. Gerrard had no connection with Worcester beyond his military service in the County.

The same remark applies to Vavassour, who, for some time after Maurice gave up the command in 1643, acted as the leader of the Royalists in the south and south-west of the County, where he did a good deal of fighting, but not so much as he should have done. He had served with distinction in Ireland and in Scotland, and had been one of that gallant band who stood round the King's standard when charged by Stapleton's cuirassiers at Edgehill. He was there taken prisoner, released on parole, which he broke, and was therefore described by the Parliament writers as one who,

"having violated his faith given, demonstrates himself to the world to be "unworthy the name of a gentleman."

While commanding in Worcestershire he appears to have looked upon the local gentry merely as means to be utilized to bring about treacherous surrenders in cases where his own exertions to that end failed, and where his fighting effected

nothing. He employed, successfully, Dowdeswell, of Pull Court,
to negotiate the surrender of Tewkesbury; he employed,
unsuccessfully, Stanford to bring about the surrender of
Gloucester. How he came to be appointed to so important a
position it is hard to say. He was profuse in promises which
he never fulfilled, and was described by Charles as being " a
man that could agree with no one in the kingdom."

Very different was his subordinate, Mynne, another stranger
to the County, He had served with distinction in Ireland,
and came over from Ireland to Bristol with troops, which he
marched from Bristol to Newent. Here he shewed the
Parliament what a clever general could do, even with a wholly
inadequate force. He possesses the great distinction of being
almost the only one of the Worcestershire leaders holding high
military rank who, during the first Civil War, fell in battle,
dying at the head of his men in the action at Redmarley.

On the side of the Parliament the most active leaders were
Sir Edward Massey, Lord Denbigh, Lord Brooke, Colonel (as
his own side called him), " Tinker" Fox (as the Royalists called
him), and Sir John Wilde. Of these Wilde and possibly Fox
were Worcestershire men,* Lords Denbigh and Brooke
Warwickshire, and Massey a complete stranger, yet he was the
person who took the most active part in the Civil War in
Worcestershire.

Edward Massey (1619-1674) was, it is said, originally an
apprentice in London, but running away he managed to get
across to Holland, where he enlisted and served in the war,
there learning the art that he subsequently practised so well.
If the story is true, which is doubtful, Massey could not have
stayed long abroad, for in 1639, when only 20, he was serving
in the Royal army against the Scotch as Captain of Pioneers.
When Charles came to York in 1642 Massey offered his
services to the King, but being somewhat rudely treated he
left the King's quarters, joined the Parliament, and was at
once appointed Lieutenant-Colonel under the Earl of Stamford.
Massey came with Stamford to Worcester in September, 1642,
and went on with him to Hereford, where he stayed until
December, when he marched with Stamford to Gloucester.
Here, in the absence of Stamford, he seems to have had chief
command, and the position of Governor of Gloucester was
formally given him in June, 1643. He was the governor
during the siege, and this, with his sorties and other operations,
made his name well known throughout all the district as one
of the best officers in the Parliament army. He remained
Governor of Gloucester until May, 1645, when he was pro-
moted to be General of the Western Association (the Counties

---

* Symonds says Fox came from Tamworth.

of Cornwall, Devon, Somerset, Dorset, and Wilts.). His last feat of arms in Worcestershire was storming the fortifications of Evesham on the 26th May, 1645. He acted with Fairfax in the west in reducing the country to the authority of Parliament. Fighting being over, in July, 1646, he took his seat in the Long Parliament as the Member for Gloucester. His brigade was disbanded on 20th October, 1646. In 1647 he was appointed Lieutenant-General to command in Ireland, but the soldiers refused to serve under him, alleging he was not a "proper man." Shortly afterwards he was impeached for seeking to raise a new civil war. He was one of the Members of Parliament excluded by Pride's Purge. He was impeached, imprisoned, but escaped in January, 1649, went abroad and entered Charles II's service. He was with Charles II. at Worcester, and commanded the troops at Upton when Lambert forced the bridge. He was severely wounded in this fight. After the Battle of Worcester he fled, but could, from his wounds, get no distance; he took shelter with Lady Stamford, but was taken and sent to the Tower. He escaped in 1652 and went abroad.

Sir John Wilde (1590-1679) was a thorough Worcestershire man, the son and heir of George Wilde, of Kempsey, an able and active lawyer, he was one of the strongest supporters of the Parliament in the County. He was, from his first entry into public life, on the side of reform. As a magistrate, in 1634, he worked at Quarter Sessions to bring about some better treatment of the prisoners in the gaol at Worcester. In some of the early Parliaments of Charles he had been Member for Droitwich, but in the Long Parliament he was elected as one of the County Members, and from the early days of that Parliament formed one of that band of lawyers who were the chief opponents of the Court. Strongly opposed to the Bishops, he acted as Chairman of the Impeachment Committee; he was very bitter against the Archbishop, Laud. As one of the Deputy Lieutenants for Worcestershire, he used his authority as much as possible in favour of the Parliament, obstructing the Commissioners of Array in levying men for the King. He obtained leave from Parliament to buy the arms of Lord Windsor, who was found to be a malignant, for his own use and for the use of the County. He was one of the Parliamentary sequestrators for the County in 1643, and his local knowledge was found of great use in dealing with malignants and their estates. When Parliament made a new great seal Wilde was made one of the commissioners. He was one of the managers of Laud's impeachment. In July, 1646, he was made Recorder of Worcester, and in October, 1646, when Parliament filled up the vacancies on the judicial Bench, he was appointed Lord Chief Baron of the Exchequer. In some way he offended Cromwell, who, when he became Protector and nominated his officers, left Wilde without employment. Wilde and Lord Denbigh form good examples of the way in which the Civil War divided families. Wilde's nephew, Robert Wilde, of the Commandery, Worcester, who was also a Barrister of the Middle Temple, was a strong Royalist, and had to pay a fine of £450 when compounding for his estate. Lord Denbigh was a Parliamentary leader. His father was killed at Camp Hill fighting for the King.

Basil Fielding, second Earl of Denbigh, was a nephew of that Duke of Buckingham who died by Felton's knife. He served as a young man in the Low Countries under Lord Wimbledon, and was present at the siege of Bois-le-Duc. In 1634 he was appointed Ambassador to Venice. On his return home in 1639 he fully expected his appointment would have been renewed. As it was not, mainly, it was said, by the influence of the Queen, whom he had in some way offended, he took violent offence against the Court and became a strong opponent of the King, while his family were all strong Royalists. When the war broke out he raised a troop of horse for Parliament, and fought under Essex at Edgehill. On the death of Lord Brooke, Denbigh was, on the 12th June, 1643, made Commander-in-Chief for the Parliament of the Counties of Warwick, Worcester, Stafford, and Salop, and the cities of Lichfield and Coventry. Although it does not appear that Lord Denbigh took much personal part in the fighting, it was in a great degree due to him and his efforts that during the years 1643 and 1644 the Royalists made no progress on the eastern side of Worcestershire, and that the County border marked the limit of the Royalist territory. So far as Worcestershire was concerned, his chief military exploit was the siege of Dudley Castle and the repulse of Wilmot's attempt to relieve it. Lord Denbigh refused to join Waller and abandon the siege of Dudley, and this was possibly one of the reasons why in the November of that year his appointment as Commander of the Associated Counties was not renewed. From his papers, which are still in existence, Lord Denbigh appears to have been a very able administrator, and to have rendered the Parliament very valuable service. From the way in which he charged and rescued Brereton in the fight before Dudley, against the advice of all his officers and men, he shewed that when the occasion required no one could exhibit more reckless courage; but he seems to have been far from popular, possibly from his proneness to take offence at every little incident.

A very different stamp of man was the other Parliamentary nobleman, "Fanatic Brooke," as he is styled by Scott. Robert Greville (1608-1643), second Lord Brooke, was

a supporter of the Parliament, not from pique, but from
principle.   At the outbreak of the war, in 1642, he joined
Essex on his march to Worcester, and was with him when the
Parliament forces occupied Worcester.   He was sent with his
regiment, while Essex remained at Worcester before the
Battle of Edgehill, to do outpost duty against the Royalist
forces who were then at Bridgnorth.   Brooke occupied
Bewdley and Kidderminster, and carried out this somewhat difficult task for newly-raised troops with success.
In January, 1643, Parliament, to better defend and organise
the Midland Counties, formed Warwick, Worcester, Stafford,
and Salop, with the cities of Coventry and Lichfield,
into an association, and appointed Lord Brooke the commander.   As such he considered it his duty to drive the
Royalists out of Lichfield, which they had occupied, fortifying
themselves in the Close.   Brooke laid siege to the place, and
was killed in his quarters by a chance shot from the walls.   His
death was a great blow to the Parliament.   It was owing to
him more than anyone else that the Parliament obtained a
controlling influence in Warwickshire and Staffordshire, and
his cool, deliberate courage would have done much to retain
and increase the influence of the Parliament.   This they felt,
as one of their writers* says :—

"His piety, prudence, and incomparable magnanimity and heroic martial
"spirit, his loyalty to his King, his fidelity to his country, deserve indelibly to
"remain engraven in letters of gold on high-erected pillars of marble."

Brooke and Denbigh represented the aristocratic side of the
Parliamentary party; there was another side, which though
not so pleasing, was certainly more influential and possibly
more effective, well represented in the County by Thomas
Fox.   The Royalists said he was by trade a tinker.   Be that
as it may, he was a colonel in the Parliament army and
rendered them good service.   Fox is a typical specimen of the
fighting Puritan, one of those men who, by a close study of
the Old Testament, brought himself to believe that he was a
divinely-selected instrument to carry out the Lord's command
on the children of wrath.   Fox organised a troop of horse,
composed of men who like himself could face any odds,
execute any service, however desperate, in the belief that
they were doing the will of God.   His influence over
these wild fanatics was remarkable.   Once when Lord
Denbigh ordered his attendance, Fox declined to come,
saying his men, if left, would either desert or mutiny.   In
the autumn of 1643 Fox took possession of Edgbaston Hall,
the home of the Royalist family of Middlemore, and made
it his head-quarters.   From there he made constant expedi-

* Vicker's "God in the Mount," p. 272.

tions all over the north of Worcestershire "to smite the Amalekite." He planted two garrisons—one at Stourton Castle, near Stourbridge, which was taken by Colonel Gerrard after a sharp fight, the other at Hawkesly, which was besieged and taken by Rupert. Gerrard attacked Fox's stronghold at Edgbaston, but was repulsed. Fox's great deed was one which reads like an extract from Dumas' novels. With a handful of men he surprised the Royalist garrison of Bewdley and carried off the governor prisoner. In his way there is no more interesting local figure in the Civil War than this military tinker. His surpassing impudence, his insatiable avarice, his cool courage, render him and his troop of horse the typical Roundheads. Later he almost disappeared from history, the Royalists say because he was the masked man, whose identity has been so often disputed, who executed "the Blessed Martyr" on the scaffold at Whitehall. It is possible that the Worcestershire poet of the Civil War, in his great poem, may have had Fox in his mind when he wrote :—

> " When Tinkers bawled aloud to settle
> " Church Discipline for patching kettle." *

On 22nd August, 1642, Charles erected his standard at Nottingham. He was disappointed at the number of persons who obeyed his call to arms. He had taken a step which amounted to a declaration of war, and found himself in dire need of all that was wanted for war—men, money and munitions. Such was his need of men that his general, Sir Jacob Astley, said :—

" He could give no assurance that the King would not be taken out of his " bed if the rebels made a brisk attempt to that purpose."†

Nothing could show his need of money more clearly than a memorandum made by Lord Herbert of an interview he had with the King on the 9th September, 1642.

" Much lieth at stake for want of a little money. Since £20,000, with what " you have, would further your Majesty's designs to a most hopeful condition, " for want whereof your Majesty is enforced to dally, though you will never " yield, and at the present you offer that which is worth £100,000 for £50,000, " besides my Lord Capel, Sir William Savile, and others of good estate, do " offer also theirs for security. Yet no want or occasion can make your " Maiesty to press my Lord, who hath already done so much, but if he and his " friends could procure £10,000, your Majesty would suddenly if it please God " to restore you, see it repaid ; and would presently, in token of thankfulness, " send my father the Garter to be put on when he pleased ; and also having " the great seal in your Majesty's own custody, you would pass a Patent of " Marquiss, of what title my father should desire and keep it private as long as " he thought fitting." ‡

As to munitions of war, Clarendon says :—‖

" All the strength the King had to depend upon was his horse, which were " under the command of Prince Rupert at Leicester, and were not at that time " in number above 800, few better armed than with swords."

---

* " Hudibras," Part I., Canto II., p. 535.   † Clarendon, II., 1.
‡ Hist. MSS. Com., 12th Rep. App. ix., p. 11.   ‖ II., 2.

The Parliamentary army was assembled at Northampton. There were at least 1600 horse, well armed and appointed, and 5000 foot, well trained and disciplined   All advantage, therefore, lay on their side.   Clarendon says :—*

"If the Parliament had marched directly to Nottingham His Majesty's few "forces must have been scattered, and himself fled or put himself in their "hands."

Such was the state of things in August, 1642.   Charles had taken up the sword, and it appeared likely he was about to perish by the sword.   He seems to have had no settled plans, and none of those about him were able to propose any.   But his opponents were much in the same position.   Essex, the general of the Parliament force, stayed in London, and each side seemed incapable of making any move.   Charles' necessities forced him into action.   Recruits came in but slowly, but recruits he must have if he was to hold his own. From the news he received from the west and west midlands, it seemed that his presence there might quicken his recruiting, so Charles decided to move westward to some place on the Welsh border, but whether to Chester, Shrewsbury, or Worcester, neither he nor his advisers could decide.   Probably this was the wisest course he could take under the circumstances, as from all that we know this was his best chance of raising an army.   In a letter of this date it states :—

"My Lord of Hertford is at Sherborne, my Lord of Bristol's, with 600 "horse and 1000 foot, as I hear.   Worcestershire, Shropshire and Herefordshire "are for the King, and others for the Parliament."

The King's plan, therefore, was to march west from Nottingham to some place on the Welsh border, using every effort to raise men, money, and munitions.   Having got together such a force as would make it possible for him to advance with safety, to push on at once to London, try if he could not get possession of the place and put down the Parliament.   Essex's object was to prevent the King reaching London.   This he was to do at all cost.   To effect this he was to keep his army to the south of the King's line of march, intercept any movement to the south, and, if necessary, fight any engagement or engagements that might be required to prevent the King getting between him and London.   Subject to doing this, Essex was to obstruct and cut off the King's communications with Wales and the west, so as to prevent him receiving the supplies he looked for, and especially to cut his lines of communication with South Wales and the country under the Somerset influence.

Such being the objects of the armies, it remains to be stated how they were carried out.   Charles was at Nottingham with some 2000 men ; about 20 miles to the south, at Leicester,

* II., 5.

Rupert was stationed with the Royal Horse, some 1000 strong; while some 20 miles further south, at Northampton, was the Parliament army, some 20,000 strong, but as yet without their general, and without orders. The first part of the campaign consisted in each of the three bodies moving to the west. Neither had as yet settled the point on which to move. Charles was undecided whether to go to Chester or Shrewsbury; Essex was waiting to follow Charles.

On the 9th September Essex set out from London to take over the command of the army. On the 13th Charles made his move, marching from Nottingham to Derby. On the 5th Rupert left Leicester and begun his march to the westward. The Royalists had got the start; for it was not until the 19th September that Essex began his march. Roughly speaking, the three forces were moving in parallel lines, the King slightly in advance, and Essex in the rear. It soon became apparent that the King was marching on Shrewsbury. No attempt was made—possibly Essex could make none—to intercept him, each continued his parallel march until events took place that settled the future movements.

Money was as pressing a need to Charles as men, and how it was to be raised none of his advisers knew. Someone seems to have hit on the idea that as the King possessed a mint at Aberystwyth—a mint controlled by a Worcestershire man, one of the Bushells of Cleeve Prior—all that was wanted was silver to be coined at it to supply the King's needs. Most of the gentry possessed plate, that could be put in the melting-pot and coined into money. It was stated to them that the King's necessities could be met by a sacrifice of the family plate, and the Royalists willingly made the sacrifice, as " Hudibras " says :—

> " Did saints for this bring in their plate,
> " And crowd as if they came too late ;
> " For when they thought the cause had need on't,
> " Happy was he that could be rid on't.
> " Did they coin —— ——s Bowls and flaggons
> " Int' officers of horse and dragoons,
> " And into pikes and muskqueteers
> " Stamp beakers, cups, and porringers.
> " A thimble, bodkin, and a spoon
> " Did start up living men as soon
> " As in the furnace they were thrown."*

To such an extent did the demand for plate extend, that a few months after, when the Court was established at Oxford, a regular form was drawn up and sent to the colleges which were supposed to possess plate. The form was as follows :—

" Charles R.

" Trusty and well beloved, we greete you well. We are soe well satisfyed

---

* Part I., Canto II., 561.

" with your readiness and affection to our service, that we cannot doubt but
" you will take all occasions to expresse the same. And as we are ready to
" sell or engage any of our land, so we have melted down our plate for the pay-
" ment of our army, raysed for our defence and preservacon of the kingdom.
" And, having received severall quantities of plate from diverse of our loving
" subjects, we have removed our mint hither to our City of Oxford for the
" coyning thereof.

" And we doe hereby desire that you will lend unto us all such plate, of what
" kinde soever, which belongs to your colledge, promising to see the same justly
" repayed unto you, after the rate of 5s. the ounce for white and 5s. 6d. for
" guilt plate, as soon as God shall enable us. For, assure yourselves, we shall
" never let persons of whom we have soe great a care to suffer for their affection
" to us, but shall take speciall order for the repayment of what you have already
" lent to us according to our promise, and allsoe of this you now lend in plate,
" knowing it to be the goods of your colledge, that you ought not to alien,
" though no man will doubt but that in such a case you may lawfully assist
" your King in such visible necessity. And wee have entrusted our trusty and
" wel-beloved Sir William Parkhurst, Knt., and Thomas Bushell, Esq.,
" officers of our mint, or either of them, to receive the said plate from you, and,
" upon weighing thereof, shall give you a receipt under their, or one of their,
" hands for the same. And we assure ourselves of your very great willingness
" to gratify us herein, since besides the more publique consideration, you cannot
" but knowe how much yourselves are concerned in our sufferings.

" And we shall ever remember this particular service to your advantage.
" Given at our Court at Oxford this 6th day of January, 1642 (1643)."

This letter is curious, as giving the value of the plate at that
time—5s. per ounce for silver, 5s 6d. for silver gilt. A very
large quantity was sent in; Jesus College gave 86lbs. 11ozs.
5dwts. The idea of getting the plate from the colleges
appears to have been, if not started, at least encouraged by no
less a person than the then Vice-Chancellor, Prideaux, the
Bishop of Worcester. He was very active in pushing this
scheme. His activity came to the notice of Parliament as
early as July, 1642, and they at once made an order forbidding
the University to send to the King at York, or elsewhere, any
of the college plate, and ordered that Prideaux and all others
concerned in the scheme should be at once arrested. For a
while the scheme dropped, as the King had no means of getting
the plate from Oxford to the local mint.

In the beginning of August, 1642, the Earl of Worcester
gave the King £5000 to set up a regiment of dragoons. This
was done, and the command of the regiment given to Sir
John Byron. Having a regiment of dragoons it was as well to
utilize them, and it occurred to someone that although the
University were unable to send their plate to the King, yet
there was nothing to prevent the King sending to the University
to fetch it. Such a service was well suited for the new
regiment, so Byron was ordered to march to Oxford, collect all
the plate he could, enlist as many recruits as possible, and then
march with his spoil to join the King. Byron set off for
Oxford. At Brackley he was set upon by the townsmen and
some Parliament troops, but he cut his way through, reached

Oxford on the 28th August, and at once began his task of collecting plate and enlisting recruits.

Meanwhile the King continued his march westwards. He stayed at Derby a night and went on to Stafford. It was then decided he should go to Shrewsbury, not Chester, a decision which was arrived at because the King was told that he could rely upon strong support from Worcestershire. This assurance was mainly due to one man—Sir Thomas Lyttelton—who had offered to raise a troop of horse and a regiment of foot for the King. This was communicated to Charles, who directed his Secretary of State (Lord Falkland) to reply.*

"Sir,

"I gave His Majesty an account of your affection and loyalty to him and "his service, with which he was fully satisfied before, and takes very kindly "now, and considering that and your knowledge of and interest in that County, "and the very great importance of those parts, desires very much to advise "with you what best may be done for their security, and hath commanded me "to signify to you that to that end you immediately repair to him at "Shrewsbury. To which I join my own desire that you will esteem me, Sir,

"Your very humble servant,

"Stafford, 19th Sept., 1642. "Falkland.

"Eight troops of horse and ten of dragoons are coming to Worcester. "Ordinance shall be sent from Shrewsbury by water."

Lyttelton went to Shrewsbury and saw the King, and was made Governor of Bewdley, where troops were to be stationed.

The Royalist plans were now developed. Charles was to have his head-quarters at Shrewsbury; Rupert with his cavalry was to occupy the country between Shrewsbury and Worcester, and it would seem, from Falkland's letter, that the Royalists then intended to occupy Worcester in force. On the day that Falkland's letter is dated (the 19th September), Essex left Northampton. Marching westward, he passed by Coventry, Warwick, and Stratford-on-Avon, where he was on the 20th, his advance guard being at Alcester.

Meanwhile Byron had pushed on with his work at Oxford. He collected much plate, he enlisted some recruits, he received a small sum of money that had been sent to Oxford for the King. So having got all he could, he determined to rejoin the King at Shrewsbury, his route being the road from London to Worcester over the Broadway Hill. It was about time he started. His visit to Oxford and the object of his visit were well known. Lord Say, the Lord Lieutenant of Oxford-shire, was mustering men with a view of capturing Byron and his convoy. A day was fixed for their assembling near Oxford. Whitelocke came " with a gallant company of horse of his neighbour's" under his command, Lord Say brought a regiment of dragoons, Lord St. John several companies of foot,

* Nash I., 499.

in all about 3000 men, when news reached them that Byron had left Oxford. He had heard of the proposed rendezvous, and promptly decided to set off to join the King, but he was in great difficulties. Encumbered with his convoy he could only move slowly. His force was no match in numbers for the Parliament forces. On his flank was Essex with the main body of the Parliament army rapidly advancing, so that there was great danger of his being cut off from the King. One thing was abundantly clear : unless he was strongly reinforced his fate was sealed, his convoy doomed. Byron accordingly sent off word to the King for help, and on the 10th September started with his convoy for Shrewsbury. He marched to Burford on his way to Worcester, but met with continual delays and difficulties as to transport and other matters, so that his progress was exceedingly slow. For the fact that Byron was escorting a rich convoy was well known, and it was the resolve of the Parliamentarians that neither the money nor the treasure should ever reach the King's hands, the convoy in some way or another must be intercepted and captured. Along his line of march Byron found all kinds of impediments, obviously made to give Lord Say time to come up. The people would not help him, but did their best to delay him. Still he pushed on. He was not able to get much over 10 miles a day out of his beasts ; the road seemed interminable. Knowing how difficult his situation had become, and how much more difficult it was daily becoming, Byron persevered with an obstinate doggedness that does him infinite credit. He despatched another messenger to the King, stating his plight, and begging for help. Meanwhile Essex was advancing, and if Essex or any considerable number of Essex's men got between Byron and Worcester all was lost. When Charles learnt of Byron's critical condition he resolved to relieve him. His horse were the only body that could do it, and to interpose his horse, leaving his flank open to the enemy, with a large and well-equipped force close at hand ready and willing to intercept them, was a most risky proceeding, that might well lead to disaster, and disaster meant ruin. Charles, however, decided that at all risks, at any sacrifice, Byron must be saved. He sent for Rupert and ordered him to go to Byron's relief, and bring him and his treasure safely to Shrewsbury. Rupert acted at once. He rejoined his regiment ; marching all night through Wolverhampton, reached Bridgnorth on September 20th. Here he halted till the 22nd. On that day he marched to Bewdley, and was now only 16 miles from Worcester, in fact, within striking distance.

Essex did not realise the rich prize he was allowing to slip through his fingers in allowing Byron to get nearer and nearer to Worcester. At last, on the 16th September—having taken six days to march 62 miles—Byron reached Worcester. Meeting with no resistance, he at once marched in and took possession of the town. Worcester now always boasts of her loyalty. At that day she was far from being a Royalist city, and the welcome she gave to Byron was by no means a cordial one. The citizens were then much exercised by the fact that at the Summer Assizes that year Wilde and Salway, the two Members for the County—both strong Parliamentarians— had appeared nominally to assist in keeping the peace ; really to put all the pressure they could on the County men and on the citizens to make them declare for the Parliament. Wilde, like all other freeholders, had been assessed by the Commissioners of Array for his contribution towards providing horses and arms. Not only had Wilde refused to pay, but had brought the matter before Parliament, and had prevailed on the House of Commons to make orders expelling three of the Commissioners who were Members of Parliament—Sir Henry Herbert, Sir John Pakington, and Samuel Sandys—and sending for another, Sherrington Talbot, of Salwarpe, who was brought up in custody to London, examined, and detained for some time in custody before he was released.

Byron's difficulties were not merely the want of sympathy from the townspeople with the King, but the much more for- midable one that his force was not sufficient to properly defend the place, while from the condition of the defences it was questionable if the place was defensible. The walls were dilapidated, and in places ruinous. The gates were old and rotten, so much so that they would hardly shut, and if they were actually closed there was neither lock or bolt to secure them. If the place had been vigorously attacked Byron could not have held it. It speaks much for his military capacity that he did his best to get the indefensible city into a defensible state.

Byron sent word to Rupert as to his condition, that he could not march out of Worcester unless help came ; that he could not hold Worcester if not strongly reinforced, should he be attacked; that he had every reason for supposing he was about to be attacked at once. Byron was not wrong in his expectation. Essex was at last roused to action, and Essex was only 25 miles away at the head of 20,000 men.

Essex had reached Stratford-on-Avon on the 21st September. Here he received the news that Byron with his convoy had reached Worcester. On hearing this the excitement among Essex's men became intense. Cries of " To Worcester ! " " To Worcester ! " were heard on all sides. So eager were some of the soldiers that one regiment of infantry, when on the march, broke into a run and kept up that pace, it is said, for two miles.* Whatever might be the enthusiasm of the troops at their first prospect of plunder, the 24 miles from Stratford-on-Avon to Worcester was too great a distance to be marched that day. By a forced march Essex managed to do 19 miles to Pershore on the 23rd. The wildest rumours were floating about : "That a battle was raging in front of Worcester," "That Rupert had occupied Worcester in force." Nothing was too extravagant to be repeated and believed.

One of the officers who was most eager to press on to Worcester was the commander of Essex's cavalry, Colonel Nathaniel Fiennes (son of that Lord Say, the Lord Lieutenant of Oxfordshire, who had tried and tried in vain to intercept Byron). The son was all anxiety to show that he, if he had only the chance, could succeed where his father failed. Fiennes was at Alcester with the advance guard of Essex's cavalry, only 17 miles from Worcester, and by his importunity he wrung from Essex, against his better judgment, leave to make a dash on Worcester, so as to cut off and capture Byron and his convoy, prevent his retreating towards Shrewsbury, and detain him at Worcester until the next or following day, when Essex and his army would arrive. The scheme was well planned, and had it been directed against a general such as Essex, would without doubt have been successful, but they had to deal with a man who recognised the importance and the value of the rapid movement of troops, especially of cavalry.

Having obtained leave to make his attempt on the evening of the 21st, Fiennes set off to march the the 17 miles from Alcester to Worcester. Among the force under him were his own troop, the 36th; that of his brother, Colonel John Fiennes, the 60th; that of Colonel John Sandys (a Kentish man, who must not be confounded with the Worcestershire family of the same name, who were as strong Royalists as the Kentish were Parliamentarians), and the 55th, commanded by Edward Wingate, a Member of the House of Commons. There is some dispute as to the total number of the Parliamentary force. Ludlow, who was then serving in Essex's Life Guards, says it was about 1000† (Clarendon, who was not present, puts it down at 500).‡ Whatever the number, the men were well mounted, well armed, and eager for action. What was more important, they had had a certain amount of military training. Attached to the force, as expert advisers, were Sir William Balfour, who acted as Lieutenant-General to the Duke of Bedford, and Colonel Brown, a Scotch officer who had seen service.

---

* Archæologia, xxxv., 327.   † Memoirs, p. 17.   ‡ II., 19.

Marching all night through Inkberrow, Upton Snodsbury, and Spetchley, about daybreak in the dawn of a dull September morning they found themselves before Worcester, facing the South, or Sidbury, Gate. It was to all appearances closed, but there being no fastenings to it there was nothing to have prevented Fiennes' men pushing it open and surprising the town. Byron's men never expected any enemy at all, least of all on that side, and kept slack guard. Fiennes' men advanced to the gate; no opposition was offered, it does not seem that the advance was noticed. Brown, who went with the advance, on reaching the gate struck at it with an axe. It was so rotten that his blow made a hole in it. Through the hole a musket was inserted and fired. The report roused the sentry, who hastened to the gate. Fiennes called on him to surrender; he refused, and ordered the guard to "turn out." Had Fiennes even now pushed on the place was lost. However, he hesitated, and his chance was gone. The guard turned out, the garrison were alarmed; not only the garrison but Fiennes' men as well; they retired from the gate in all haste. On reaching the main body they also retreated at once. Byron's men promptly rode out to the attack, but by the time his leading files had got clear of Sidbury Gate Fiennes and his men had disappeared. Byron was too good a soldier to allow his men to be scattered looking for the enemy, so, keeping his force in hand, after a short search he retired into the city, being able to say, as he did say afterwards, that the Parliament troops had tried to surprise the gate and had been repulsed.

Fiennes had failed in the first part of his task, to take Worcester, and had failed wholly by his want of enterprise and dash. He was by no means disconcerted. He had still the second part of his duty to carry out, to cut off Byron's retreat towards Shrewsbury, and by stationing his men so as to intercept any such movement, place Byron in a position that he must on Essex's advance on the next day, or the day following, find his only escape would be surrender. Essex would advance up the east side of the Severn; to reach Shrewsbury Byron would cross the river and go up the west bank. Fiennes' duty was, therefore, obvious : To cross the river, remain on the west bank until the head of Essex's column should appear on the east, and then place himself on the Shrewsbury road in the line of Byron's retreat, meanwhile keeping watch on the Shrewsbury road to intercept any movement of Byron before Essex appeared. The plan was carefully thought out, and was probably the best one that could have been designed under the existing circumstances. By it Byron was placed in a trap, and Fiennes had only to wait for the arrival of Essex to compel Byron to surrender.

To carry out his plan Fiennes gave orders to his men to march south down the Severn so as to cross to the west bank. Except that a part of his force crossed at Upton, over the bridge, it is not clear where the rest passed the Severn. There were fords at Pixham, Cleveload, and the Rhydd between Worcester and Upton, and it is very likely that some of Fiennes' men crossed at these fords. But wherever they crossed, the whole of Fiennes' force passed the Severn by the afternoon and marched up the west bank to Powick, a village three miles from Worcester. Here Fiennes halted. Whoever selected the spot, Fiennes or his expert advisers, shewed considerable tactical knowledge, for the post was a strong one, commanding good views of Worcester and the Severn Valley, and one from which as soon as Essex's arrival was seen there would be no difficulty in intercepting Byron on the road to Shrewsbury. The evening of the 22nd passed off quietly, Fiennes and his men were not disturbed. In some way, how does not appear, the fact that Fiennes had occupied Powick was well known in Worcester, for on the 23rd the Worcester people walked out in some numbers to Powick, if not to show sympathy with Fiennes, at least to see the soldiers and what was going on. Among those who went was Richard Baxter, who tells us he walked out to Powick to see the soldiers out of curiosity. His curiosity might have cost him dear. While he was at Powick, possibly " improving the occasion," someone, who it was does not clearly appear, but it was afterwards said to have been a citizen, who was paid to treacherously betray Fiennes to his ruin, came in all haste from Worcester with the news that Byron's men were mounting and preparing to set off. Strange as it may seem the news was true, Byron was on the move. Fiennes and his men at once jumped to the conclusion, the very natural conclusion, that hearing of the advance of Essex, Byron was making a desperate dash to get his convoy off towards Shrewsbury. This is what he anticipated would be done ; this he was there to prevent. As the fact became known among Fiennes' men the excitement grew to be intense. They were most eager to set off at once and get in front of Byron on the Shrewsbury road. Fiennes was, however, not left without wise counsels. It was suggested that the news was false, and only invented to get him to leave his advantageous position at Powick, possibly to draw him into an ambush, or to lead him off so as to leave the way clear for Byron to escape. No one ever seems to have suspected the real reason of Byron's sudden movement. Fiennes would not listen to the advice that he should remain at Powick until Essex came. He urged that he had been sent to intercept Byron, that his force was superior to Byron's in discipline, in numbers, in arms, and in equipment, that if once

Byron was allowed to escape he would never be caught again. Brown, Fiennes' expert adviser, strongly urged an immediate advance should be made. In this view Fiennes cordially concurred, and ordered it to be carried out. This decision was, doubtless, the right one with the knowledge that Fiennes then had of the Royalist force in his front. He believed he had only Byron to deal with, and if that was so, as Byron was not reinforced (and Fiennes had no reason to believe he was), if he left Worcester his fate was settled.

Fiennes ordered his men to mount and fall in on a large meadow just below the village, known still as Powick Ham. Across this meadow runs the road from Powick to Worcester, the road that Fiennes would have to take to intercept Byron. On falling in Fiennes allowed his troopers to indulge in singing a psalm. This ended, they were ordered to march down the road towards Worcester.

About three quarters of a mile from Powick the road crosses the River Teme by an old narrow brick bridge, so narrow (it is only eight feet wide) that not more than two men could ride over it abreast. Fiennes' leading files crossed the bridge, and following the road, which was little better than a lane, with high hedges on each side, concealing anyone going up the road from sight, passed a public-house, called "The Chequers" (which has long since disappeared), on up the lane to the point where it entered on a large open field, called Wickefield. From here, which is comparatively high ground, on one side, Worcester is visible ; the other over- looks the bridge and the lane leading to Powick. This lane which, even to our own day, was called "Cut Throat Lane," but which, regardless of the past and its associations, modern affectation or vanity has re-named "Swinton Lane," after crossing the field, passed on to the left, leading into the main road from Worcester to Bransford at a point about a mile and a quarter from Worcester. Near the point where the lane from the bridge opened out into the field there then stood a large thorn tree.

Probably Fiennes' men from their eagerness to push on, and from the narrowness of the bridge over which they were passing, got somewhat out of formation, and while passing up the lane did not regain it. They were going somewhat care- lessly, never expecting to see anyone but Byron and his men trying to escape. They had not as yet got nearly far enough on their way to hope to see them; all they expected to do was to re-form when they gained the open field from the lane. Some of them reached this point. Those who did so saw a sight that was to them a somewhat startling surprise.

As has already been said, Rupert reached Bewdley from Bridgnorth on Thursday, 22nd September. He then knew, if he did not know before, that if Byron was to be saved instant action was necessary. He was 16 miles from Worcester, Essex with his whole army was at about the same distance. Rupert set off from Bewdley very early on the 23rd. Marching through Astley, Shrawley, Holt, and Hallow he reached St. John's, the western suburb of Worcester, about mid-day. Here he halted, probably hearing that some of the Parliament troops were at Powick. On this he divided his force, sending a detachment into Worcester to help Byron to get all ready for a start. It is probable that the preparation that Byron made for this was the origin of the news that was brought to Powick and led Fiennes to march to intercept him. Rupert, with the main body of his men, marched up the Bransford Road, turned down "Cut Throat Lane," into Wickefield. Whether it was that he held the Parliament troops in supreme contempt, or whether it was carelessness or forgetfulness it is impossible to say, but on arriving in the field a halt was ordered. After their long march the men were allowed to dismount, no reconnaissance was made, no sentry posted. The day was hot, the men were tired; in a few minutes after the order was given to dismount officers and men were resting on the ground. Had it been a time of profound peace there could not have been greater slackness nor a greater disregard to all ordinary military rules.

It is not easy to say what was the actual strength of the force under Rupert in Wickefield. As he had sent a detachment to Worcester he had not the full strength with which he marched from Bewdley. Whatever its actual number, most writers agree it was an inferior force to that led by Fiennes, both in number, equipment, and discipline. But it had one priceless advantage which more than compensated for all these. It was the crack force of the King's army, composed not only of gentlemen accustomed to the use of the sword, but also of some of the bravest men in the Royalist ranks. Rupert and his brother Maurice were present, Wilmot, the Commissary General of the Royalist army, Lord Digby, whose courage was as perfect as his conduct was imperfect, Sir Lewis Dives, and others whose names were soon to be historic as Royalist leaders. Sitting quietly under the thorn tree, surrounded by his officers, the last thing Rupert thought about was the near presence of the enemy. Something attracted his attention, causing him to look up towards the end of the lane, and there he saw emerging from it the leading files of Fiennes' cavalry. Rupert was fairly caught, and caught as the result of his own carelessless and neglect.

Probably Fiennes was equally surprised with Rupert. Had he possessed any military knowledge or spirit he would at once have ordered his men to charge. If he had done so Rupert was lost. But Fiennes was not of the stuff out of which generals are made. He was too utterly astonished to realise the gifts the gods had given him if he would only take them. He let his chance go, he was not given another.

Rupert, whatever his faults, knew how to act on an emergency. Without waiting to order his men to mount, he leaped on his horse and, calling out " Charge," rode right into the advancing troopers. As quickly as they could his officers followed him. Before their men were in their saddles Rupert, followed by Maurice, Wilmot, Digby, and Dives, were in the midst of the Parliament cavalry. The fighting was sharp, as is shewn from the fact that with the exception of Rupert all the other officers were wounded. But they had redeemed their folly. Fiennes' men, taken at the moment they were emerging from the lane, were too surprised to fight. Turning their horses they tried to regain the lane. The confusion caused by this prevented the possibility of any formation being attempted. The dreaded Rupert was in their midst. Disconcerted, discredited, discouraged, they tried to get back down the lane. They blocked its entrance, forced back those behind them, who in their turn tried to escape. Thus before Rupert's men came up, the lane was filled with a struggling, frightened mass of horsemen, riding over each other in their efforts to get away. As the leading files turned and tried to get back, so did the rear files. Even without any pressure from the Royalists the rout was complete if the fugitives could not be rallied. Colonel Sandys and his Quarter-Master Douglas, Fiennes, and Wingate drew across the lane and tried to shew a front to the Royalists, but Rupert's troopers were now coming up, and cutting their way into the terrified Parliamentarians drove them back on their officers, who were ridden down by their own men. The fleeing, struggling mass pressed on for the bridge. The confusion was hopeless. What with those carried away in the rush, those cut down by the Royalists, those unable to control their horses, a rally was impossible. The Parliament officers would not believe it to be so. At the bridge Balfour and the two Fiennes faced about, and drawing across the road tried to turn their men. It was not to be, the men were past rallying. Pressed on by panic, they rushed through the line of the officers on to the bridge. Here things became worse, for the road narrowed. Some fell over into the water, some were trodden down by the horses, some were cut down by the soldiers, some got across the bridge into the road. But still the stampede continued across the Ham up into Powick village, through the village, along the Upton road. Beyond the village Rupert · did not continue the pursuit. Baxter, who says he was near enough to see the whole affair, states the pursuit was not continued " much beyond the bridge." Possibly the fact of their long march in the morning, and the knowledge that to bring Byron into safety there must be another long march in the evening, for once made Rupert prudent; or possibly he did not know but that he might "blunder unawares" on the whole army of Essex. Whatever it was Rupert recalled his men. He had, however, done his work so effectually that no pursuit was needed. Fiennes' troopers had the fear of Rupert before their eyes. Along the seven miles of road from Powick to Upton, over Upton Bridge, along the eight miles across Defford Common to Pershore, these men went as fast as they could get their horses to go, too much alarmed to turn aside or halt. They reached Pershore just as the advanced guard of Essex's army was marching into it. Seeing these frightened troopers galloping wildly into their midst, Essex's men also turned and went back as quickly as possible, thus causing alarm and terror even to the main body of the Lord General's army Ludlow, who was present, serving in Essex's body guard, the crack corps of his army, describes the effect of the appearance of Fiennes' troopers on the best of the Parliament troops :—

" The body of our routed party returned in great disorder to Pershore, at " which place our Life Guard was appointed to quarter that night. When we " were marching into Pershore we discovered horsemen riding very hard " towards us, with drawn swords, and many of them without hats, from whom " we understood the particulars of our loss, not without improvement by reason " of the fear with which they were possessed, telling us that the enemy was " hard by in pursuit of them, whereas it afterwards appeared they came not " within four miles of that place. Our Life Guard, being for the most part " strangers to things of this nature, were much alarmed with the report. Yet " some of us, unwilling to give credit to it until we were better informed, " offered ourselves to go out upon a further discovery of the matter. But our " Captain (Sir Philip Stapleton) not being then with us, his Lieutenant, one " Bainham, an old soldier (a generation of men much cried up at that time), " drawing us into a field, where he pretended we might more advantageously " charge if there should be occasion, commanded us to wheel about ; but our " gentlemen, not understanding the difference between wheeling about and " shifting for themselves, their backs being now towards the enemy, whom they " thought to be close in the rear, retired to the army in a very dishonourable " manner, and the next morning rallied at the head-quarters, when we received " but cold welcome from the general, as we well deserved."*

Halting his troops at Powick, Rupert collected his men, took up his wounded, marched back to Worcester. His detachment that had gone into Worcester earlier in the day had made all the preparations for the convoy to move. A halt of a few hours was all that Rupert allowed, the private soldiers who were taken prisoners were released on their promise not to serve again against the King, the wounded were left in Worcester, and in the evening Rupert was ready to set off for Shrewsbury with the convoy. They left Worcester that evening, marching back along the road they

* Memoirs, p. 18.

had come in the morning, through Hallow and Holt. They turned off by the Hundred House, over Abberley Hill to Tenbury, halting in the morning at Burford, having marched some 20 miles. They rested on the Saturday, the 24th, after their exertions on the previous day. On Sunday, 25th, they had a short march to Ludlow, and on Monday, the 26th, at last, after all its dangers and perils, Byron brought his convoy safe to its destination, Shrewsbury.

Such was the Battle of Powick Bridge, or Wickefield, the first real fight of the war. It shewed two things. First, that much of the fighting would be done, as all of it was done here, with cold steel. It proved completely—

"   .   .   .   What perils do environ
" The men that meddle with cold iron."

The fight could not have lasted more than a few minutes—a quarter of an hour at the outside—but at the most moderate estimate some 50 of Fiennes' men were put *hors de combat*, killed, wounded, or drowned. Among them were Colonel Sandys, his Quarter-Master Douglas, and Captain Wingate. The Royalists had no officers killed, but, except Rupert, every one of those who rode into the Parliament ranks was wounded. Maurice had two cuts on the head, Wilmot a cut on the arm. A number of the Royalist rank and file were wounded, some as much from the kicks of the horses in the struggle as from the soldiers' swords. One of the future historians of the war, who was serving under Rupert, gives his experience, which was probably that of others. Bulstrode's horse, frightened at the novel situation, bolted, carrying its rider into the midst of the struggling crowd. He felt he was lost, but says that they were all so occupied in trying to escape that they took no notice of him, so he rode safely through the Parliament force, coming out unhurt, spared to write his " Memoirs and Reflections."

Clarendon says* that—

" Wingate and two or three Scotch officers were taken prisoners, with six or " seven cornets, many good horses, some arms, as those who ran away made " themselves as light as they could."

The second result of the fight was to lead to the belief that " Cavalry, if well led, were irresistible," a belief that survived for two centuries, and to some extent still exists. At best, Powick was only a cavalry skirmish. Had it taken place in 1643 or 1644 it would have been " unhonoured and unsung." Its importance was not the number of killed or wounded, the military trophies taken, or even the rescue of Byron's convoy. It was the lesson it taught the Parliamentary leaders. This is well put by Clarendon.*

---

* II., 20.

"This renconter proved of great advantage and benefit to the King, for it
"being the first action his horse had been brought to, and that party of the
"enemy being the most picked and choice men, it gave his troops great
"courage, and rendered the name of Prince Rupert very terrible, and
"exceedingly appalled the adversary, insomuch as they had not in a long time
"after any confidence in their horse, and their very numbers were much
"lessened by it. For that whole party being routed, and the chief officers of
"reputation either killed or taken (though the number lost upon the place was
"not considerable), there were very many men who never returned to the
"service, and, which was worse, for their own excuse, in all places talked
"aloud of the incredible and irresistible courage of Prince Rupert and the
"King's Horse."

But it is quite open to question if the result was not equally,
in another way, as disastrous to the Royalists, for it encouraged
and supported the idea that one charge of cavalry well pressed
home was all that was required to win a victory, an idea which
spelt disaster at Edgehill, Marston Moor, and Naseby.

But whatever were the results of Powick, nothing should be
said to detract from what was one of Rupert's most brilliant
feats of arms. With a force inferior in numbers and discipline,
at best a cavalry brigade, to march 20 miles, attack and defeat
a cavalry force of greater strength, supported by the main
army some 20,000 strong, and bring off in safety a valuable
convoy, was an achievement that any soldier might have
regarded with pride. Baxter probably only expressed the idea
of very many others when he said :—

"This sight quickly told me of the vanity of armies, and how little confidence is to be placed in them."

From Burford on Saturday, the 24th, Rupert sent to the
King his despatch of the fight.

"Sir,
"The bearer hereof will with all circumstance tell your Majesty of our
"proceedings at Worcester. I shall only say this : that upon your Majesty's
"commands to succour the town we went thither with our forces, and found the
"rebels on both sides of it. No ammunition, nor anything fitting to maintain
"so great a force as the Lord Essex would have brought that night, but all
"things in so great a disorder that certainly we had all been lost had we not,
"by a great chance, met with ten troops of their horse and five of their
"dragooners, which we did entirely rout and killed most of their chiefest officers.
"The manner and the names I leave to the bearer to tell you.

"Your Majesty will be pleased to accept this as a beginning of your officers
"and my duty, and I doubt not as (certainly) they behaved themselves all
"bravely and gallantly, that hereafter your Majesty shall find the same
"behaviour against a more considerable number. Of this your Majesty may
"be very confident, as also of the endeavour of,

"Sir,
"Your Majesty's most obedient
"From Bobfort,   Nephew and humble servant,
"Sept. 24th, 1642.   Rupert."*

Stories of the fight are very numerous. Most of them differ
in the details, but in all the main facts are as above stated.
One of the letters may be quoted :—

* Rushworth, V., p. 24.

" The variety of reports of the fight at Worcester is so confidently affirmed,
" on both sides, of the great and small loss on the Parliament side, that being
" not an eye-witness I cannot boldly report of either. Some of the troops that
" did run or come away from the fight report 300 or 400 were killed, and many
" wounded and made unserviceable. The like were of their horses. But the
" report of this town is still but 38 slain, and of note only Captain Douglas
" slain. Mr. Sandys is recovering, and past danger. I hear not of any men of
" note of the King's side slain. Sir John Strangeways' son was taken prisoner,
" who is exchanged for Captain Wingate. Prince Rupert and Prince Maurice
" were both hurt, and so were Mr. Wilmot and Sir Lewis Dives. . . .
" Yesternight, I do now (as I am writing) hear, came a letter to my Lord
" Wilmot from his son, and he that did read it did tell me to this purpose. . . .
" We met at Worcester with the Parliament force of equal strength, 10 troops
" of horse and 500 dragoons a piece. In a short time we overthrew 400 of the
" flower of their horse, and did take between 60 and 80 prisoners, which we set
" again at liberty with their promise not to take arms against the King. I
" was hurt in the back, Sir Lewis Dives in the shoulder, and Prince Maurice
" two cuts in the head, but none dangerous to any of us."*

The Parliament were greatly angered and disappointed at
their defeat. This is shewn most clearly in the steps they took
to hide it. Rupert's retreat on the same night with Byron's
convoy was cited as evidence of his defeat, and their writers
tried to keep up the spirits of the party by claiming a
victory for their forces. Nor did they rest here, Parliament
issued

" An ordinance directing thanks to be given to Almighty God in all churches
" and chapels throughout the land for the great success of the army at
" Worcester."

Lord Falkland, in a pamphlet, gave an account of the fight
in terms far from flattering to the Parliamentary troops. This
action of the Secretary of State Parliament strongly resented,
and ordered the pamphlet to be burnt by the common hang-
man. Nor were the Parliamentarians slow to put out their
own accounts. One of these given by Vicars, that Vicars who
is immortalised in " Hudibras " as being inspired " with ale or
viler liquors,"† was professed to be written and " faithfully
recited " to

" let the world see what desperate liars and faithless and shameless crackers
" the Cavaliers are to boast of these things and acts of theirs, whereof they have
" far juster cause to be ashamed and blush to speak of having bled so much for
" the same, especially at the issue hereof, also, which is without all question a
" contradiction, they having been forced to flie and forsake both the field and
" the City of Worcester, also, which they had in their possession but durst not
" abide in it ; the most noble and renouned Lord General being come tither
" with his forces and taken the said city without the least resistance or
" opposition."

The accuracy of Vicars' account will be seen by two extracts.
He alleges that the Parliamentarians were outnumbered by the
Royalists and compelled to retreat to the bridge, and con-
tinues—

" which (the bridge), notwithstanding all this great strength whereby we were
" so over-matched with numbers, we, in despight of all this power, made good

---

* M.H.R., XII. Rep., App. 2, p. 322.   † " Hudibras," Part I., Canto I., line 645.

" most resolutely, and forced them to a hasty retreat, yea, even to fly back three
" times, and killed at least ten of the Cavaliers dead on the place, besides many
" in the fields, whom they, as their ordinary trick is, conveyed away suddenly."

The other gives the account of Rupert's leaving Worcester :—

" Many of their soldiers and Cavaliers, being fled into Worcester before the
" end of the skirmish, were seen in the streets most woefully cut and mangled,
" some having their ears cut off, some the flesh of their heads sliced off, some
" with their very skulls hanging down, and they ready to fall down dead, their
" pistols and carbines being hewed and hacked away in slices, which it seems
" they held up for guard of their heads.   And about ten of the clock that night
" all Prince Rupert's forces as was toucht before fled away, together with many
" malignants of the city, both men, women, and children, to Ludlow, leaving
" behind them great stores of arms, even all (as 'twas verily believed) which
" they stole from Kidderminster and Bewdley, and more, too, yet they had dis-
" armed Worcester before the flight."[*]

Fiennes himself wrote two accounts of the fight.   The one—

" A true and exact relation of both of the battles fought by His Excellency
" Robert Earl of Essex and his forces against the Bloody Cavaliers, the one on
" the 23rd October last, near Kyneton, the other at Worcerter, 4°, 1642."

This " piece justicatif " may be judged from the title the attempt to compare Edgehill and Worcester.   The other,

" A narrative of the late battle before Worcester, taken by a gentleman of the
" Inns of Court from the mouth of Martin Fiennes, 4°, 1642,"

did not tend to clear up matters.   Powick had give Fiennes a holy horror of Rupert, a horror which was displayed when next they met, and Fiennes surrendered Bristol to him, an act for which he was rightly brought to a court-martial.

Curiously enough, the Parliamentary accounts have long been taken as the real version of the Powick fight.   Nash[‡] says the action is confusedly described by Clarendon and Ludlow.   He describes it in half-a-dozen lines very inaccurately, and quotes Baxter, Vicars, and " Mercurius' Rusticus."   Green[§] gives a still more misleading account, describing a battle on Pitchcroft which never took place, and making out that the battle at Powick was but part of a much larger fight.   But his authorities are only the newspapers of the time, which contained accounts more inaccurate, if possible, than the Russian newspapers now give of the Japanese War.   This is not by any means the only fight that depends for its existence on the fact that it is

"   .   .   .   registered by fame eternal
" In deathless pages of Diurnal."

The unfortunate thing is that all subsequent writers have copied Nash and Green, so that their erroneous versions have been accepted as history.   It was not until 1879, when " Webb's Civil War in Herefordshire" was published, that a

---

* " Jehovah Jireh," p. 166.   ‡ II., p. 264.   § I., p. 270.

true version of the Powick fight appeared, a version the accuracy of which is admitted and adopted by Mr. Gardner in his history.

Essex reached Pershore on the 23rd September. On Saturday, the 24th, he marched the nine miles to Worcester, arriving before the city about noon. No resistance or opposition was made to his entry, so he at once marched in and took possession of it. The fighting of the previous day had made the Parliament troops furious, and Worcester was treated precisely as if it had been taken by storm. The city was now to learn what a military occupation by a hostile force really meant. Neither Essex nor his men were likely to show any mercy. The town was not in the good graces of either. It was supposed to have helped the King; an example of what would be done to those towns who did this was necessary, and " this base town and country " was to furnish the example. The mayor was made to go down on his knees and beg the Lord-General's pardon for betraying the city. The troops had to be quartered; the first step, therefore, was to billet them on the citizens. Soley (the mayor) and Alderman Green were at once arrested and imprisoned, their offence being having surrendered the city to Byron without striking a blow. They were shortly afterwards sent up to London under a strong guard. Byron's convoy of plate had escaped, but Essex collected or took all he could lay hands upon in Worcester, including all that could be found in the mayor's house, making in all a waggon load of 2200lbs. of plate, as is said, and sent it up with the mayor and alderman as an offering to Parliament. An offering was also prepared for Essex himself. The city accounts shew :—" Paid for hogshead of Gascoyne wine and sugar loaves given to the Earl of Essex, being in the city with his army, £8."

Sunday, September 25th, the day after Essex arrived in Worcester, was long remembered there. The parochial clergy were made by force to surrender their pulpits to the so-called chaplains of the various regiments, persons who the Royalists called " Military Levites," and from them the Worcester citizens had a pouring out of the Word. If nothing else their sermons were long. It is true Baxter speaks highly of their discourses, but he is almost the only person who does so. But while the Word was poured forth, and the preachers were explaining that Essex's men had already

> "   .   .   .   done enough to purchase
> " Thanksgiving-day among the churches,"

the soldiers looked at more carnal matters. The choice was given to the parish churches to pay or to be spoiled of their goods. In the accounts of St. Michael's appears this entry :—

"Given to captain and soldiers for preserving our church goods and "writings, 10s. 4d."

And this is probably only a specimen of the treatment served out to all.

The parish churches, however, fared well in comparison with the Cathedral. The fanatical bigotry of the Puritan party in this their first great triumph led them to commit acts of which even they were afterwards ashamed. The organ, the service books, the vestments, the windows, in fact everything that however remotely bore the mark of the beast, were ruthlessly destroyed. But they did not rest satisfied with merely destroying the survivals of so-called Papistical idolatry, the Cathedral was put to military uses. In the nave horses were stabled, camp fires lit, military courts held. The choir and aisles were used as latrines for the soldiers. Rings and staples, the traces of which still remain, were fastened to the recesses in the cloisters, for tethering the horses in the places where the monks had worked. This may have been done on the ground of necessity, as there would be difficulty in finding accommodation on so short notice for several thousand horses. Even we in our own days have known churches and places of worship used for quarters for troops and horses. But no such excuse is possible for the bigoted joy of the Puritan soldiers in the open dishonour of all holy things. Dragoons put on the surplices and vestments of the Cathedral clergy, and danced in them about the streets; books were burnt; profane imitations of religious services gone through. Essex allowed his soldiers to indulge in these excesses without any remonstrance. Making every allowance for the strong anti-ecclesiastical feeling that was then so rife, to the fact that the mass of the people believed, and honestly believed, that Charles was doing his best to introduce into the country the religion they hated, that Worcester was the first town that had been taken, and that the Puritan soldiers were thirsting to shew their "zeal for the Lord," still it is a disgrace to Essex that he made not the smallest attempt to keep in check the religious excesses of his men. There can be little doubt that this was the time when all the injury to the Cathedral at Worcester was done, yet with a strange injustice all these ungodly acts of the godliest soldiery are always ascribed to Cromwell, who was nowhere near Worcester, and Essex's name is never even mentioned. Cromwell has much to answer for, but the ruin and spoil of the ecclesiastical buildings and ornaments of Worcester should not be laid to his charge.

Rupert had conveyed both his own wounded and some of those of the Parliament from Powick to Worcester, not being able to take them with him to Shrewsbury they were left at Worcester. Among them was the Kentish Colonel, Sandys, who had taken a leading part in the Powick fight. Whether from neglect or some other cause his wounds, which had first been considered as curable, became rapidly worse; blood poisoning set in, and his case became hopeless. Lying there dying he was the subject of a violent theological controversy. He was first attended by a Royalist chaplain, to whom it was said Sandys expressed regret at having taken up arms against his Sovereign. Gratified by this proof of the success of his ministrations, the chaplain rushed into print and published the dying speech and confession of the expiring penitent. With Essex's army there was serving as chaplain to Holles' Regiment Obadiah Sedgewick, one of the most fanatical of the fanatics of that day. He at once took steps to bring back the wanderer to the fold, and, having got from the dying man what he considered a satisfactory assurance of his faith, like his Episcopalian rival, he published for the edification of the world the record of his success. The Royalist was not to be beaten; he again took Sandys in hand. A war of pamphlets followed. The surgeons in Essex's army seemed only to keep the wounded man alive that he might serve to shew the bigotry of the two parties. All the month Essex remained in Worcester the contest raged. Each party told Sandys that his sufferings were on account of his sin in listening to the other. An extract from a Royalist account will shew the spirit of the controversy:—

"In his thigh the flesh did daily rot and putrefy, and was cut away by "degrees even to leaving of the bones naked, and stunk in so loathsome a "manner that as he was a burden to himself so to his friends, too, and "those that were about him being hardly able, for the noisomeness of the "smell, either to come near him, or to do the office of necessary attendance, or "so much as to endure the room where he lay, so intolerable was the stench and "so offensive."*

"Master Cotterell, an orthodox, godly minister, parson of St. Andrew's, Worcester," and "Obadiah Sedgewick, a scandalous, seditious minister of Essex," quarelled over the dying man, as to whether he was fit to receive the sacrament. Their difference being on the view they took of the sin and guilt of rebellion, Cotterell accused Sedgewick of having brought "the dog back to his vomit." The Royalist account does not give Sedgewick's reply; it was most likely forcible and scriptural. The doctor advised a third minister (Mr. Halsetor, the rector of St. Nicholas) to be sent for, but the Royalist account says this man drove Sandys mad, and he died raving. The saddest matter followed. On hearing of his wounds his wife with her son came to nurse him. Small-pox had broken out among the wounded. She and her son took it, and she died. Sandys and his wife were buried in the Cathedral; the Royalist writer

---

* "Mercurius' Rusticus," p. 126.

calling attention to the fact that as Sandys' grandfather had
been Bishop of that Church, that Sandys' death was the result
of failing to " look to the Rock from whence he was hewn."

Essex settled his quarters at Worcester, and from there
directed the movements of his troops. One of his early orders
was to set up in the Market Place a gallows, on which the
citizens who took over to Powick, on the 23rd September, the
news that led Fiennes to advance to his ruin should be hung.
As Essex wanted money, the citizens were required to pay a
contribution of £5000. The soldiers who were billeted in the
town were not great respecters of property, and did a good
deal of damage, besides what they took from the citizens. In
the St. Michael's accounts there is an entry of a payment of
17d. for repairing " Widow Ward's chimney broken down by
the soldiers." But Essex did not rest content with plundering
the citizens. He considered it necessary to put the city into
a state of defence, to have the old fortifications repaired
and new ones erected. So the citizens were made to
work on them. Forced labour on fortifications was a
new experience for the Worcester men, not much to their
taste; there was much grumbling. But they did not stop at
grumbling. According to one of the tracts of the time, a wonderful gunpowder plot was devised against Essex at St. Peter's
Church, Worcester. It was, however, discovered. In order to
prevent help being sent to the King—at least, this was the
reason given—the houses of suspected malignants were
searched for arms. Steps were taken for properly securing
and arming the militia. Parliament appointed a committee of
12, drew up rules for their procedure, and directed them so to
manage the County as to bring it under the control of the
Parliament. The Corporation was reformed; the Royalist
members were turned out and their places supplied by
supporters of the Parliament. The two County Members,
Sergeant Wilde and Salway, with the great Herefordshire
Parliamentarian, Sir Robert Harley, were sent down by Parliament to advise and assist Essex in carrying out and executing
whatever would be of service to the Parliament. As Essex
was only at Worcester for a month, it will be seen that he was
far from idle, as in addition to the civil work he had all the
work of the army to do as well.

There is an account of the proceedings of Essex's army at
Worcester, written by one of his soldiers, Nehemiah Wharton.
He had been an apprentice to Mr. George Willingham,
merchant at the Golden Anchor in St. Swithin's Lane,
London, and was probably one of the 5000 Londoners who
"listed themselves " under the Earl of Essex on the 26th July in
Moorfields, when they were distributed into regiments.
Wharton writes a series of letters to " his late master and

honoured friend," and his letters give details of the service, and a picture of the life in the Parliament army that no other account supplies. The following is his account of Worcester :—

" Worcestershire is a pleasant, fruitful, and rich country, abounding in corn, " woods, pastures, hills, and valleys. Every hedge and highway beset with " fruit, but especially with pears, whereof they make that pleasant drink called " perry, which they sell for a penny a quart, though better than ever you tasted " in London. The city is more large than any I have seen since I left London. " It abounds in outward things, but for want of the Word the people perish. It " is pleasantly situated, exceeding populous, and doubtless very rich, on the east " bank of that famous river, the Severn. The walls in the form of a triangle ; " the gates seven. There is a very stately Cathedral, called St. Mary's, in " which there are many stately monuments ; among the rest in the middle of " the choir is the monument of King John, all of white marble, with his picture " thereon to the life. Sir, our army did little think ever to have seen Worcester, " but the providence of God hath brought us thither ; and had it not, the city " is so vile, resembles Sodom and is the very emblem of Gomorrah, and doubt- " less it would have been worse than either Algiers or Malta— a very den of " thieves, and a receptacle and refuge for all the hell hounds of the County."*

While Essex had been settling matters in Worcester, the Royalists had been pushing on their preparations. Reinforcements were daily arriving at Shrewsbury, not only from Wales but also from Lancashire.

" The King is expecting the forces of my Lord Marquis Hertford and my " Lord of Derby,"†

Wilmot writes to his father. The report in London was that the King

" intendeth to advance towards this town this week, but hath fortified Shrews- " bury and Bridgnorth, and intendeth to leave garrisons in them. His army, " horse and foot (as information cometh), 20,000, some say well armed, others " report not at all to be so, and for his further strength he expecteth my Lord " Marquis Hertford, and my Lord Strange, with their troops, both of horse and " foot. My Lord-General is reported to have 16 regiments of horse and foot, " and all well armed and well paid. £20,000 went down on Saturday last unto " him, convoyed by Captain Rigby's troop of horse."†

In order to put Essex off his guard, a report was set on foot that Charles intended to advance to London by way of Worcester. This made it necessary for Essex to take some steps to prevent it. Rupert was sent to Bridgnorth, and as a counter move Lord Brooke was sent with his regiment to occupy Kidderminster, and he detached Lord Wharton to Bewdley. Essex, sending troops to Kidderminster, made people believe that he intended to advance and attack the King. It was said that Essex was hastening from Worcester into Shropshire,

" that the rest of the King's forces that were at Worcester are retired to Bridg- ' north, where it is thought the Earl of Essex will not let them rest long."

But Essex had no such intention. From a letter of Lord Mandeville's to Pym, if he had had such an idea he might

---

* Archæologia, xxxv., 328.   † H.M.R., xii. Rep., App. 2, p. 323

not have been able to carry it out. Lord Mandeville·
writes :—

"We are still at Worcester, watching what the King will do. It is rumoured
"that he will march towards London on Monday next ; others think that he
"will advance towards us, which may be probable, because he hath sent 2000
"foot into Bridgnorth. I pray, haste down the Scotch Commanders. There is
"some suspicion that our artillerymen are not as they should be. If this prove
"a truth we are but in ill condition for action."

Parliament were impatient that something should be done.
They ordered the bailiffs and officers of Droitwich to keep the
magazine of arms at Droitwich, and directed that £300 should
be collected in Worcestershire for "coat and conduct money."
As the King was daily increasing in strength, and as that
strength mainly came from Wales, Essex was ordered to do all
in his power to intercept it. Accordingly, on the 30th
September, a column of 900 foot, three troops of horse, and
two guns, under the command of the Earl of Stamford, were
sent to occupy Hereford. With Lord Stamford was Massey
and also Nehemiah Wharton, who complains that they had to
stand in the mud for a long time before Hereford. The
difficulties that Stamford met with appear to have been caused
far more by the state of the roads and the state of the weather
than from any Royalist opposition. What difficulties there
were did not long detain him. Hereford was occupied without
opposition. Stamford had thus placed himself on the line of
the King's communication between Shrewsbury and South
Wales. Edward Reed wrote to Sir John Coke from London,
on the 10th October, 1642 :—

"Your neighbour, by Loughborough, my Lord of Stamford, hath taken
"Hereford, and is in it now, unto whom the town and country hath given a
"contribution in monies, and so hath the town of Worcester, £3000 as I hear.
"Bewdley is not as yet taken by either party."

In this last item of news the writer was wrong; Lord Brooke
had sent Lord Wharton on to Bewdley, and he was occupying
it. Some statements say that he drove out Sir Thomas
Lyttelton, who was appointed governor of it for the King, and
was said to be holding it for him, but it is not clear if Wharton's
garrison went in before or after the King moved from Shrewsbury. In the Kidderminster register of burials there is an
entry under the 14th October :—

"Buried, one Thomas Ringe, a Pliament souldier, that brake his necke,
"falling down the rocke towards Courfield into the Holloway that leads to
"Bewdley."

In the Bewdley accounts for 1642 are the following
entries :—

"Paid for candles when the soldiers did watch	o	o	6 "
"Paid for a drum by Mr. Bayliffe, Application	o	11	6 "
"Paid for wine and sugar for Sir Thomas Littleton	o	3	8 "

A garrison was also placed at Stourbridge.

It was not only to the north of the County that Essex directed his attention. A garrison was placed at Tewkesbury to close the line of the Avon, keep open his communication with Gloucester; to keep his troops in readiness for work the County was scoured by detachments, who went nominally to search the houses of malignants for arms, but in reality to plunder and carry off all they could. Two instances, one of a party of Parliamentarians from Gloucester, the other of some of Essex's men from Worcester, will shew what persons who dwelt in the County had to endure.

Mr. Bartlett lived at Castle Morton, a man so popular in his district that if any other day than Ledbury Fair day had been selected for a search of his house it is said all the country side would have come to his defence. As it was everyone was at Ledbury Fair. Some soldiers from Gloucester and Tewkesbury, taking advantage of this, came to Castle Morton, secured the village and road, and surrounded Mr. Bartlett's house. Their commander, Captain Scriven, was the son of an ironmonger at Gloucester. On Scriven entering the house, Bartlett inquired what he came for. Scriven replied to search for arms. Alas! said Bartlett, you are like to lose your labour, for Justice Salway (the County Member) has already been here, but adding, you had better see if you can find any gleanings after the other has had the full vintage. Bartlett gave them some beer. While sitting drinking, Scriven saw Bartlett's sword hanging up on the wainscot, and asked if that was not arms ? Bartlett replied :—

"No more than is necessary for every honest man to defend himself on the "highway."

Scriven took possession of Bartlett's sword, and also of his son's. When the son came in Scriven noticed a ruby ring on his band string, and took it from him. Scriven then searched Bartlett's pockets, and took all the money he could find, between £2 and £3. Bartlett was wearing a scarlet "Gippo." Scriven took a fancy to it, and ordered Bartlett to take it off, but he declined, asking that he should not be robbed both of money and clothes. Scriven then asked Bartlett where he kept his money and plate, threatening to kill him if he did not say at once. As Bartlett declined, Scriven's men seized his housekeeper, and to make her tell presented a pistol at her breast, while others of the soldiers pricked her with the points of their swords. As she refused to say anything they searched the house. Scriven began with Mrs. Bartlett's room, took her watch, broke open her trunk and took out of it £600, all her linen, money, plate, jewels, bracelets, and amongst other things a "Cock Eagle's Stone, for which 30 pieces had been offered by a phissition and refused." Having got all the plunder he cared for, Scriven allowed his men to take what they liked.

" In a confused tumult they rush into the house, hunt from the
" parlour to the kitchen, from thence by the chambers to the garrets.
" Besides Mr. Bartlett's, his wife's and children's wearing apparel, they
" rob the servants' clothes, and carry off whatever they can put their
" hands on. They found Mr. Bartlett's sweetmeats, but scattered them
" upon the floor, not daring to taste them, as they feared poison. Except
" bedding, pewter, and lumber, they left nothing behind them, for besides two
" horses laden with the best things—Scriven's own plunder—there being 150
" rebels, each rebel returned with a pack at his back. As for beer and perry,
" what they could not drink they spoilt, pouring it out on the ground. They
" wound up with saying they had learnt Bartlett a lesson, and left him not
" worth a groat."*

Some days after a party of Essex's men from Worcester
visited Bartlett and searched his house for arms.

" They took away a good store of bacon from his roof, beef out of the
" powdering tub, the pots, pans, and kettles, pewter to great value, all the pro-
" visions for hospitality and housekeeping, and then broke the spits as
" unnecessary utensils. They sold his bedding, carried away in carts, which
" they compelled to work for them, all chairs, stools, couches, and trunks."

Within the next year Bartlett's house was searched three
times more for arms. The searchers carried off all his kitchen
stuff, five horses,

" abusing Mrs. Bartlett in beastly, immodest, scurrilous language, offensive to
" Christian ears."

On one of these searchings the officer in command was asked
to join in eating a stubble goose, which one of the soldiers had
plundered. He refused, as he could not eat what was
stolen, but taking Mr. Bartlett's mare from the stable rode
away upon it.

Among the plunder were some partridges, which they were
asked to leave as they were kept for a lady about to be
confined. They refused, saying if they could get her they
would soon make her so she would not need partridges, as
they had killed old men, women, and children.

" And so," the account continues, " boasting himself in his sin and glorying in
" his shame, without regard had to the dangerous longings of a pregnant
" woman if not satisfied, took them away. So truly is that of the prophet
" verified in these miscreants. ' They declare their sin as Sodom, they hide
" it not. Woe unto their souls, for they have rewarded evil unto themselves.' "†

Such is a Royalist account of Parliamentary plunderings.
How far it is true may be doubtful, but it shews at least that
the search for arms was only the pretext—the real object was
plunder.

Nehemiah Wharton gives the other instance of a search for
arms at Sir William Russell's, at Strensham. It is interesting
as being a typical account of the spirit in which plundering was
carried on :—‡

" Tuesday, our soldiers, by commission from his Excellency, marched seven
" miles to Sir William Russell's house, and pillaged unto the bare walls.

---

* " Mercurius' Rusticus," p. 188.   † " Mercurius' Rusticus," p. 191.
‡ Archæologia, xxxv., 330.

"Wednesday, we fasted, and Mr. Obadiah Sedgewick preached unto us, whom
"the Lord extraordinarily assisted, so that his doctrine wrought wonderfully
"upon many of us, and doubtless hath fitted many of us for death, which we all
"shortly expect. Thursday, his Excellency proclaimed that whoever had any
"of the goods of the Cavaliers in custody should forthwith surrender them this
"day. . . . . I have nothing of worth to present you with, but I have
"sent you the gods of the Cavaliers enclosed. They are pillage taken from Sir
"William Russell's, of which I never yet got the worth of one farthing, for it is
"constantly the prey of the ruder sort of solders, whose society, blessed be God,
"I hate and avoid."

The time had now come when Essex's plundering expeditions
had to cease. Charles had collected and equipped such a force
as enabled him to take the field. This the Parliament heard
of, and at once became excited as to the result. A letter of the
11th October, 1642, from London shews this :—*

"The news here is that the King is coming hither, and there is order from
"the Parliament to all counties to make all preparations for their defence.
"Here is great watch in the city night and day by the train bands, and beyond
"us as far as the Charter House there is a court of guard of the train bands
"watches every night."

On the 15th October another letter from London says :—

"Little news is here stirring, our expectations being from the armies, which
"they say are advanced one towards the other. His Majesty to Bridgnorth and
"the other to Bewdley, both resolving to put the difference to a speedy issue."†

Meanwhile, as he was getting ready to fight, a last attempt
had been made by Charles to negotiate. On the 27th
September, at Chester, he issued a declaration pointing out the
refusal of the Parliament to treat with him for the relief of
the kingdom. He goes on to refer to the

"barbarous, sacrilegious inhumanity exercised by the Parliament soldiers in
"churches, as in Canterbury, Worcester, Oxford, and other places."‡

This the Parliament felt required an answer, so they drew
up a petition, which they sent by Sir Philip Stapleton to
Essex, and ordered him to send it on to the King. Charles was
at Bridgnorth. Essex sent a messenger to the King from
Worcester, asking for a safe conduct for the officer who
would come to present the petition. This Charles refused,
as he declined to receive a petition from rebels. As a
last resort Essex sent Fleetwood (then only a private
in the cuirassiers) to Bridgnorth to deliver the petition.
Charles refused to see him, or to receive anything from
a horseman whose sword was drawn against his King. The
Earl of Bedford, who was at Worcester, on hearing of
this, wrote to the Committee for the Safety of the Kingdom, saying that the King refused to receive any petition
from the Lord General, he being declared a traitor. This
decision was said to be "a most high indignity and scorn
on the authority of Parliament, and destroying all chance of
peace."

---

* H.M.R., 12 Rep., App. 2, p. 323.   † Ib.   ‡ Rushworth, v., p. 7

The petition had done its work. Charles was ready to move, all his preparations were complete, and he began his march on London. His object was to out-manœuvre Essex, get between him and London, and march direct on to it. As a blind, and to make Essex believe that the advance was to be upon Worcester. Rupert was ordered to march from Bridgnorth towards Kidderminster. This was quite successful. Lord Brooke and Lord Wharton at once fell back to Bewdley and Kidderminster without attempting to fight. To out-manœuvre Essex, Charles extended his left and marched direct on London. To keep the King's march secret and Essex employed for a day or two was the object of Rupert's march, and this object was very effectually carried out. Rupert marched on Monday, October 10th, from Shrewsbury to Shifnal, on the 11th to Wolverhampton. Here he stayed the 12th. On the 13th he marched to Mere, Mr. Moseley's, in Enville Parish; on the 14th to Mr. Foley's, at Stourbridge, where he remained for three days, threatening the flank of Lord Brooke's brigade, thus causing him and Lord Wharton to fall back.

"On Tuesday letters came from my Lord Wharton, that he had made a "soldier-like retreat from Kidderminster, excusing himself not fighting with "Prince Rupert in regard to the inequality of numbers, but it is commonly and "confidently reported by others that for haste and fear he left some waggons "and three or four pieces of ordnance behind him. There came last night "from Worcester 3200 weight of plate."

"There came a post this day at noon, that the £400,000 sent to his "Excellency was come safe to Worcester. It was a booty Prince Rupert "aimed at, but his intelligence or his tribe was not good."*

Meanwhile the King had started from Shrewsbury on his march for London, Essex and his officers being completely deceived by Rupert's march, expecting Charles to advance from Shrewsbury to Kidderminster and to Worcester.

On the 17th October, while this movement was going on, Lord Coventry sent up a petition to Parliament, submitting himself to the House,

"is sorry to have offended in not replying to their Lordships' summons, but he "had also received His Majesty's summons to attend him at York."

This is of importance as shewing the unreliability of the usual statement that Lord Coventry had been in command at Worcester when Byron was there, and had taken part in the resistance to Fiennes when he came before it.

It is not quite clear when Essex learnt of Charles' advance and that Rupert's move was only to blind him. Rupert stayed at Stourbridge till Monday, the 17th October, when he marched across to King's Norton. On Tuesday, 18th, he went to Solihull, the King arriving on the same day at Meriden Heath,

---

* H.M.R., VII., p. 530.

and, it is added, "where we had the first appearance of an army." Charles had marched by Aston, where he slept on the 16th. On the 17th, as he passed through Birmingham, the inhabitants seized some of the Royal carriages containing plate and other valuables, and sent them off to the Parliament garrison in Warwick Castle. They also cut off all stragglers and small parties, sending them prisoners to Coventry. Hence, says Hutton,* the origin of the expression, "Sent to Coventry." This attack on his carriages greatly enraged Charles, and, it is said, led him to give Rupert instructions next year to teach the people of Birmingham their duty.

If any reliance is to be placed on a tract of the time, Rupert's march on October 17th from Stourbridge to King's Norton did not pass without fighting. The tract, which contains the only record of the fight that has survived, is entitled:—

"A true relation of a great and cruel battle fought by the Lord Willoughby,
"of Parham, with 800 horse and foot, who were going to the Lord Generall,
"against Prince Robert, with 9 troops of horse and 300 foot, near Brumegum,
"in Warwickshire, October 17th; declaring also the manner of the Lord
"Willoughbie's obtaining the victory, killing about 50 of the Cavaliers and
"taking 20 prisoners, with the loss of 20 men. Sent in a letter from his
"Excellencie to the House of Commons, and read in the said House October
"18th. Printed for Richard West, October 20th. A renouned victory
"obtained by the Lord Willoughby, of Parham, against Prince Rupert, within
"three miles of Brumegum, October 18th."

The passage relating to the battle is as follows:—

"It is also informed by divers letters from Brumegum that the Lord
"Willoughby, of Parham, with about 800 horse and foot, in his march towards
"the Lord Generall, met Prince Robert, with 8 troops of horse and about 300
"foot two or three miles from Brumegum, and gave him battle, which was very
"fierce and cruel on either side, but at length the Prince's soldiers retreated
"and fled, there being slain of the malignants about 80 and 20 taken prisoners,
"and of the Lord Willoughbie's side about 17. The fight being ended, the
"Lord Willoughby, with his forces, marched forward to his Excellency, with
'whom he hath now joined himself."

What was the locality of the fight it is difficult to say beyond this: if fought on the 17th it was somewhere between Stourbridge and King's Norton, and so in Worcestershire. Wherever it was, each party, when it was over, made their way to their destination—Rupert to join the King, Lord Willoughby to join the Lord General. If he did not know it before, Lord Willoughby may have conveyed Essex the news of the King's march. Essex knew it on the 17th, or the 18th at latest. On

"Wednesday, the 19th, Essex marched from Worcester, upon intelligence that
"the Royal army was removed from Shrewsbury and Bridgnorth, and
"bending southwards. Our train of artillery was so unready through want
"of draught horses, and through other omissions of Monsieur Du Coys, that

---

* Hist. of Birmingham, p. 48.

" we were forced to leave it behind to follow us, and with it the regiments of
" Colonel Hampden and Colonel Grantham."

Possibly Viscount Mandeville's surmise about the artillery* was
correct.

Charles' manœuvre was quite successful.   He had got
between Essex and London, and gained two days' march
upon him.   All he had to do now was to press on; there was
no force between him and London.   He was, however, advised
to give up this advantage, and not leave an unbroken army in
his rear; so he halted, turned round and faced Essex, and on
Sunday, October 23rd, the Battle of Edgehill was fought.

The result of Edgehill was to remove the main portion of
the war from Worcestershire.   With this exception at first
there was no great change.   The Parliament still held Hereford,
Gloucester, Tewkesbury, and Worcester.   But Sir Thomas
Lyttelton took possession of Bewdley for the King, and very
soon afterwards Sandys took possession of Evesham.   Colonel
Thomas Essex, with his regiment, was sent to Worcester, he
being appointed governor.   He had no easy task before him,
in spite of a sort of welcome that was given him, the churchwardens of St. Michael's providing him with "a bottle of
white wine and sugar" at the Talbot; the Worcester people
were not best pleased with the treatment they had received
from the Lord General and his soldiers.   Even if they had
been, the positions of the governors in the West Midland
garrisons had become difficult.   The Parliamentary army had
been withdrawn from this district to the neighbourhood
of London, and there did not seem to be much prospect
of their returning.   Supplies were difficult to get, and the
force at the governor's disposal was but small.   The garrison at
Worcester was, if not in a hostile, certainly not in a friendly
district, so it had become a grave matter to consider not
only if any real good could be gained by its maintenance, but
if maintained could its safety be provided for.   Colonel
Essex felt the full force of these considerations.   He soon
found that Worcester had become no place for him, and that
it was very doubtful if he could maintain himself there if
attacked.   The way to retreat was now open; how long it
might remain so it was impossible to say.   Gloucester would
for many reasons be a safer and better quarter, so to Gloucester
he determined to go.   His stay at Worcester was very brief.
He arrived at the end of October, early in November he, with
the troops who formed his garrison, marched off to Gloucester.
He got the citizens to pay him £40 at the time of his
departure to free the city from plundering.   His landlord,
or rather the man who owned the house where he had his

---

quarters, was paid £5 "for the spoiling of his goods by entertaining the governor, Essex." With Essex's abandonment of Worcester the last Parliament garrison in the County was withdrawn. So far as any military force went the County was now held entirely for the King. In November, 1642, Sir William Russell took possession of Worcester on the King's behalf, hoisted the Royal Standard, and from that date until July, 1646, Worcester remained a Royal garrison.

The evacuation of Worcester by Colonel Essex had isolated Hereford, and made Lord Stamford's position there untenable. It soon came home to him that it was quite impossible for him to hold it. He wrote to the Parliament:—

"I am confident had I not kept this unworthy city, a torrent of Papists and "malignants had fallen down, which might have augmented the adversaries to "an infinite number. Now, my Lord, we have as much heart and courage left "us as ever we had, but we have neither money nor credit for bread ; our hay and "provender being very scant. Yet so long as I can find any means of "subsistence I shall remain here. The country, as well as this vile city, are "so base and malignant that although the roguish army of the Welsh Papists "and other vagabonds that were beaten in the first battle in Warwickshire do "plunder, kill, murder, and destroy men and women, take away all their goods "and cattle, yet such is their hatred to our condition that they would rather be "so used than be rescued by us."*

Such being Stamford's account of his own position at Hereford, it is hardly to be wondered that he took the first opportunity to relieve himself from it. Finding that Colonel Essex had come to the conclusion that Worcester was no longer tenable, Stamford decided that Hereford was even less so. To make matters worse, a Royalist force from Monmouthshire was advancing on Hereford, under Sir Richard Lawdey. Stamford was practically his own master. A commission was about to issue, appointing him

"Commander-in-Chief of all the Parliamentary forces in the Counties of "Hereford, Gloucester, Salop, and Worcester, with the power of appointing "officers, and making his residence anywhere in any of those counties, or in "the Principality of Wales, according to his convenience as Governor of the "whole."†

If he was to be of any use to the Parliament he should be at head-quarters, not at an outlying garrison. So he determined to abandon Hereford and retire on Gloucester. On the 3rd December he marched out. He had held it from the beginning of October—for over two months—in circumstances of considerable difficulty. He could hold it no longer.

Stamford's evacuation of Hereford did for Herefordshire what Essex's evacuation of Worcester had done for Worcestershire. It placed the whole county in the King's hands. It was a great success for the Royalists. The road was once

---

* Webb's Civil War in Herefordshire, Vol. I., p. 204.   † Lord's Journals, Dec. 13, 1642.

more open and undisturbed for the King to draw his supplies from Wales. A letter dated the 13th December states :—

"One from Worcester has informed me that on Sunday the Earl of Stamford "went away from Hereford, having plundered and burnt several houses there. "News had come to Worcester that their carriages could not pass, but that "they were all in a dirty lane in the way towards Gloucester. The Hereford "people sent 700 horse after them, but with what success is not known. "Hopton came into Ledbury with colours and drum, and called on the men to "join him. One answered him that he had received His Majesty's word to "the contrary, and he should not be a traitor. Others answered to the same "manner, so he went out of Ledbury, and his colours and drum were taken "from him. It is said that Hopton has since come to Worcester and turned "to the King's part."*

How important it was for the King to have the road to Wales open was very soon to be demonstrated. A letter dated 2nd January, 1643, says :—

"My Lord Marquis Hertford and my Lord Herbert are now with the King "at Oxford with 4000 men, and 3000 they have left at Worcester, and some at "Hereford. Being left the day before by my Lord Stamford, before my Lord "Marquis his coming hither."†

As Russell had occupied Worcester, so Lawdey now occupied Hereford for the King. Thus the whole of the two counties —Hereford and Worcester—had returned to their allegiance.

Charles, after the affair at Brentford, made his head-quarters for a time at Reading. At the beginning of December he removed from Reading to Oxford, which place was for the future the head-quarters of the Royalist party. No further fighting took place in Worcestershire during the rest of 1642. At no time during the war did the King's prospects appear more hopeful than at the end of December of that year. The district had been swept clear of the enemy, and Charles was again, so far as Worcestershire went, "over all persons and in all courses, as well ecclesiastical as civil, supreme."

---

* H.M.R., V. Rept., p 142.   † H.M.R., XII. Rept., pt. 2, 329.

UPTON-ON-SEVERN BRIDGE.

PULLED DOWN 1852.   THE ARCHES UNDER THE CHURCH ARE THOSE DESTROYED IN 1651.

Reproduced from "Hanley Castle," by permission of the Publisher, Wm. North, Tewkesbury.

CHAPTER II.

1643.

In January, 1643, the King's position was as favourable as possible, far more so than could have been expected. His communications with Wales were uninterrupted; his forces held the Thames Valley as far as Reading; all the Severn Valley to Gloucester was in his hands. A glance at the map will shew what the Royalists had to do. To clear the Parliament troops from the Cotswolds, so as to open the road to the west, with an alternative route to Wales, to press on up the Thames Valley, and threaten, if they did not attack, London. Except so far as they directly affect Worcestershire, it will not be necessary to say anything about the movements outside the County. Some mention will have to be made of those that concerned Worcestershire.

In Worcestershire Sir William Russell held Worcester for the King, Colonel Leveson held Dudley, Colonel Sandys first and then Colonel Washington Evesham, Sir Thomas Lyttelton Bewdley. It is not quite clear if there was then a garrison at Hartlebury. The same may be said of the other Worcestershire garrisons.

In Gloucestershire it was different. Lord Stamford had left Hereford in December for Gloucester. Soon after arriving there he had been ordered to the west, and had left Massey in temporary command. Massey at once acted on the offensive, and proceeded to occupy Tewkesbury, making it into a garrison. The importance of this town is shewn by the number of times it was taken and re-taken. Placed at the junction of the Severn and the Avon, it at once commanded the way into South Worcestershire and also into the Cotswolds. It also controlled the Avon Valley. Had it only had a bridge over the Severn it would have been the most important place in the district. There was a bridge over the Avon, but nothing over the Severn nearer than Upton on the north and Gloucester on the south. Although it was garrisoned for the next three years, it does not seem ever to have been a walled town, or to have had any regular works to protect it. This is probably the reason it changed hands so often.

About 10 miles from Tewkesbury is the town of Winchcombe. This was on the road into the hills, and was in possession of the Royalists. Sudeley Castle, which is close to Winchcombe, was then garrisoned by Lord Chandos for the King. Further away in the hills was Cirencester, a fairly strong town, held by the Parliament in force. Parties from here were able to march out, foray, and disturb the Royal troops at Burford, Chipping Norton, and Stow-on-the-Wold.

Warwickshire was as strongly Parliamentary as Worcestershire was Royalist. Coventry, Warwick, and Kenilworth held garrisons for the Parliament.

The Parliament had a considerable following in Staffordshire, but so had the King. Stafford was held for the Parliamen*, Lichfield for the King.

In Shropshire, also, the Parliament had a large following. They held Ludlow, Bridgnorth, and Wem, the King holding Shrewsbury.

Parliament, seeing the importance of having some officer who would take the command and look after their interests, proceeded in the beginning of 1643 to "associate" the counties, that is to unite them under one officer, who should have very large power, both military and civil. The counties now associated were the County of Warwick, the City and County of Coventry, the County of Stafford, and the City and County of Lichfield. This was done by the Ordinance of Association, which directed that the Lord Lieutenant and the committee named in the ordinance

"should associate themselves to protect the counties, raise horse and foot, "money and plate, give battle, fight, and levy war, put to execution of death, "and destroy all who should levy war against the Parliament."*

They were to obey the Lord General Essex, and next after him their Lord Lieutenant Lord Brooke, who had already served in Worcestershire, holding Kidderminster and Stourbridge during the time Essex was at Worcester. Brooke was also appointed general of the forces of the two associated counties of Stafford and Warwick. So on the north and the east of Worcestershire the Parliament had a responsible organization under a skilled officer to look after their interests. There was, however, nothing of the kind in the south and west. There everything depended on one man, who was in a subordinate position, Mássey; but he was a host in himself, and did more for the Parliament than any association could have done.

Lord Brooke at once got to work, raised some forces, and determined to dislodge the Royalists from the position they had taken up in the Close at Lichfield. He laid siege to the place, but was killed by a shot from the walls. The Close, however, was afterwards taken. Later on in the year the Earl of

---

* Rushworth V., 103.

Denbigh was appointed to succeed Lord Brooke as head of the association.

The Royalists had no officer in supreme command at the beginning of the year except Lord Capel. The want of such a person was keenly felt, so at the end of March Prince Maurice was appointed to the post.

Such being the positions of the two parties, their general ideas, so far as they had any, were, on the part of the Royalists, to clear the Cotswold country of the Parliament troops, and thus having secured their right flank and rear from attack, press on against Essex, drive him back on London on their left, and press on into the west on their right. If these plans were carried out the main movements of the war would be entirely removed from Worcestershire. The Parliament plan was that the two wings of their army, under Essex on the right and Waller on the left, should drive back the Royalists from the Severn and Thames valleys, unite near Oxford, force back the King into Wales, so cut him off from the north-west and London, in fact, entirely isolate him, and compel him either to leave the country or surrender.

In pursuance of the Parliament's plan, Sir William Waller was appointed to command the Parliament forces in the west, with his head-quarters at Bristol.

Wilmot had already, in December, 1642, stormed and carried Marlborough, and the Royalists were only waiting for reinforcements to proceed with their plan.

The Parliament generals, to carry out their scheme of operations, had first to take Reading Until this was done they could make no general move in the Thames valley. Pending this, all they could do was to extend the authority of the Parliament in the highlands of Gloucestershire and the Cotswolds. This they did by harassing and annoying the Royalist posts on the line of march that reinforcements in men or supplies for Oxford would take. This imposed on Massey at Gloucester a double duty. (1), To do all he could to keep the Welsh occupied in Monmouthshire and South Wales. (2), To prevent them sending any reinforcements, but if, in spite of his efforts, reinforcements were sent, to do all in his power to harass them on their line of march. Using Gloucester as a centre, Massey had two favourite places for intercepting men and supplies; the one which may be called the line of the Leaddon, the district that forms the south-western border of Worcestershire, through which the Ledbury and Gloucester railway now passes; the other the district between Evesham and Oxford, very roughly indicated by the present line of the railway between those places. This accounts for the fact that there was so much fighting on the south-west border of the County, and shews how Campden became so important a garrison for the King. Gloucester was the centre from which the forays up the Leaddon valley were made. Cirencester was the place from which the Parliament troops· set out to intercept the line from Evesham to Oxford. For the present Gloucester could not be attacked, but it was quite possible to take Cirencester, and the Royalist generals decided that it must be taken. All that was wanted to do it were men.

It is very difficult to estimate the forces at the disposal of either party at this time. The Royalists had about Burford the reinforcements from Wales that the Marquis of Hertford had brought up at the end of December, and there were a certain number of men from the garrison at Oxford who were available for forays and "beating up quarters;" but a field army, in the sense of a number of troops beyond the men in the different garrisons, the Royalists did not possess. The garrisons were continually recruiting, but they do not appear to have done much more than make good their losses from casualties and desertions ; it seems that any available field force had to be drawn from the different garrisons, they from time to time recruiting to keep up their numbers.

It was much the same with the Parliament. Any force they had for offensive operations had to be drawn from their different garrisons. They had no field army, but their garrisons were more numerous and more fully manned than those of the Royalists, therefore they could put a larger force in the field.

As far as can be learnt, numbers were not the only advantage the Parliament possessed. Their troops were better paid, better drilled, and better armed as a whole than the Royalists, and although there was not much to be said as to the discipline of either party, yet the discipline was better among the godly Puritans than among the godless Cavaliers. It was, however, very weak on both sides. Fiennes, the officer who had commanded at Powick, was now the Governor of Bristol. Two of his regiments deliberately disobeyed his orders, and on being called to account questioned the right of any man to give orders to the servants of the Lord. Lord Grey, son of that Lord Stamford who had been Governor of Hereford, gave a soldier some order that displeased him; the soldier followed the officer and cut him on the head with a pole-axe. These acts of the Parliament troops were all justified by their men by reference to the Old Testament, and to the case of some hero of Hebrew history; this they considered not only sufficient excuse, but obligatory on the servants of the Lord to follow.

The Parliament soldier only disobeyed orders on conscientious grounds, the Royalists disobeyed them out of pure lawlessness. One case, which shews the state of things in the Worcester garrison, will prove this. Among the officers there was a Colonel Hide, who was in command of a regiment of foot. He had seen service abroad, and on the strength of such service considered he was entitled to treat all who had not some such experience with the most supreme contempt, and especially the governor (Sir William Russell) and his two chief officers, Sir James Hamilton and Sir Francis Worsley, both of whom were in command of dragoon regiments forming part of the garrison.

The Mayor of Worcester (Henry Ford) in January, 1643, gave a New Year's feast, to which he asked the governor and his officers, including Hide. On sitting down to dinner, Hide took up his napkin from the trencher, looked under it, and seeing nothing, observed, " Mr. Mayor, I expected a New Year's gift," and then began to abuse the mayor in no measured words for not paying his (Hide's) soldiers, On this being arranged, Hide proceeded to drink with the Mayoress, and a fresh quarrel broke out because the lady declined to drink as many beer glasses of wine as Hide asked her to take. On the mayor desiring to protect his wife's sobriety, Hide threw his trencher at him. Sir William Russell, on this, intervened, trying to make peace, but Hide became so very violent that Russell had to put him under arrest. Hide then left the room. On getting into the street he imagined that two women insulted him, so with his sword he cut one over the head and the other over the shoulder. One of the women went to the mayor to complain. Hide followed, beginning to abuse the city magistrates. To stop the disturbance, Russell ordered Hide to his quarters. With some difficulty Sir James Hamilton got Hide to his lodgings. He then became most violent, abusing Russell, and telling the soldiers he wondered they submitted to be ruled by such a coward as the governor, and declared his intention of at once shooting him. A guard was placed at Hide's door, confining him to his quarters, but he broke out through the guard, struck several officers, caused the alarm to be beaten, and nearly raised a serious disturbance. Russell sent a report of Hide's conduct to head-quarters at Oxford. Hide was sent there under a guard, tried by court-martial, but discharged, as Russell did not appear against him.

Hide's, though a bad case, was by no means an isolated one. The old soldiers who, Ludlow says, were made much of, were grossly insubordinate, and desperadoes of the class of Hide, who, on the strength of their knowledge of military matters, were given commands, brought into England the worst features of Continental military licence. What made matters worse was that the strict military discipline which had prevailed abroad was wholly wanting here, so these men became terrors, not only to the garrisons to which they belonged, but also to the country, and did more harm to the Royal cause than anything else, shewing to peaceable, God-fearing Englishmen the class of men Charles Stuart, if successful, would place to rule over them. It is easy to suppose that Worcester, with desperadoes like Hide, with canny Scots like Hamilton, and with a governor unable to preserve order or discipline, could not, in 1643, have been an ideal place of residence.

These ruffians of the Hide class had their use. They were instances of what the professional trooper might degenerate into at the lowest end of the scale. What he might be improved into was seen at the other end in the commander of the Royalist cavalry, Prince Rupert. He was only a glorified trooper, and possessed much of the spirit of these men. It is usually said that Rupert's cavalry were composed of English gentlemen, ready to give their lives and fortunes for the King. That there were many such is true, but there was also a leaven of men of the Hide class, who gave Rupert's Horse their reputation for plundering as well as for fighting. At this period of the war Rupert's reputation was of the greatest value to the King. Powick had sunk deep into the minds of both friends and foes; the lesson taught by Powick had been confirmed at Edgehill, and Edgehill had been enforced at Brentford,* so it was believed to be the fact that

" Rupert never comes but to conquer or to fall ; "

that the troops of the Parliament could not stand before the cavalry of the King, the reason being well put in the remark Cromwell is said to have made to Hampden :—

" You never will get on with a set of poor tapsters and town apprentice
" people, fighting against men of honour."†

Now, as always, Charles' great want was money, and the difficulty was to raise it. It was much more difficult to get the money to pay the men, than to get the men. Worcestershire answered well to the King's demands. At the Epiphany Sessions, 1643, the Grand Jury directed a levy of £3000 a month to be made on the County,

" to be paid monthly towards the payment of His Majesty's forces sent and
" raised for the defence of the County of Worcester."‡

John Baker, gentleman, was appointed

" collector to receive the money and pay it over to Sir William Russell, High
" Sheriff of the County and Governor of the City of Worcester."§

At the Easter Sessions, on the 4th April, Baker certified that the money ordered to be paid at the Epiphany Sessions " was for the most part yet unsatisfied."‡

---

* See the account of Charlgrove Field, cited by Frith.—*Cromwell's Army*, p. 135.
† Carlyle's Cromwell's Letters and Speeches, I., 167 ; ed. 1845.
‡ Sessions Records, I., p. 701. § Ib., p. 710.

A motion was then made in open court for the continuance of the payment of £3000 a month for a longer time:—

"Thereupon, we of the Grand Jury, taking it into our consideration, do "think fit the same should still be paid, according to the said order, for three "months longer, until further order be taken herein at the next General "Sessions of the Peace by the Justices of the Peace and Commissioners of the "County."*

The fact that this order for taxing the County was made at the Epiphany Sessions and renewed at the Easter, shews perhaps more than anything else that the King's influence was now predominant in the County. It may be said that a Royalist Sheriff like Sir William Russell would take care that a Royalist Grand Jury should be returned. This may be so; but having regard to the difficulties that were met with in 1642 by the Commissioners of Array, and also the strong Parliamentary leaning that is shewn in the Sessions Presentments, for instance, the presentment against Catholics,† the order of 1643 shews a considerable advance of the power of the Royalist party.

The presentment of Easter, 1643, goes on to give directions about the County; obviously Massey's raids were beginning to be felt. It says:—

"Further, we of the Grand Jury, do [present] that the outmost parts of the "County, which be [the] nearest unto danger, may speedily be se[cured] by "troops of horse and other necessary assistance, and that we may be freed "from giving free quarter, hay, or provender without money."

This shews that already Rupert's system of allowing his men to live at free quarters was resented. This, in fact, is the first muttering of the storm that afterwards broke out into the Clubmen of the County. The people of Worcestershire do not appear to have objected to the taxes, but to being both taxed and plundered, and they gradually gravitated to the side that was able to give them some security against enduring both.

The presentment proceeds:—

"And that in assessing the said £3000, the same shall be assessed according "to the taxing of the £400,000 by Act of Parliament, and according to the "order of the . . ."

This £400,000 had been raised by the Statute 16 Car. I., c. 32.‡ It was to be paid by two equal payments; the County of Worcester to pay £5802 10s. 6d., and the City of Worcester £356 4s. 9d. Aliens and Popish Recusant convicts were to pay double. The first moiety was payable before the 20th May, 1642, the second before the 20th November, 1642. The Commissioners to levy it for Worcestershire were:—

"Sir Walter Devereux, Sir Thomas Rous, Baronets, Sir John Rous, Knight, "John Wilde, Serjeant-at-Law, Humphrey Salway (these two last were the

---

* Sessions Records, I., p. 710.   † Ib., p. 698.   ‡ Statutes of the Realm, V.

"County Members of Parliament), Edward Pitts, Edward Dingley, William
"Jeffryes, of Ham Castle, John Savage, Henry Ingram, Henry Townsend,
"John Nanfan, Edward Vernon, William Childe, Thomas Good, Robert
"Wilde, of the Commanders, John Winford, Esq., George Lench, Philip
"Brace, Roger Lowe, John Colding, Esqs., Henry Dison, Edward Barret and
"Nicholas Gower, of Droitwich, John Hailes and Francis Gilding, of
"Bewdley, Daniel Dobbins, Esq , the Bailiff of Kidderminster for the time
"being, the Mayor of Evesham for the time being, Francis Harwell, Thomas
"Chresheld, gentleman."

This list is interesting as shewing the trend of feeling. Both
the County Members, Sergeant Wilde and Humphrey Salway
(who were Parliamentarians), were appointed. The Members
for Evesham were Richard Chreshold and the Hon. John
Coventry; neither of them were appointed, unless, as is likely,
"Thomas" should be "Richard Chreshold." William Sandys,
who had been the member, was expelled the House in January,
1641, as a monopolist; his monopoly being the patent to make
the Avon navigable, and for dues on goods carried on the river.
In his navigation scheme he was most bitterly opposed by Sir
William Russell. How they got on together afterwards does not
appear. Coventry took his place, but in 1643 was disabled from
sitting as a Commissioner of Array. Richard Chreshold was
a Serjeant-at-Law, Recorder of Evesham, and a commissioner
to compensate the Avon proprietors for damage done by
Sandys' scheme of navigation. He was of a Norfolk family,
and is probably the person here meant. Droitwich was represented by Endymion Porter and Samuel Sandys. By a vote of
the House in February, 1642, Porter, who was one of the
Grooms of the Bedchamber, was removed, being "one that is conceived to give dangerous counsel." In August, 1642, Sandys, as
a Royalist, was disabled from sitting in Parliament. Sir Henry
Herbert was Member for Bewdley. It will thus be seen that
the only Members of Parliament on the Commission were the
two opposition Members for Worcestershire, and, if Thomas
Chreshold is the same as Richard Chreshold, the opposition
Member for Evesham.

The Commissioners for Worcester City were:—

"The Mayor for the time being, John Coucher, Roger Gough, John
"Hanbury, John Nash, William Norris, George Street, Aldermen Francis
"Street, Esq , Richard Heming, Humphrey Vernon, gentlemen."*

John Coucher, who was member in 1642, was then 81, and, it
is believed, never took his seat.

John Nash, the other member, was a strong Parliamentarian,
commanded a troop of horse for the Parliament, and was
afterwards, in 1644, one of the Assessment Committee for the
County.

The presentment went on:—

"We also desire that Sir William Russell may forthwith give an [account]
"to the Commissioners for the Defence of the County how he has disbursed

---

* Statutes of the Realm. V., 157.

"the money by him r[eceived], according to the former order and His
"Majesty's instructions."

From some papers of Sir William Russell's it would appear
that he had spent money, probably "the money so received,"
in various ways.   For instance :—

"Vicisimo die, Aug.
"Whereas Sir William Russell's Regiment of Horse did quarter in
"* bberley in May and June last, Sir William Russell hath [al]lowed unto
"me, Constable,   said town, out of the contribution,
"   moneths, the sum of ffowertiene pounds, tenn shillings, nyne pence,
"in discharge thereof.
                                                  "John Ford, Constable."†

Other vouchers are :—

"Received of Sir William Russell the sum of one hundred pounds towards
"the payment of my Regiment.   I say, received the sayd some the 24th
"December, 1642.
                                                  "John Owen."†

"10th die Feb , 1642.
"Received, the day and yeare abovesaid, of Sir William Russell, the sume
"of forty shillings for casting of iron ordinance.   I say, received the some of
"40s.
                                                  "Brian Newton."†

"16th Feb., 1642.
"Received then, of Sir William Russell, Baronet, Governor of Worcester
"and Teuxbury, the sum of 20li., for payment of his own company of
"dragoons here at Teuxbury.   I say, rec. the sume of £20.
                                                  "Tho. Maylard."†

From these it would appear that all the money received was
not disbursed for the defence of the County, but generally for
the King's needs.

The presentment goes on :—

"And whereas it was ordered by the Ri[ght] Arthur Lord Capell and the
"Council of War, that the £3000, and what other money was formerly
"collected or due for horses, coat, and conduct money in the County, with
"the putting out of which money Sir [Walter] Devereux, Sir William
"Russell, and [Sir John] Rous were entrusted for the County . . .   now
"due to the County by bond from . . .   Hill, surveyor, shall, together
"with the in[terest] thereof owing, be forthwith paid to C[olonel] Samuel
"Sandys, towards the payment of several billets and debts of his regiment,
"and the maintenance of his soldiers, and that the . . . Sir Walter
"Devereux, Sir William Russell, and Sir John R[ouse] . . . stand
"thereof utterly discharged, as by order . . . produced to us appeareth,
"which said or[der] we approve of, and do desire the same . . . at this
"Sessions be so ordered, and that the Clerk of the Peace shall deliver up Mr.
"Hill's bond . . ."‡

Coat and conduct money was the sum paid to a recruit for
his uniform, outfit, and journey to his post.

There is a fragment of a presentment in 1642, by the Grand
Jury, among the Worcestershire Papers, which speaks of

" . . . payment of the money unto Colonell Sandys, all which we have
"in the . . . of His Majesty's Commissioners appointed for the safety
"of the County of Worcester.   We likewise think well that Mr. Kimberley
"shall have fifteen shillings out of the three pounds which is in the fund."‖

---

* This may be "A," or "Cu.   † Russell Papers, W.H.S.
‡ Sessions Records, I., p. 710.   ‖ Sessions Records, I., p. 700.

Samuel Sandys was appointed in 1643 to command the horse of the County. He raised a regiment of infantry and a troop of horse for the King, and the payments here mentioned must refer to some outlay for them.

The Sessions' order for the £3000 a month is of interest from several points. It gives some clue as to the strength of the Royalist forces in the County. From Sir William Russell's accounts it appears that the pay per troop was £20 a week.* Assuming the whole of the £3000 went in pay, this would represent 150 troops, and, at their full strength of 100 men a troop, about 1500 men. This agrees very nearly with the account given by Symonds of the number of men in the garrisons in the County in June, 1644,† who puts it between 3000 and 4000.

What the tax was may best be understood if it is contrasted with one at the present day—police. £36,000 a year is not quite what the police force now (1904) costs the County. Spread over the whole County that represents a 5d. rate. On this assessment it must have been, if it is assumed money is now worth nearly five times more than then, a 2s. rate, but the assessment then must have been much less than a fifth of what it is now.

To raise £36,000 on that would mean a 5s. rate. It is not to be wondered at if on these figures the people of Worcestershire resented the payments they had to make, besides having troops living on them at free quarters, to say nothing of the plunderers on both sides.

It will be as well to mention here a list given by Symonds in his diary‡ of the troops raised in the County for the King. He says, writing in 1644 :—

"Since the Civil War in this kingdom these regiments have been raised out "of this County (Worcestershire) *pro rege*, which consists only of 150 'od' "parish churches."

"Sir James Hamilton, about May, 1643, raised three regiments—one of "horse of 400 or thereabouts, one of foot, near 1000, one of dragoons; all at "the charges of the County. These captains were under him of this County :

OF HORSE.

"Captain John Blunt, of Soddington, son of Sir Walter Blunt.

"Captain William Welch.

"Captain Colt.

"All these and his regiment were cut off and taken prisoners about or near "the Devizes. These captains aforesaid are now in town.

"His regiment of foot lost there, so was his dragoons.

"Henderson, a Scot, was his lieutenant.

"Colonel Samuel Sandys, of Ombersley, four miles from Worcester, about "the same time raised three regiments, one of horse, one of foot, one of "dragoons, all at his own charge. He hath £3000 per annum.

"The horse consisted of between 6 or 700.

"John Sandys, his uncle, Captain-Lieutenant.

---

* Russell Papers, W.H.S.   † p. 12.   ‡ p. 11.

" Mr. Windsor Hickman, Lieutenant-Colonel.

" Captain Savage, of this County.

" Captain Langston.

" One regiment of foot of about 1000.

" Captain William Sandys, his uncle.

" Captain Frederick Windsor.

" Captain Fr. Moore, of this County.

" Captain Heling.

" Regiment of dragoons not perfected.

" Captain Thomas Symonds, of Claynes, in this County, nephew to Mr.
" Williams, of Worcester.

" Colonel Sandys gave up his regiment of foot to Knotsworth, who was
" now Governor of Evesham, of the County of Warwick, about April, 1644,
" when Prince Rupert was here.

" Sir William Russell, of Strensham, in this County, raised, not long after,
" one regiment of horse, consisting of about 300, now in being about this
" city.

" One regiment of foot, consisting of about 700. About 300 still, the rest
" gone for want of pay.

" Colonel Sandys, younger brother to Sandys which was killed here on the
" rebels' side, raised a regiment of horse in this County.

" In the City of Worcester the Governor, Sir Gilbert Gerard, hath
" a regiment of foot, Lieutenant-Colonel—Major Bishop, Captain Gerard, and
" one regiment of horse.

" Colonel Martin Sandys, uncle to Mr Samuel Sandys, hath a regiment of
" foot of the townsmen, consisting of about 800."

Nothing is said in this account of Sir Thomas Littleton and the troops he raised. Possibly the fact that Littleton had just been taken prisoner, and was then in the Tower, may account for this.

It is somewhat difficult to get the names of those who raised troops for the Parliament, but among them were:

Sir Walter Devereux, of Leigh Court, a relation of the Earl of Essex, whom he succeeded in the title. He bought Leigh Court from the latter, and was a very active Parliamentarian. His house at Leigh was burnt by the Royalists.

Sir John Rous and Nicholas Lechmere.

Sergeant John Wilde subscribed for two horses and their maintenance.

Charles began to find the great advantage that Worcester-shire was to him. Not only the Welsh reinforcements came through it, but stores of various kinds reached him from it, brought by carriers on pack horses and by waggons. So much was this the case that Parliament issued an ordinance on January 16th :—

" That no carriers or waggoners whatsoever shall be permitted hereafter to
" go to Oxford without special license from the Parliament."*

The troops the Marquis of Hertford had sent reached Worcester at Christmas, 1642, and soon after the New Year arrived at Stow and Burford. Here they halted. Lord Falkland had an estate near there, Great Tew, and provided for their

---

* Rushworth, V., p. 117.

wants. As soon as Massey learnt of their arrival he began to
harass them and beat up their quarters. This was too much for
Rupert. Taking the Welsh, his own regiments, and those of his
brother Maurice, on the 7th January, he marched to Cirencester, attacked it, but was repulsed. Massey, encouraged by
his success, attacked the Royalist garrison at Sudeley Castle,
which was held for the Earl of Chandos by Captain Brydges.
The attack was repulsed, but Massey, gaining possession of the
garden, set fire to a quantity of hay and straw, and planted his
guns to fire on the Castle, which so alarmed the garrison that
they surrendered.

These Parliamentary successes quite upset the Royalist plans,
which could not be carried out until the Cotswolds were
cleared. To do this Cirencester must be taken, and it was
decided again to attempt it. But it was not now so easy a
task; the fortifications had been strengthened, and the garrison
increased; four great iron guns had been sent up from Bristol,
a brass gun from Gloucester. In spite of all this the Royalist
generals resolved it should fall. Rupert had gone off on
one of his foraying expeditions through Northamptonshire
and Warwickshire. Orders were sent to him to march on
the place; reinforcements would be sent, and he must take it.

On the 29th January Rupert was at Shipston-on-Stour. On
the next day (Monday) he marched to Winchcombe. He encamped in a field at Hulling, near Sudeley Castle, but made no
attempt on it. On the 1st February he reached Northleach;
here his reinforcements joined him. He now found himself at
the head of some 4000 horse and foot, with which force he was
to make the attempt to take Cirencester. On the 2nd
February he marched to the place, and after some hard fighting
took it.* 1100 prisoners, 5 guns, 13 muskets, and 14 colours
were the spoils of his victory. Tying the prisoners two and
two, he marched them towards Oxford.

" Among them was a proper handsome man, with a very white skin, where it
" could be seen for the blood of his wounds. He not being able to go, was
" set naked on the bare back of a horse, his wounds gaping and his body
" smeared with blood; yet he sat upright upon his horse with an undaunted
" countenance, and when near the King a brawling woman cried out after
" him, ' Ah, you traitorly rogue, you are well enough served.' He, with a
" scornful look towards her, answered, ' You base woman,' and instantly
" dropped off dead from his horse."†

The capture of Cirencester was really a great success. It was
a serious check to the Parliament in the Cotswold district, and
gave the King the upper hand there.

" It brought," says Clarendon,‡ "almost that whole County into contribu-
" tion, and was a great enlargement to the King's quarters, which now
" without interruption extended from Oxford to Worcester, that important
" city, with the other of Hereford."

---

* Rushworth V., 131.   † Whitelock, 64.   ‡ II., 97

It had other results. Massey at once began to concentrate his forces in Gloucester. He abandoned Sudeley, withdrew the garrison from Tewkesbury, which Russell took possession of and garrisoned early in February, 1643. Russell was governor for a short time himself, but later he appointed Sir Nathan Carew. Rupert did not delay. Cirencester was taken on the 2nd February; on the next day his men were before Gloucester, and summoned it to surrender. Massey refused, and Rupert therefore determined it should be besieged.

Lord Herbert, who had succeeded the Marquis of Hertford in the command in South Wales, brought up some 2000 Welshmen, and to them the siege of Gloucester was entrusted. Sir Richard Lawdey, the Governor of Hereford, brought further reinforcements. He was put in command of the infantry, the command of the cavalry was given to Lord John Somerset.

Massey was not to be shut up without an attempt to beat off his foes. He marched into the Forest of Dean to meet the Welsh. A skirmish took place at Coleford, in which Lawdey was killed, shot, it was said and believed, by a silver bullet. His place sa commander of the infantry was taken by Sir Jerome Brett, who marched at once to Gloucester and occupied Highnam and the Vineyard. Surrounding Gloucester, on Massey again refusing to surrender, he immediately began the siege. Nothing shews Massey's ability as a soldier more than this siege, with a much inferior force, he throughout assumed and kept the offensive, and at last was able to attack the besiegers on their own ground near Highnam. Even if relief had not been at hand, Massey would probably have been able to hold out. As it was, he was able to do far more. On hearing of the approach of the Welsh, Massey sent to Bristol, the head-quarters of his Divisional General, informing him of what was taking place, and of the way he proposed dealing with it. The Severn had to be crossed, and to cross the Severn with an army anywhere below Gloucester is no easy task. Massey, however, had collected a number of boats at Framilode, lower down the Severn, sufficient to convey the troops across. Once they had crossed they had only to advance on to Highnam, take the Welsh in the rear, while he (Massey) attacked them in front. The scheme commended itself, as any bold and daring scheme would do, to the general commanding at Bristol, for that general was Sir William Waller (" William the Conqueror," as his friends called him; " The Night Owl," from his bold and successful movements by night, as the Royalists called him), the Sergeant-Major General* of the

---

* That is the Commander-in-Chief of the infantry of Parliament army.—See Frith, *Cromwell's Army*, p. 61.

Parliament army, who was now to make his first appearance in the West Midlands.

At that time no Parliamentary general had a greater reputation, and no Parliamentary general better deserved it. His successes in the south had placed him in the very foremost rank of the Parliamentary leaders. When Waller left the University he entered the Venetian service, fought in the Bohemian Wars against the Emperor, took part in the English expedition to defend the Palatinate. He came back to England in 1632 and married. In consequence of a quarrel with one of his wife's family, who was about the Court, to whom Waller gave a sound and deserved thrashing, Waller was prosecuted and severely fined. This set him against the Court. A zealous Puritan, he was elected for Andover in the Long Parliament as a member of the opposition. On the war breaking out he was appointed colonel of a regiment of horse, and given the command of the troops sent to take Portsmouth. This he did. In December, 1642, Waller took Farnham and Arundel Castles, Winchester, and Chichester. For these services he was made Sergeant-Major General of Gloucester, Wilts, Somerset, and Bristol, with head-quarters at Bristol. Five regiments of horse and five regiments of foot were to be raised to serve under him. He took up his command on the 21st March. He out-manœuvred Rupert and took Malmesbury by assault on the 23rd. He then marched to Framilode; utilising Massey's fleet of boats he crossed the river without difficulty, marched past Huntley, drawing up his men at Highnam in the rear of the Welsh troops,

Massey had attacked them in front, sallying out from Gloucester. His attack had not been altogether successful; the Welsh stood their ground well, not merely withstanding Massey's efforts, but in their turn attacking him. While the issue was in doubt Waller's guns were heard firing on the Welsh rear. Massey's men, on this, again advanced to the attack, carried an earthwork, made the garrison prisoners; then, to quote Waller :—

"Before the enemy had any notice we fell upon their backs, and in a short "time, without the loss of above two, they rendered up the place upon "quarter, when we had 1444 common prisoners, well armed, commanders and "gentlemen about 150, many of the chief of Wales and Herefordshire."*

As soon as the Welsh found they were attacked both in front and rear, in spite of their officers urging them to make an effort to break through the lines, they refused to fight, and nothing remained but to surrender. The Welsh were angry and sullen, considering they had been deserted by their general, Lord Herbert, who had gone to Oxford,

"leaving," says one account, "all his Welsh behind him, which made them

---

* Sir William Waller's letter to Parliament. "Bibliotheca Gloucestrensis," pp. 29, 195.

"' swear by St. Taffy they would never fight for him again, unless he will pass
"' it under his hand and seal that he will stand it out."*

They had some grounds for their belief that they were
deserted. Lord Gerrard had marched off with all the cavalry
to Tetbury. He might have prevented Waller passing the
river at Framilode if he had had any dash, but he never even
attempted to strike a blow, and left Brett and the Welsh to
their fate. The defeat and the disgrace could not be denied.
The only thing to be done was to explain it away. The
Royalists, therefore, ascribed it to a breach of faith on Waller's
part. After describing his march, his passage of the Severn,
and his attack on the Welsh rear, the Royalist account goes
on :—† Waller

" met with such resistance that he lost 400 of his men, and so gave over for
" that time. Finding the next day that the King's forces were willing to
" admit of parley, he hearkened unto it and entertained a treaty with them,
" having lost so many of his men in the former onfalls. But while they were
" in debate upon the conditions, and almost come to a conclusion, some of
" the men, perceiving one of the outworks to be but meanly manned (most of
" his soldiers being withdrawn in confidence of some fair end by the present
" parley), gave in upon the same and won it, and from this set upon the rest,
" that the horse, both troopers and dragoons, seeing how little hope of safety
" there was if they should abide it, went fairly off and saved themselves for
" better times, leaving about 300 of their foot behind them, who were had
" prisoners into Gloucester, besides 300 or thereabout which were killed in
" defence of the works."

This view is to some extent borne out by the fact that when
the Gloucester and Ledbury Canal was cut a number of bones
were found about the spot where the fight took place. A
tradition had long existed about Barber's Bridge that if certain
mounds near there were opened the bones of the Welsh killed
at the siege of Gloucester would be found. In filling up a pool
in 1868 one of these places was opened, disclosing a large
number of bones. It is said that these are the bones of the
Welsh who had fought at Highnam, driven back, and
met at the brook by another body of soldiers, there surrounded and killed, so that the brook was called, as it still is,
" Red Brook," because it ran red with their blood, that
" Barber's Bridge " is a corruption of " Barbarous Bridge," and
the name was derived from the barbarous massacre of the
Welsh.‡

Whether gained by treachery or by fair fighting, Waller's
triumph was complete. He had avenged Cirencester ; 1300
foot and three troops of horse were marched prisoners into
Gloucester.§ Lord Herbert never forgot or forgave the loss of
his men, Years after (1666-7) he wrote to Charles II. :—‖

" How was His Majesty recruited at Gloucester siege, even after the defeat

---

* Perfect Diurnal, 27th March to April 3rd, 1643.   † Mercurius' " Aulicus."
‡ See a Paper by Captain Price, read at a meeting of the Cotswold Club, 1871, p. 14.
        § Clarendon II., 119.   ‖ H. M. R., xii., app. 9, p. 60.

" given by Waller to my men ? God forgive them of the King's party who
" were the occasion that 1500 gentlemen were surprised and I not despatched
" from Oxford till the day after! Yet at 14 days' warning I brought 4000
" foot and 800 horse to the siege of Gloucester, paying them £6000 down
" upon the nail at Gloucester."

Waller's succcess raised the hopes of the Parliament. Their
favourite general had again proved his right to the title of
" Conqueror." Worcestershire and Herefordshire were now
to see what a really active general could do. The Royalists
felt something must be done, and that a man should be
sent to take the supreme command who should be a match
for Waller. The King's ideas in military matters never went
much beyond his nephews. Waller had out-manœuvred
Rupert at Malmesbury, so it was not well to send him;
there only remained Maurice. The choice was singular. A
young man of 23, who had seen no service to speak of, who
had never had any experience as a leader, was sent to meet
the best general the Parliament had as yet found. The very
impudence of the thing made it deserve to succeed, and it
succeeded. Maurice was appointed early in April to the
supreme command in Worcestershire. Rupert was sent on a
special service elsewhere.

Maurice at once set out from Oxford to take up his new
command. On reaching Evesham he heard that Waller had
raised the siege of Gloucester; that Sir Matthew Carew, the
Governor of Tewkesbury, on hearing that Massey was advancing against the place, had abandoned it ; that within 12 hours
Massey had re-occupied and was now in possession of it, and
had appointed Captain Fiennes Governor. Maurice determined to re-take it; unless he could do so he was powerless
against Waller. Lord Grandison was at Cheltenham with the
remains of Lord John Somerset's horse which had been absent
at the Highnam surrender. Maurice ordered them to join him
before Tewkesbury. He sent to Worcester and the other
garrisons for men, and collected a considerable force out
of the commands of Sir William Vavassour, Sir Walter Pye,
and Colonel Wroughton. With these he set out from Evesham
to meet Lord Grandison. Scouting was never the Royalists'
strong point. Had either Lord Grandison or Maurice taken
ordinary precautions they could probably have taken Tewkesbury and its garrison without any difficulty. Marching
leisurely towards Tewkesbury, down the Cheltenham Road,
when about a mile from the town Lord Grandison met a
countryman coming from Tewkesbury. He asked the man
what force was there, what was its strength, and who commanded it ? The man, mistaking them for Parliament troops,
and wanting to shew his zeal for their side, told them of the
great number and strength of the Parliament force, and how
impossible it would be for any Royalist force to take it.   This

so alarmed Lord Grandison that he proposed to turn back and retreat to Cheltenham. But that some of his men chanced to see Maurice advancing from Evesham, he would have done so. On this Grandison plucked up courage to advance, and reached Tewkesbury just in time to see the rear of Fiennes' force making a hurried departure along the Gloucester Road. But for this cowardly delay nothing could have saved the Tewkesbury garrison from capture.

Maurice at once occupied the place. His force amounted to about 2000 men. They remained there for some days. Maurice employed his men in building a bridge of boats across the Severn, while he waited to see what Waller's next move would be. He had not long to wait; Waller determined to complete the Welsh discomfiture by a raid on that side. Accompanied by his favourite officer, Sir Arthur Haselrigge, the Member for Leicester, one of the celebrated five members, whose well-known regiment of cuirassieurs from their armour and red jackets were known as "Haselrigge's Lobsters," Waller set out for Ross, passing on to Monmouth and Chepstow. As soon as Maurice heard of this he crossed the Severn on his way to Ledbury and Ross, partly by his bridge of boats and partly by the bridge at Upton. His object now was to shut up Waller in the corner between the Wye and the Severn, and force him to fight, with an impassable river in his rear, so that if defeated he must surrender. To carry out his encircling movement he placed his force in a line from Ross to Newnham, making Little Dean his head-quarters. Maurice's strategy was fairly successful; Waller found that he could not extricate himself from this corner without a battle, and that any battle he might fight would be under considerable disadvantage, so he decided to send his foot, guns, and baggage across the Severn by the old passage from Beachley to Aust, and with his horse make a dash through Maurice's lines to regain Gloucester. He sent his guns and baggage away, leaving Chepstow at night; at daybreak next morning he was at Little Dean. Again Maurice's bad scouting lost him his chance. Waller was not expected; the Royalists turned out, but Waller got his men through Maurice's lines with but very small loss and brought them safely to Gloucester. Waller now determined to assume the offensive, and compel Maurice to retreat. The next day he advanced to Tewkesbury,

"where lay a garrison of Sir William Russell's, the High Sheriff of "Worcestershire, upon intelligence of whose approach, so terrible was the "name of Sir William Waller in those parts, the garrison presently with only "two drakes* fled away towards Worcester, and left the town to noble Sir "William, who presently entered it without any resistance."†

Waller made Colonel Cooke Governor of Tewkesbury. He

---

* Small Cannon.   † "God in the Mount," p. 294.

destroyed Maurice's bridge of boats, and sent a detachment to Upton to secure and break down the bridge. If this was done Maurice's retreat would be cut off.

As soon as he found Waller had broken through his lines at Little Dean, Maurice began to retreat on Tewkesbury. He was not aware what Waller had done, nor of the trap set for him. Maurice proceeded at his leisure to Upton, and, on arriving there, to his surprise found it in the hands of the Parliament. It then dawned on him that his safety lay in an instant attack on the place and capture of the bridge. Maurice attacked at once. The Parliament men said they were too weak to hold the place against Maurice's force, so at once retreated over the river. They did nothing to destroy the bridge, and Maurice's men at once took possession of it, while his cavalry pushed on after the retreating Parliament troops. When the Parliament men reached Ryal some fresh troops from Tewkesbury joined them, and it was determined to make a stand. Ripple, like so many other places in the County, consisted of a village with enclosures round it, and a large open field. From Ryal the field was reached by a long lane with high hedges on both sides; this lane formed the only road for cavalry. Waller had come up while his troops halted. He was too late to save the bridge, but not too late to teach Maurice a lesson. In numbers Waller was slightly the weakest, but the two forces were on fairly equal terms. Waller lined the enclosures round Ripple with troops, and drew up his main body in the large open field at the end of the lane, his idea being that if his men were driven out of the enclosures Maurice would follow up the lane. As soon as he got out of the lane into the field Waller would charge, and then Powick would be repeated, and Maurice be driven back in disorder over Upton Bridge. The only thing required to ensure the success of Waller's plan was that he could rely upon the steadiness of his men. If that failed he was lost. It did fail. Maurice attacked furiously, not only in front, but on each flank, driving Waller's men out of the enclosure into the lane. There the Parliament troops soon became a disorganised rabble, as into the lane Maurice's cavalry charged, breaking in over the hedges at the sides, shewing no mercy, giving no quarter. On seeing this Waller tried to cover the retreat and stay Maurice's cavalry. He ordered " Haselrigge's Lobsters " to shew front to the enemy and charge. To some extent this checked, at least for a time, the Royalist pursuit, and enabled the infantry to recover, escape out of the lane on to the open ground, and reform. To use the words of a Parliament writer, the bold conduct of Massey, who had come up with some fresh troops, and the steadiness of Haselrigge's men, " in some part took off the foulness of that retreat." When the open field was reached Massey tried to reform his men and induce them to stand up against the Royalist cavalry. This was, however, asking too much of them.

"They stood in a maze, and on a sudden ran ' flock meale,' with the enemy "on their backs."*

Maurice reformed his men as they emerged from the lane and charged the enemy again. This time they were delivered into his hand. No rally was possible ; they broke and fled, carrying the others with them. It was no longer a fight—it was only a butchery. It was only the fact that strong rein-forcements, hurried up from Tewkesbury, were drawn up on the high ground in front of the town, whom Maurice did not think it prudent to attack, that saved the residue of the routed men. But for this, Maurice might have re-taken Tewkesbury and destroyed the Parliamentary force. On Maurice's men halting, Waller, glad of the respite, at once retired into Tewkesbury. After a short time Maurice drew off, marching with his men, wounded, and baggage, to Evesham.

Such was the fight at Ripple. Although no direct results came from it, yet it was not without its effect. The great Sir William Waller had been fairly beaten, and, what is more, routed. The superiority of the Royalist cavalry had again been proved. Although things were almost precisely as they had been when Maurice came to Evesham, so far as position went, yet it was something to boast that Waller's career of victory had been checked. As he said afterwards, "Worcester-shire was not a lucky place for him."

The slaughter at Ripple had been considerable. The "Lobsters," who saved the day, suffered very severely: out of a strength of 70 at the beginning of the fight, only 20 went back to Tewkesbury. The Royalist loss was small. Waller returned to Gloucester. Essex ordered him to return to Bristol, but Waller did not obey ; he wanted to restore his reputation before leaving the district. Haselrigge went to London to recruit his regiment.

On Maurice's arrival at Evesham he found orders recalling him to Oxford. Rupert was already there. Matters had become critical at Reading, and Charles was vainly casting around to find means to help him out of his difficulties.

Before turning to these matters the proceedings of Rupert should be stated. It has already been said he was ordered on a special service when Maurice was sent into Worcestershire. Rupert went into the north of the County.

The Royalists had occupied the Close at Lichfield ; Lord Brook, at the head of the Warwickshire and Staffordshire

---

* Corbet, Bibliotheca Gloucestrensis.

levies for Parliament, had besieged and taken the Close ; during the siege Lord Brook had been killed. Charles was very desirous that Lichfield should be re-taken and turned into a Royal garrison. He was also in considerable need of ammunition, his chief supply of which was drawn from the northern counties. The convoys had, however, to pass through districts well affected to Parliament, where

"the enemy was much superior in all the counties between Yorkshire and" "Oxford, and had planted garrisons so near all the roads that the most "private messengers travelled with great hazard, three being intercepted for "one that escaped,"*

while a party little inferior in strength to an army was necessary to convoy any supply of ammunition from Yorkshire to Oxford. It was, therefore, resolved to establish a Royalist garrison at Lichfield, thereby forming a centre from which escorts could be sent to convoy whatever was required.

One characteristic of Charles was the small acts of vengeance in which he indulged. Among the orders given to Rupert for the Lichfield expedition was that he should teach Birmingham a lesson for their disloyalty, especially for the insults they had put on the King in October, 1642, before the battle of Edgehill, in plundering the Royal Coach. Clarendon adds that Birmingham was then

" A town of as great fame for hearty, wilful affected disloyalty to the King as "any place in England."†

Rupert's mission was, therefore, threefold. Punish Birmingham, garrison Lichfield, and clear the country as far as possible. To do this he was given a force of 1200 horse and dragoons and 600 or 700 foot.

On Wednesday, 29th March, Rupert left Oxford, reaching Chipping Norton that evening. On Thursday he was at Shipston-on-Stour, on Friday, 31st March (Good Friday) at Stratford-on-Avon, and on Saturday, April 1st (Easter Eve), at Henley-in-Arden. Here he spent Easter Sunday, and on Easter Monday, April 3rd, set out for Birmingham to execute the first part of his task. Clarendon says:‡

" Birmingham was never made a garrison by direction of Parliament, being "built in such a form as was hardly capable of being fortified. Yet they had "so great a desire to distinguish themselves from the King's good subjects "that they cast up little, slight works at both ends of the town, and "barricadoed the rest, and voluntarily engaged themselves not to admit any "intercourse with the King's forces."

So Rupert found it when, on the 3rd April, he marched there from Henley-in-Arden. After passing Shirley the road enters Worcestershire, then proceeding northwards along one of the great main roads leading out of Birmingham, now called the Stratford Road, it is joined at Sparkhill, near where

---

* Clarendon, II., p. 180.   † II., p. 180.   ‡ II., p. 181.

" The Mermaid " now stands, by the road to Warwick.   Here
the further approach to Birmingham was barred by some of
the slight earthworks which had been thrown up.   The men
of Birmingham possessed a very inadequate force to defend
these works.   In the town were stationed a small company
of foot, under Captain Greaves ; the Lichfield garrison had
sent in a troop of horse, but their united strength did not much,
it at all, exceed 200 men.   Rupert did not believe that his large
body would be opposed by so inferior a force.   He therefore
sent his Quarter-Master forward to take up his lodgings, and
to

" assure the townsmen if they behaved themselves peaceably they should not
" suffer for what was past.   But they had not consciences good enough to
" believe him, and absolutely refused to let him quarter in the town, and from
" their little works, with mettle equal to their malice, discharged their shot
" upon him."*

In was about three in the afternoon that Rupert, to his
surprise, found that " the sturdy sons of freedom,"† as the
local historian calls them, were determined to fight.   This
determination was opposed to the opinion of the Parliamentarians—not only of the military, but also of the civilians—the
ministers of Birmingham, and the leading men of the town ;
but the " middle and inferior sort" of people, expecially those
that bore arms, insisted on resisting, so at last they all resolved
to fight.   Finding such was their case, Rupert gave the order
to attack their defences at once.   The defences were only a
bank of earth, behind which the handful of musketeers was
placed.   As the Royalists advanced they received so heavy a
fire that on reaching the works they could not stand up against
it and had to retire.   A second attempt met with a similar
repulse.   Things were getting serious ; it would never do for
Rupert to be defeated by the inhabitants of Birmingham.   Yet
there was little chance of carrying the works by a direct attack.
Some of Rupert's men saw that it might be possible, by
going across the fields, to ride round and get into the rear of
the works, and from there charge the defenders.   This was tried
and proved successful.   The defenders of the works could not
stand being attacked front and rear, so abandoned the works
and fled into the town.   Rupert's troopers followed them.
From the houses a desultory fire was kept up on the Royalist
troopers as they advanced up the street.   On this the troopers
set fire to the houses from which they had been fired on, and
the town was soon ablaze in several places.   Pushing on the
resistance became less ; those who had fought fled and
scattered.

But the fight was not over.   Greaves rallied his troop of
horse, and drawing them up at the further (the Lichfield) end

* Clarendon, II., 181.   † Hutton, p. 48.

of the town, wheeled them round, and charged the scattered Cavaliers. Little expecting any resistance, the Royalists gave way. Lord Denbigh, who was leading them, was severely wounded, knocked off his horse, and left for dead; he died shortly after from his wounds, and his men fled back helter-skelter till they came near their own colours, when they formed up in the rear of the Royalist lines. Greaves, having carried out his object, which was by his charge to give time for his foot to get away, and to prevent them being pursued, did not press his success further. He had himself in his charge received no less than five wounds. Reforming his men he faced about, and drew off towards Lichfield. He had saved his soldiers, but he left the unfortunate townsmen to the tender mercies of Rupert's troopers. Irritated by the resistance, and especially by Greaves' charge, Rupert's men were not inclined to be merciful. They rode desperately round the town, leaping hedges and ditches to catch the townsmen; those they caught they slew. If the lists given are to be trusted, tradesmen, labourers, women were all cut down indiscriminately. Two cases even then called for notice. Some of the troopers riding up to an inn, the ostler came out to take their horses, he was cut down and killed. A minister slain in the street. The Parliament men said he was mistaken for the minister of Birmingham, a violent supporter of the Parliament, and was therefore murdered. The Royalists said that he told the troopers that

" the King was a perjured, Papistical King, and that he would rather die than " live under such a King,"*

and that the troopers, on hearing this, cut him down. The Parliament men alleged he had long been a lunatic, held Jewish opinions, and had laid in Bedlam and other prisons, some said 16, some 22 years, and was only lately come out. On him were found a number of " idle and foolish papers," which the Parliament said proved him mad, the Royalists said proved him immoral. Like other foolish people he kept a diary, and entered in it a number of matters that might well have been left out.

" 28th March. A comfortable kiss from Mrs. E., with some moistness.
" A cynamon kiss from a noted woman.
" A kiss from a girl of 14 years old."*

Nothing could shew better the feelings of both parties. It may or may not have been in accordance with the laws of war to have cut down a preacher making disloyal speeches, but to kill in cold blood a man who had in his pocket a journal with doubtful entries was a disgrace even to those wild times.

It also proves how strong feeling was on the subject, that in the account Clarendon gives of the affair,† he says that Rupert

---

* See "A Letter from Walshall concerning Birmingham." † II., 181.

"took not that vengeance upon them they deserved, but made them expiate
"their transgressions by paying a less mulct than might have been expected
"from their wealth if their wickedness had been less."

He then justifies the death of the clergyman:—

"He was killed at the entering of the town, after he had not only refused
"quarter, but provoked the soldier by the most odious revilings and
"reproaches of the person and honour of the King that can be imagined, and
"renouncing all allegiance to him; in whose pockets were found several papers
"of memorials of his own scurrilous behaviour, in such loose expressions as
"modest ears cannot endure. The man was the principal governor and
"incendiary of the rude people of that place against their Sovereign. So full
"a qualification was a heightened measure of malice and disloyalty for the
"service that it weighed down the infamy of any other vicious behaviour."*

Clarendon adds† that if it had not been for the death of the
Earl of Denbigh he should not " have mentioned an action of
so little moment as this of Birmingham." He deplores it,
because

"of the dismal inequality of the contention in which always some earl or
"person of great honour or fortune fell when, after a most signal victory over
"the other side, there was seldom lost a man of any known family, or of
"other reputation than of passion for the cause in which he fell."†

This was especially true here. It was not the mere death of
the Earl of Denbigh; it was the fact that his son and successor
(Basil Fielding) was a strong Parliamentarian, and the death of
the Earl meant the transfer of the family influence, which was
considerable, from the King to the Parliament.

The battle of Camp Hill was remarkable from the fact
that an armed mob—they were nothing more—twice repulsed
assaults of the best troops in the Royalist army, who attacked
them in overwhelming numbers. That less than 300 men
should keep some 1800 at bay, even for a short time, was an
act that deserved to be recorded; that they, an untrained mob,
should have checked the dreaded Royalist cavalry, was a still
greater achievement. The Parliamentarians were delighted,
and they had reason to be. Captain Greaves, probably a local
man, a member of the family that lived at King's Norton, who
commanded the Parliament troops, might well be proud of his
men's achievement.

Nothing that had taken place in the war produced more
controversy than the way in which Rupert treated Birmingham. It was certainly harsh, but by the laws of war as
understood on the Continent, in the school in which Rupert
had been brought up, there was nothing illegal or improper in
it. If the owners of a house allowed firing from that house
on the soldiers of the other side, the soldiers fired on
were justified in destroying that house. Burning has always
been one of the recognised means of destruction. If Birmingham had been a Continental town nothing would ever

---

* Clarendon, II., 181.   † Ib., II., 181.

have been heard of it; but because the Continental laws of war were applied to an English town the outcry was terrible.

The organs of the Parliament extolled the Birmingham bravery and the Royalist cruelty—their wanton cruelty—in burning houses. The Royalist organs rejoiced at the just judgment which had befallen the disloyal town, and the punishment it had pleased the Lord to inflict on the inhabitants for their rebellious views.

Three accounts of the fight were published. The first, a Parliamentary account, gives their idea of the affair. Its title is:—

" A true | relation | of | Prince Rupert's | barbarous cruelty | against the | "towne of Brumingham | to which place on Monday, April 3rd, 1643, he "marched with | 2000 horse and foot, 4 drakes and 2 sakers, where | after "two hours' fight, being twice beaten off by the | townsmen, in all but 140 "musqueteers, he entered, | put divers to the sword and burnt about 80 "houses | to ashes, suffering no man to carry away his goods | or quench the "fire, and making no difference between | friend or foe, yet by God's "providence the greatest loss fell on the malignants of the town | and of the "Cavaliers were slain divers chief commanders | and men of great quality, "amongst whom was | the Earl of Denbigh, the Lord John | Stuart, and, as "they themselves | report, the Lord Digby. | London, | printed for John "Wright in the Old Bailey, | April 12th, 1643." |

This title sets out the grievances of the Parliament against Rupert's action. The pamphlet contains two reports, one signed "R. P.," who, it is usually said, was R. Porter, a maker of sword blades of some celebrity, whose mill was afterwards burnt by the Royalists because he declined to make or sell sword blades to any but those who fought on the side of the Parliament. He is said to have known not only how to make, but also how to use a sword when made, and that he used his own sword with some effect on that 3rd April, being one of those troopers of Captain Greaves who took part in that charge against the Royalists towards the close of the fight near Smethwick, in which the Earl of Denbigh was killed. The other account is signed " R. G.," possibly Richard Greaves himself. There is one interesting passage in it :—

" The plunder was over £2000, of which Mr. Peake lost £1300. Mr. Jennens "lost much."

This was probably one of the Jennens family, whose large estates in and around Birmingham have given rise to so much litigation even down to our own day.

The second pamphlet is a Royalist production :—

"A | letter | written from | Walshall | by a worthy gentleman to his "friend in Oxford | concerning Burmingham. | Printed in the year "MDCXLIII." |

This brochure tries to defend Rupert from the load of abuse showered on him for this Birmingham business.

The third is a strong Parliamentary production, possibly the most savage of all :—

" Prince Rupert's | burning love to | England | discovered in | Birmingham
" flames, | or, | a more exact and true narrative of Birmingham's cala | mities
" under the barbarous and inhuman | cruelties of P. Rupert's forces, | wherein
" is related how that famous and well-affected | Town of Birmingham was |
" unworthily opposed,
" insolently invaded,
" notoriously robbed and plundered,   By Prince Rupert's forces.
" and most cruelly fired
" in cold blood the next day
" Together with the number of Prince Rupert's forces, | his considerable
" persons slain or mortally wounded, | the many abominable carriages in and
" after the taking | of the town. The small strength which Birmingham | had
" to maintain their defence, the names of their men | slain, the number of
" houses burnt, and the persons thereby | destitute of habitation, with divers
" other considerable passages. | Published at the request of the Committee
" at Coventry, | that the kingdom may timely take notice what is generally |
" to be expected if the Cavalier insolencies be not speedily | crushed. | ' A
" righteous man regardeth the life of his beast, but the | tender mercies of the
" wicked are cruel '—Prov. xii. 10. | London.   Printed for Thomas
" Underhill, 1643."

The titles of these tracts shew clearly what the grievances of
the Parliament were against Rupert.   His defeat of the men
of Birmingham was resented, but still more so was his application of the rules of war to unfortified towns.   For long after
the Parliamentarians never ceased to speak in the strongest
terms of the Birmingham Butcheries.

All traces of Camp Hill fight have passed away.   The ground
has been all built over, and the site of the Birmingham earthworks is covered by streets.   A relic, which has also now
disappeared, remained until a recent date.   The public-house
at Camp Hill, known as the " Old Ship," was, according to
local tradition, the head-quarters of Rupert on the afternoon
of that Easter Monday.   It was at one time known as the
" Anchor."   Before it was destroyed the last owner published
a history of the old inn and the events connected with it.

Rupert made no stay in Birmingham to enjoy the fruits of
his triumph.   On Easter Tuesday, April 4th, he marched from
Birmingham to Walsall; on the Wednesday, the 5th, he
reached Cannock.   He halted there until Saturday, 8th, when
he marched on to Lichfield.

Rupert at once summoned the city to surrender.   Colonel
Russell, the governor, sent back the following answer:—

" I have heard there is a man who goes by the name of Rupert, who has
" burnt near four score houses at Birmingham, an act not becoming a gentle-
" man, a Christian, or Englishman, much less a Prince, and that that man
" has not in all the King's dominion so much as a thatched house ; and if
" this be the same man, I do not intend to deliver the King's places of
" strength unto him, let him pretend what authority he pleases for the having
" thereof."*

Rupert accordingly began the siege.   After a week's work, on
Sunday, April 16th, the breaches were considered practicable.

* Webb, I., 305.

Rupert assaulted the place, but was repulsed. The siege was continued until Friday, 21st April, when Rupert again assaulted the place and took it, by means of a mine—said to have been one of the earliest used in England—blowing up part of the wall of the Close. On this taking place the garrison surrendered on terms; they were allowed to march out with bag and baggage, and sent under a convoy to Coventry.

Rupert had now completed his task, and took steps to return to Oxford. He did not stay long at Lichfield. The day after the surrender he set out on his way back, and on Monday, the 24th, was at Oxford. Here he found the King most anxious that steps should be taken to relieve Reading, and wanting Rupert's help. But the fates were unkind—Rupert got no chance of helping. On Thursday, the 26th, the news reached Oxford that the Royalist governor (Colonel Fielding) had surrendered the place to the Parliament.

This marks a point in the war. The Parliament were now masters of the Thames valley. Nothing remained to prevent them carrying out their original idea of a dash on Oxford, provided Essex and Waller joined forces. To prevent them doing this was the task now set Rupert; this entailed his marching to the West of England.

As has been stated, after the battle of Ripple Waller retreated to Tewkesbury, and on to Gloucester. When there he found orders to repair to his head-quarters—Bristol. This he delayed to do, probably thinking it was necessary to do something to maintain his reputation. There was no love lost between him and Essex. His bad luck in the operations against Maurice rendered it necessary for him to achieve something really brilliant before he returned to Bristol. He accordingly did not obey his orders, stating it would not be safe for him to leave Gloucester until Hereford and Worcester were reduced. He, therefore, set to work to carry out this task.

From his spies he learnt it was possible, if a bold and sudden attack was made, that Hereford might be taken. Such work Waller loved, and he determined to try. With about 2500 men he set out from Gloucester, and at daybreak on the 24th April appeared before Hereford. Some desultory fighting went on during the day, at times rather sharp, but the garrison had no heart in their resistance and deserted, so that there was nothing for Sir Richard Cave, the governor, to do but to surrender. This he did, and on April 25th Waller entered Hereford in triumph. He was entitled to every credit that belongs to a bold and successful leader, and had more than restored his reputation as a conqueror. He had struck unexpectedly, and struck hard, with the result that he had dealt a blow where least expected, and one which was of considerable tactical importance, as he had severed the King's line of communication with Wales. Maurice, on his return to Oxford, had brought with him as a trophy of his triumph over Waller one of his colours, probably taken at Ripple. The Royalists boasted that Maurice had made Waller a negligible quantity by what he had done. Maurice returned in triumph on 7th April ; not more than 14 days had elapsed and Waller had not only undone all that Maurice professed to have accomplished, but also upset the future plans of the Royalists. They were naturally furious. Hereford surrendered on April 25th, Reading on April 26th. The two governors were each brought to a court-martial, but both were acquitted. Secretary Nicholas, writing to the Marquis of Ormond, says:—

"There hath lately been two very considerable towns rendered to the "rebels here, as is strongly suspected by treachery, for we hear that since "they cannot prevail against His Majesty's forces, they say they will make "trial what they can do by corrupting some of our commanders."[*]

Parliament made the most of their triumphs. Their feelings were expressed in lines which speak more for their joy than their poetry.

> "Reading yielded is,
> "Hereford taken is,
> "Hopton beaten is,
> "Malignants grieve I wis."

The third line referring to another Royalist disaster, the defeat of Hopton, near Launceston, by Major-General Chudleigh,[†] on the 25th April. Nor did they confine themselves to poetry. Their preachers ascribed their successes to the direct interposition of God. Waller's entry into Hereford was said to be "as great a deliverance as the Israelites passing the Red Sea."[‡] Essex taking Reading was "no less a miracle than the razing down the walls of Jericho with pitchers and rams' horns."[§]

There was cause for their exultation. These were the first really important successes the Parliament had gained in the Midlands, and if they had been able to hold Hereford and reap the fruits of their victory the war would doubtless ended sooner. But the difficulty was to find men to garrison both Gloucester and Hereford. Waller had a force with which to raid the County, but not a sufficient force with which to garrison it. All he could do was to send out forays from Hereford to secure such supplies and plunder as could be secured, and bring in all arms and money that could be brought in. For instance, a band went to Holm Lacey, Lord Scudamore's place, near Hereford, and were paid £10 15s. to

---

* Carte MSS., E., 119.   † Rushworth, V., 267.   ‡ Burrough's Sermon.
§ Sedgewick's Sermon at Reading

go back. The depredations were not confined to raids from Hereford. Waller's soldiers may have been saints, they were certainly thieves. In an account book of a lady who then resided in Hereford are these entries:—*

"April 24th, 1643, he came, and 25th, Wednesday, he entered the city.
"Paid John Baddam for mending the tiles over my new closet, which Sir
"William Waller's soldiers brake down to shoot at Widemarsh Gate when he
"besieged Heriford,   4d."
"Paid Richard Winnye Smith for mending locks and keys at Heriford,
"which the plunderers broke,   16d."
"Paid Maud Pritchett for a cheese when Sir William Waller was in
"Heriford, for his soldiers, that I kept,   18d."

Having got all he could, Waller saw it was useless to continue to hold Hereford, so resolved to return to Gloucester with his force, in order to carry out the remaining part of his plan and occupy Worcester. Probably his movements were hastened by the knowledge that the Royalists were making preparations to re-take Hereford. On May 18th Waller set out for Gloucester; on May 20th Hereford was again occupied by the Royalists.

The fate of Hereford had put the Worcester garrison on the alert. The Governor (Sir William Russell) had gone to Oxford, Colonel William Sandys was acting as Governor. Russell, as Sheriff, had called out the *posse comitatus*, all between 16 and 60, to come in and serve the King, but it does not appear that the summons had been largely obeyed. There was a good deal of insubordination among the Worcester garrison, and the supply of money and of provisions was far from regular. There was consequently much discontent. This had been kept alive by the fact that bands of Waller's raiders had come fairly near the town; they had been seen at Upton, and probably at Powick, and some communication was kept up between the discontented party in the city and the Parliament troops outside. Essex had appointed various persons who were favourable to the Parliament to offices in the Corporation during the time he had held the town in October, 1642. By a Royal warrant of the 15th March, 1643,‡ these persons had been removed and their places filled with Royalists. The removed men were still in Worcester, and did not regard the ruling power with favour. All this was told to Waller, and he was informed if he only appeared before the walls he would thereupon be joined by a strong party from within the city. Waller therefore determined to attack Worcester at once.

Worcester, in May, 1643, was in a very different state from what it had been in September, 1642. The walls had been re-built, the fortifications re-made, Dud Dudley says, under his direction and supervision. Whether that was so or not, the

---

* Archæologia, XXXVII., 210.   ‡ Harl. MSS., 6802, 21.

place was now too strong to be carried without a regular siege. A force of some 300 volunteers had been raised and trained from among the citizens. The garrison, about 1500 strong, was in readiness, and expected to be attacked, for Waller's raiders had been noticed at Malvern and elsewhere. Sandys believed all was prepared for Waller whenever he liked to come, and that he could hold the city if it was attacked.

On the evening of the 28th May handbills were scattered about the streets of Worcester:—

" To all gentlemen, and other inhabitants of the City of Worcester.

"As many of you as are sensible of the danger of your religion, your "persons and goods, and the privileges of your Corporation, are desired to "declare yourselves sensible of them at this opportunity. It being my errand "(by the help of God) to rescue them from the oppression of your present "governors. And I promise that all such as shall appear willing to welcome "my endeavour shall not only be received to free quarter, but protected to "the utmost of my power.

" May 29th, 1643.   William Waller."

This invitation was cleverly worded, and was meant to appeal to all classes of the discontented. "Religion" referred to the lecturers who had been displaced for the parish clergy; "persons and goods "to the state of martial law and billeting that prevailed in a garrison town, to say nothing of the plundering of lawless ruffians like Hide; "privileges of the Corporation" to the displacement of the members by the Royal warrant. Waller appealed to all the parties who were aggrieved, and he believed he should not appeal in vain.

Naturally, Sandys considered this handbill was the prelude to an immediate attack, so the troops were mustered, the gates closed. He was right; with the morning came Waller. Leaving Gloucester on the afternoon of the 28th May, marching all night through Tewkesbury, Severn Stoke, and Kempsey, he reached Worcester about daybreak on the 29th. He had with him a considerable force, about 3000 strong, and 8 guns. It comprised all his cavalry, including the celebrated Gloucester Blue Regiment. It was obvious that he had come in earnest to deliver the oppressed. On arriving on the south side of the town he halted his men on the high ground above Diglis, sent his trumpeter to the Sidbury Gate to demand the surrender of the place. Colonel Sandys told him, in answer to his demand, that " he was not at Hereford," and had better be off. The trumpeter replied, rightly, that such an answer was most uncivil, and not such as he would take back to his general. Sandys on this told him very peremptorily to be off, and having said so Sandys returned to his quarters. The trumpeter would not leave, refusing to stir, basing his refusal on the fact that he was by the laws of war entitled to a civil answer to take back to his general. The sentry thereupon sent to Sandys asking for orders. Sandys returned not in the best of tempers, accompanied by one of his officers, Captain Beaumont, who commanded one of the regiments that formed the garrison. Sandys again asked the trumpeter why he did not go. The reply was short, decisive, and insulting. On this, Beaumont ordered the guard to fire at the trumpeter. One of them did so, hitting him in the thigh. He fell from his horse mortally wounded.

A great and heated controversy arose over this "regrettable incident," the Parliament writers and speakers contending with some truth that the Royalists had deliberately violated a flag of truce, and killed, while doing his duty, a messenger under its protection, an act opposed to the laws of war; an outrage on civilization. The Royalists contended that the trumpeter, having discharged his mission received his answer, and, refusing to leave when ordered, had by such refusal forfeited all the protection a flag of truce gave him, and might be, and ought to be, as he had been, shot down like a dog.

Whatever might be the rights or wrongs of the question, the death of his trumpeter was more than Waller could stand; it hastened his action. It was now about 6 a.m. Waller ordered the attack to be begun. Placing his guns in position they at once opened on the place. A long artillery duel followed. Some accounts say it lasted all day, some 16 hours (from 6 a.m. till 10 p.m.); but this can hardly be so, having regard to the rest of the operations. Waller's guns were not able to keep down the fire from the city forts, still less to obtain the ascendant. One account says:—

"The city cannoneer-in-chief, with his cannon from the city, together with "the musketeers, all proved good firemen."*

An assault towards Friary Gate was repulsed with heavy loss to the assailants. In front of Diglis Waller fared better. After some hard fighting he carried a house just outside the walls near the Castle Hill, belonging to Mr. William Berkeley. This afforded Waller cover, from which he could fire on the city with safety, "annoying it and likewise the Friary." Sandys determined to dislodge Waller from this post, and after some severe fighting succeeded, not only in doing so, but also in burning the house, so that it was no longer tenable by Waller's men.

A sortie was made from St. Martin's Gate against Waller's right flank by a party of the Royalist horse. They drove the Parliamentarians back on Waller's centre, near Greenhill, and cleared the east side of the city. The fighting was severe. Waller lost some 60 or 70 men. It was said that among them was Sir Robert Cooke, of Highnam, a strong Parliamentarian, who had married the widow of George Herbert, the poet, but as

---

* Townshend M.S., Nash Sup., p. 87.

this Sir Robert Cooke wrote a letter to Speaker Lenthall after the fight, describing it for his information, it could not have been the same man.

The result of this sortie, and the failure of his attack on the Diglis side, led Waller to consider his position. A report arrived urging the garrison to resist, as Lord Capel was on the way to their relief. This was untrue, but it was true that Maurice, wanting to shew what he could do against Waller, had set out from Oxford with three regiments of horse to cut off Waller's retreat to Gloucester. With his troops discouraged by their defeat, encumbered with their wounded, Waller was in no position to resist an attack by Sandys on his front and by Maurice on his flank and rear, besides having the Avon to cross in case of disaster. So Waller determined to retreat while he could. To get rid of the encumbrance of his wounded he collected all the boats round Worcester, and placing his wounded, baggage, and guns on board, sent them by water to Gloucester. He searched round Worcester to get horses, and is said to have been careful to send out as far as Ombersley to carry off all those belonging to Colonel Sandys, the Governor of Worcester, and Martin Sandys, who was helping him. Having collected all he could, about 1 a.m. on the morning of the 31st Waller began his retreat towards Tewkesbury.

His loss in this attack on Worcester was heavy ; five or six captains and 160 soldiers were killed; the wounded filled several barges. But the fighting had been sharp, sharper than usual, especially round Diglis, and this accounts for the casualties.

Sir Robert Cooke, on his return to Gloucester, sent the Speaker the following account of the fight.*

" Gloucester, 2nd June, 1643.

" The success of Sir William Waller's late design upon Worcester was not " so prosperous as to hasten an account, especially the opportunity of sending " it being wanting, yet not so ill as perhaps report may render it. Sir " William, finding a necessity of drawing his forces from this part, was " desirous to leave in as good condition as he might this country, afflicted on " the one side with the Worcester garrison, and the rather because it was " impossible for him to march away with a convenient strength unless he " withdrew the garrison from Tewkesbury, consisting, with officers, near 1000 " horse and foot. In this regard he held it both necessary for the country, " and of great consequence to the main to attempt the taking in of Worcester, " that as the works being slighted it might not remain a strength for the Par- " liament's enemies and give assurance to their chief body of retreat upon " occasion of disaster. Upon Monday morning he presented his force before " it all that day, assaulted it, and especially at two gates, Sidbury and St. " John's [sic. q. Martin's]. The cannon played on both sides all day, the " defence was obstinate, yet within less than four hours we had beaten the " enemy out of all their outworks, and had gained the suburbs, and had " lodged our musketeers at the very ports, and were in so fair a way in so

* Hist. MSS. Com., XII. Rep., app. 1, 709

"short a time of gaining the town as could be.   But Sir William Brereton's
"force not coming in according as was expected, and Sir William Waller
"being called away by no less than five packets that evening out of the west,.
"exclaiming that all would be lost there if he did not immediately advance
"that way, it was held necessary to rise to attend that service as of greater
"importance.   What their loss was we cannot certify, but we are credibly
"informed, a sergeant-major and a cannoneer besides others were slain.   We lost
"the day before Captain Lane, killed by scouts ; that day Captain Ball, an
"ensign, and in all about 16.   Sir William Waller's trumpeter, after he had
"delivered his summons, was unsoldierly shot in the thigh by one Sterm, at
"the animation of the Governor, Colonel Beaumont.   On Tuesday morning
"Sir William Waller drew from thence to Tewkesbury, and so to Gloucester,.
"leaving orders with me to throw down as much of the works as the conveni-
"ence of my time would afford, which I believe is so done that they are made
"unuseful, though not fully slighted, and to withdraw the force from
"Tewkesbury to Gloucester, from whence he had sooner departed had not
"the impossibility of either marching without money, or getting it without
"the employment of his troops to collect it, a little hindered his speed.   The
"country is much troubled at his departure, and unless my Lord General's
"motions shall direct the other force they fear the worst."

This letter gives a fair account of Waller's defeat.   He had
been disappointed that there was no help from Worcester
itself or from outside ; Waller evidently feared an attack, or
he would not have retired so quickly, or evacuated Tewkesbury
so hastily.

The Worcester garrison stated, obviously untruly, that their
loss was only two men and three women.   The gunners were
said to have used 11 barrels of powder and 200 great
shot.*

The great point in the defence was the conduct of the
Worcester women.   All accounts say that they worked hard
at the defences to relieve the soldiers.   Nor did their labours
end with the day's fighting.   Waller had been able to make
his attack with much greater effect from the cover and shelter
he obtained against the fire from the walls by the trees, hedges,
mounds, and fences outside the city walls, especially round
Diglis, and also by the houses.   It was decided that all the
fences and mounds should be levelled, and also all houses and
buildings situated like Mr. Berkeley's houses near the walls,
which could be used by the enemy, removed.   This it was
decided should be done at once, in case Waller might return,
so

"the ordinary sort of women, out of every ward of the city, joined in
"companies, and with spades, shovels, and mattocks did begin to work on
"Tuesday last, the 30th day of June, who were to the number of 400 on a
"day, going in a warlike manner like soldiers, and did so behave themselves
"there in levelling all such fortifications as were left by the Earl of Essex,
"and throwing down ditches, that by their own industry and free service in
"imitation of the citizens of London, as they within one week perfected the
"levelling of the same, which was done the rather by the reason some of them
"were killed in the siege, though casually ; also to ease the soldiers, who,
"being weary of their late hot service, desired some rest, and to prevent

---

* Townsend MS., Nash, Supplement, 87.

" Sir William Waller's approach near if he should return suddenly against " them."*

They need not have feared, Waller would not return ; he was in no state to do so. As Cooke's letter shews, his position was far more serious than the Parliamentarians were willing to admit. Excuses were made for him. It was said that his zeal and his successes had made him attack a fortified city with an improper, insufficient, inadequate force. The Lord General, who had long been jealous of Waller's popularity and reputation, improved the occasion by a severe censure. Waller had no answer to make; he had blundered, and blundered badly. To Worcester is due the honour of having checked the victorious career of the most popular, and hitherto the most successful, of the Parliamentary generals. From a Worcestershire man, a few weeks later, he was to receive that crushing blow that ruined his reputation as a general. Truly Waller said " Worcestershire was not a lucky place for him."

On the 31st May Waller reached Gloucester. He at once took steps to comply with his long-neglected orders. Mustering all the forces at Gloucester and in the district, he got together all the recruits and supplies he could lay hands upon. On the 9th June, with all his horse, nine regiments of infantry, and 22 guns, Waller marched out of Gloucester for his head-quarters, Bristol. Before he left he did one thing that had an important bearing upon the war in the district. He obtained for Massey a commission as Governor of Gloucester and installed him in the post. But Waller did much to prevent Massey doing any useful work in his new position; he left him only a single regiment to garrison Gloucester, a force wholly insufficient for the place, and which put an end to any hope of assuming the offensive until he was reinforced.

The Royalists, if they knew, which is doubtful, how weak Massey was, were still afraid of him, and considered it necessary to have a new general to command in the Leaddon Valley. After some little hesitation the Royal choice fell on Sir William Vavassour, a soldier who had served not only in the present war, but also in Ireland and Scotland, as Colonel of the 13th Regiment of Foot.

Vavassour, as a general, was not fit for the place; he was distinctly inferior to Massey. Charles himself said of him, " that he was a man who could agree with no one in his dominions." His letters shew he was far more profuse in promises than in performances. He was for a time the leading spirit on the Royalist side in all the fighting that took place in the south-west of the County. His head-quarters were at Hereford.

Before further fighting on any considerable scale took

---

* Townsend MSS., cited by Nash, Supplement, p. 87.

place in Worcestershire great events were to happen, and
Massey's hands were far too full for any thought of raids
or skirmishes.

The capture of Reading had laid the left flank of the
Royalists—the Thames Valley—open to the Parliament. On
the right flank there had been a good deal of fighting, on the
whole in the Royalists' favour. Now the time had come
when it was to be decided who should hold the highlands of
Gloucestershire, Wiltshire, and Somersetshire. The Marquis
of Hertford commanded for the King, with Prince Maurice
acting under him, and it was against them that Waller was to
try to redeem his reputation. The plan adopted was that
Waller, whose head-quarters were at Bristol, should engage,
defeat, and, if possible, crush the Marquis of Hertford; having
done this he should move at once towards Oxford, join Essex,
who would advance up the Thames Valley to meet him, and
then with their united forces march on Oxford.*

In pursuance of this plan a good deal of skirmishing took
place round Wells, and at Marshfield, in Gloucestershire,
but Waller was not able, as he wanted, to bring on an action
under conditions favourable to himself. At last, on the 5th July,
a desperate fight took place between the two armies at
Lansdowne, of which Waller had certainly the worst. Yet
the Marquis of Hertford decided to retreat towards Oxford,
thus playing Waller's game. Waller at once followed, out-
manœuvred Hertford, completely cutting off his rear-guard at
Devizes and quickening his retreat. So sure was Waller that
the Royalist troops that were cut off must surrender that he
wrote to Parliament, boasting that his work was done, and that
the next day he would forward a list of the names and quality
of his prisoners.†

The main body of the Royalists reached Oxford. Things
looked serious for the King. If Waller captured the rear-guard
and joined Essex Oxford must be evacuated. Could this
be prevented? It was a forlorn hope; probably the most
desperate of all the desperate things done in that war,
but it was the only chance. Essex was at Thame, only
10 miles away, and Waller might be in front of Oxford
the next day. It was decided to risk everything in an attempt
to prevent this. All the Royalists could spare were 1500 horse
and two guns. These were handed over to Wilmot, and he
was ordered, if he could, to prevent Waller joining Essex and
rescue the King's forces. Wilmot set off the same night,
marching with all speed on Devizes, about two miles outside
the town on " a fair hill," known as " Roundaway Down,"
Wilmot halted; with "all the insolence of assured success"

---

* Clarendon II., 215.   † Clarendon II., 223.

Waller marched out to crush him. Within half-an-hour the Royalists had won their greatest victory in the Civil War. Waller's army was dispersed, disorganised, defeated. Waller himself, with an escort of scarce 100 men, was fleeing, a fugitive, to Bristol, bearing the news of his own rout. With his 1500 men Wilmot had engaged a force of over 5500, with a large train of artillery, and defeated them so utterly and completely that Waller himself admitted that after the fight his cavalry—that force which included "Hazelrigge's Lobsters," and was his pride,—

"was so crippled that a corporal with an ordinary squadron might have taken "them all!"

Waller was crushed. Roundaway Down was fought on 13th July; on 27th July Rupert entered Bristol in triumph. The whole country between the Thames and the Severn was now in Royalist hands. With the single exception of Gloucester they held the whole of the Severn Valley. If Gloucester was reduced, then the Royalist plan of campaign for the year would have been carried out. On its fall all the Royalist energies could be given to the north and west, and then they could march in triumph on London. Gloucester was, therefore, the turning point of the war.

On August 1st Charles came to Bristol, on the 8th to Cirencester, on the 9th to Painswick. On that day Gloucester was summoned. It was in those days considered to be a matter of duty to summon a town before attacking it. Massey, in spite of the terrific odds against him, determined to resist to the last. To His Majesty's most gracious message he replied :—

"That we do keep this city according to our oath and allegiance to and for "the use of His Majesty and his royal posterity, and do accordingly conceive "ourselves wholly bound to obey the commands of His Majesty, signified by "both Houses of Parliament, and are resolved, by God's help, to keep the "city accordingly."*

The garrison was only 1400 men at the outside; "50 barrels of powder was all their store, a mean and slender artillery, works of a vast compass and not fully perfected."

Massey's first act shewed he was terribly in earnest. He burnt the suburbs, destroyed all shelter and cover round the place, including Higham House (the residence of Sir Robert Cooke). On the 10th August the siege began. From all parts men were drawn for the siege. Vavassour came with the Welsh and Herefordshire levies; Russell brought men from Worcester. They were quartered at the Kingsholm, and at Longford, on the north side the city. Vavassour made a bridge of boats across the river to join up with the troops on the west. On the east was the King and Sir Jacob Astley, on

---

* Rushworth V., p. 287.

the south, between Llanthony Abbey and the walls, Lord Ruthven. This completed the investment. The Royalist hopes were high, as the King told Massey's messenger who brought the refusal to surrender, "Waller is extinct, Essex cannot come." No wonder the King was astonished at a handful of men daring to defy the whole Royalist force. He could not understand how they ventured to do it. The answer was simple—they had Massey. With an enthusiasm that never failed, the besieged set to work to strengthen their entrenchments. Women and girls worked, bringing in turf in face of the King's horse and under the fire of the King's guns. Massey had at once to abandon two forts on Alney Island, as he had not men with which to garrison them. This enabled the Royalists to cut off the water supply, which also drove the town mills, so the besieged had to rely on the river for drink, and to grind their corn as best they could.

Massey kept making constant sorties at all points, keeping the Royalists on the alert. On the 12th August Captain Gray headed a sortie against the Worcester men on Kingsholm, burnt their main guard, killed Captain Ramsay with eight or nine soldiers, took five prisoners and some arms, and returned without losing a man. On the 16th another sortie was made against the Worcester men, resulting in an exceeding hot skirmish for about half-an-hour, the cannon and muskets on both sides playing very furiously. On the 18th Massey himself led an assault on the Worcester men, got behind their guns and breastworks, fell on their main guard, killed several officers, soldiers, and two gunners, took a lieutenant prisoner, spiked the guns, and retired with the loss of only two killed and four prisoners.

On the 24th a letter was sent into the town, that Mr. Bell, of Sandhurst, and Mr. Hill, of Tewkesbury, both lawyers, had something of importance to communicate. It was only to advise the garrison to surrender, considering the great force against the place and the impossibility of relief. Massey refused to listen to anything of the kind.[*] Stubborn as was Massey's resistance, his condition was getting desperate. His men were running short—his powder shorter. Unless relief came surrender was only a question of days. Would relief come? The heroism of Gloucester had roused even Essex. Parliament were rapidly reaching fever heat on the question : they determined that Gloucester should be relieved. They ordered volunteers to be enrolled for its relief ; 2000 men were to be pressed for its succour. Volunteers did not come in, pressing was not successful, Gloucester was not relieved.

---

[*] Rushworth V., p. 289.

Parliament became helpless.   The City of London came to their relief.   They resolved that Gloucester must be rescued, and determined to

"send forth from the city some speedy aid for the relieving of the City of "Gloucester, now in great distress by reason of the enemies' army wherewith "they are besieged."

All shops were ordered to be closed until Gloucester was succoured   Lots were drawn by the men of the different trained bands which should go on the service.   On August 24th a general muster was held on Hampstead Heath of the men to go on the expedition, and on the 26th Essex set out on his march to relieve the city.   Essex was in earnest. Writing, on 30th August, to the Committee of the County of Northampton, he says :—

"I am marching for the relief of Gloucester, and shall go to-morrow, God "willing, to Bicester, where I desire those horse and foot of my Lord of "Denbigh's which are with you may be, and they shall have money from me, "and when that business is done they may go their intended way, which will "be but little out of their way. . . If the foot cannot come timely I desire "the horse only may come."*

As soon as the Royalists heard of this march, Rupert was sent with the cavalry to oppose and delay Essex.   It had now become a matter of hours how long Gloucester could hold out; every delay, however short, was essential.   Any time Gloucester might fall even if Essex was not delayed; in a short time Gloucester must fall if Essex was delayed.   Wilmot, who went with the cavalry, desired to do all that could be done to harass and obstruct Essex, and keep him on the road; Rupert wanted to bring Essex to action, fight a battle, and prevent him ever arriving at Gloucester.   If either plan had been carried out it would have been successful, but neither was persisted in.   Wilmot was not allowed to delay and harass Essex as he might have done ; Essex was determined not to fight a battle.   Skirmishes took place at Bicester, Stow-on-the-Wold, and other places, but Essex, " by marching orderly and circumspectly," pressed on, not so rapidly as he would have liked, but still steadily, and Gloucester held out. Marching on, Essex daily reduced the distance, the long length to be traversed got less and less, the opportunities to delay him fewer and fewer.   It is true Essex was in greater force than Rupert, but if ever rashness would have been justified this was one of the occasions.   Neither Rupert nor Wilmot did anything effective to stop Essex.   On the 5th September Essex reached Presbury Hill.   From there he looked down on Gloucester.   He saw that Gloucester still held out, for the Parliament colours were flying over it, but to his surprise the siege was raised, there was no besieging army before

---

* Hist. MSS. Com., IV. Rep., p. 263.

it, nothing but the burning huts of the Royalist camp. Charles had raised the siege. Massey's bravery had received its reward.

The Severn had risen and filled the approaches with water, compelling Charles to draw off his men to the north. The King went on the 5th to Painswick; on the 6th the Royalist army drew up on Birdlip Hill in order of battle. Essex had no intention of fighting, That night the King went to Cubberly, the next to Sudeley Castle, Rupert going to Mr. Stratford's at Farncote. On the 11th Charles went on to Evesham, Rupert to Sheriffs Lench. On the 12th both Charles and Rupert were at Pershore, and on the 13th Rupert went on to White Ladies Aston on the road to Worcester. Charles and Rupert both considered that Essex would follow them northwards, and a great battle would be fought somewhere in Worcestershire.

Essex had no such intention. He or the Severn had done the work, his object was now to get back to London as soon as possible. He only remained at Gloucester three days to revictual it as well as he could, and to replenish its arsenal with such stores of powder and shot as he could spare. To deceive the Royalists Essex marched from Gloucester to Tewkesbury. Here he levied a contribution for the use of Gloucester. Better to outwit Charles, he spent his men's time during the five days of his stay in making a bridge over the Severn. This he finished, and sent out men to occupy Upton. Charles was completely deceived. At night, on the 14th September, Essex suddenly marched from Tewkesbury. Crossing the hills he was by morning in front of Cirencester. The place was too surprised to resist, and Essex occupied it. The importance of Cirencester as a garrison, from what had taken place, had greatly declined, but its capture was a serious loss to the Royalists, as it was the magazine of their army, and by its fall all their stores fell into the hands of Essex. He had now obtained the object for which he had been manœuvring : he had reprovisioned his army, secured an open road to London, and gained two days' march on the Royalists. All this had been done and Gloucester relieved without a battle. Essex was congratulating himself on his good luck and good management as he marched leisurely back to London.

The news of Essex's retreat from Tewkesbury must have reached Charles at Pershore, if not on the same evening it took place, not later than the next morning. Charles at once set off to get between Essex and London. He left Pershore the same day, marched to Evesham, sending on the news to Rupert at White Ladies Aston, with orders to follow as rapidly as possible. Rupert set off that evening, but did not get beyond Charlton. He started very early in the morning of the next day (Saturday), marched all that day and night and most of Sunday. Pressing forward on Monday, he came up with Essex's rear-guard on Auldburn Chase, an open down between Hungerford and Newbury. Here a sharp cavalry skirmish took place, which terminated in favour of the Royalists. Rupert, still pressing on, reached Newbury, so placing himself on the London Road in the direct line of Essex's march. He had gained his end, intercepted Essex, and placed him in a position where he would be forced to fight.

Charles had not been able to keep up with Rupert. On the 16th he left Evesham, rested for some hours at Broadway, but pushed on in the evening. On the 19th he reached Newbury, joined Rupert, and on the 20th September the first battle of Newbury was fought. On the 23rd Charles marched back to Oxford.

One incident of the stay of the army in the County is very characteristic of the times, and should be mentioned. Sir Richard Crispe, one of the farmers of the customs, was colonel of a regiment of horse. His regiment was one of those that Essex had surprised at Cirencester. Crispe had acted as escort to the Royalist siege train on its journey from Oxford to Gloucester. After the siege was raised he left his regiment, going with the King into Worcestershire. While quartered at Sheriffs Lench, on the 15th September, he had a quarrel with another officer, a Northamptonshire man, Sir James Enyon, with the result that they fought with swords, Crispe killing his man with a thrust. Crispe was brought before a court-martial, reprimanded, and discharged on the ground that he only acted in self-defence.

With the Battle of Newbury the main operations in the Midlands for 1643 ended. Although Charles had failed to take Gloucester, he had done a good deal to strengthen his position. All the Vale of the Severn except Gloucester was now his, Bristol gave him a port for Ireland, and he had certainly the upper hand in the West Midlands. Had Charles taken Gloucester, it is likely that the war in Worcestershire would practically have been over. As it was the County had to suffer three years more of fighting, suffering, and misery.

The autumn of 1643 was mainly occupied by fighting on the south-west border. In other words, Massey was again active. His reputation had been, and had rightly been, largely enhanced by his defence of Gloucester. The House of Commons passed a resolution :—

"That Colonel Massey have £1000 betowed on him as a reward and "acknowledgment of his services, whereof £500 to be paid in present, and "that it be recommended to my Lord General to prefer him to some place of "honour and profit, and that the Committee for Advance of Monies take care "that this £1000 be paid with all convenient speed. That the arrears of the "garrison of Gloucester shall be forthwith paid, and that the officers and soldiers

" of that garrison shall have a month's pay bestowed upon them as a reward
" of their services."*

It was easier to resolve than to perform. Neither Massey
nor the garrison ever saw the £1000, the arrears, or the
month's pay.

A letter of thanks from the Speaker was also sent to Massey,
with promises of men and money; but they remained promises.
500 men were enlisted, but when mustered they dwindled
down to 50, and even these did not come for some time.
Powder, muskets, pistols, and carbines were ordered to be sent
but never came. After some months' delay a small supply of
ammunition was forwarded, but nothing like a proper quantity.
No money was ever sent. Massey was thus to a great degree
handicapped.

Vavassour fared better. He was reinforced to some extent,
ordered to occupy Tewkesbury, garrison it, and harass
Gloucester from the Welsh side. These orders Vavassour
carried out, with the result that Massey was in difficulties
about food. Vavassour now elaborated a scheme by which,
with the aid of the governors at Cirencester, Bristol, Sudeley,
and Berkeley Castles, he could blockade Gloucester and starve
out Massey. With their help Vavassour kept the right bank of
the Severn fairly safe, and protected the district practically
from the Malvern Hills to Bristol

To carry out any real scheme against Gloucester Tewkesbury was essential. No town, certainly no unfortified town,
had in the course of the war been taken and retaken with
greater frequency. In the last 12 months it had changed
hands at least seven times. Vavassour now determined to
again take it for the King. With this object early in October
he set out from Hereford with 700 horse and foot. Crossing
Upton Bridge he reached Tewkesbury and occupied it. He
promised the townspeople that, " as their governor, he would
behave with moderation," and asked the townspeople for a
little help. But Massey was not going to part with Tewkesbury without a struggle. He sent up on the tide a boat load
of soldiers from Gloucester. These on their landing, caused
Vavassour considerable alarm. On the arrival of Massey's
soldiers Vavassour's men mutinied, demanding their pay.
Vavassour had no money to give them, so the soldiers
took themselves off over the Avon Bridge, past Ripple and
Upton ; once over the Severn they dispersed to their homes,
eaving Vavassour in Tewkesbury with no force but his officers.
With these he could not resist an attack by Massey, so nothing
remained for him but to abandon the place and march off
with his officers. This he did, taking the road to Upton,
crossing the bridge, and returning to Hereford.

---

* Rushworth V., p. 295.

Massey's despatch to Essex, describing the affair, clearly brings out matters.*

" 5th October, 1643.

" Monday last there being marched into Tewkesbury 400 foot and 3 or " 400 horse. Report is also that considerable numbers are marched into " Sudeley and towards Evesham, and their full resolution are to lie at Stroud, " Painswick, and Cheltenham, on the forest side at Newnham, Mitcheldean, " and Newent, and nearer also, so that your Excellency well knowest how im- " possible it will be for us to maintain this garrison without supply of " strength, many of the townsmen here being weary of the service, and the " country already desire not or will not look upon us, being also likely to lose " our markets, since we are not able to defend them from the enemy's seizure. " To remedy all this I am bold to make this address to your Excellency, by " whose favour of a speedy order and command our succour may be full and " timely, which, if delayed till they settle and fortify themselves in their " winter quarters, it will be a thing of much hazzard and difficulty to relieve " us."

" *Postscript, October 6th.*—I am truly advertised by my scouts that those " foot which were at Tewkesbury, being of the Welsh forces, are all marched " away yesterday upon an alarm my troop of horse gave them, that they cried " out, 'the enemy from Gloucester was coming with 4 pieces of ordinance and " 2000 foot and horse,' and so in much confusion and haste quitted the town, " and some, being of the Welsh force, that the Lord Herbert should never " make them slaves again, nor bring them out of their own country on any " pretence whatsoever, so took the way over Upton Bridge, and no persuasion " of Colonel Vavassour or other officers, nor the force of their horse, would " constrain them to stay and fortify Tewkesbury, as this day they should have " begun ; and now not one left there, I know that the enemy will do what " possibly they can to take Tewkesbury for their winter quarters if we can " prevent them not, for we expect others in the room of the Welsh, whom I " persuade myself will hardly ever be brought so far again upon any service " whatsoever. We hear nothing of Sir William Waller, but hope our supply " is cared for. Sir John Winter's house in the forest is fortified, and a large " number of soldiers allotted to garrison there. Sir Ralph Hopton is said to " be at Berkeley Castle, and hath brought with him 3 or 400 men to garrison " there."

This letter of Massey's shews what difficulty he had to maintain himself at Gloucester, even with Tewkesbury in his possession. One of his great dangers was his communications with London. His only source for supplies and his only route was across the Cotswolds to Blockley, then to Warwick, Newport Pagnell, St. Albans, and London—a long way round. Sudeley Castle being a Royalist garrison, and near the line of route, formed a basis from which parties were constantly sent to intercept his messengers and convoys. If a party got past Sudeley they had then to run the gauntlet of the Campden garrison, which had become a very strong post, as it lay on the Royalist lines of communication between Oxford and Worcester, as well as on the Parliament lines between Warwick and Gloucester. The Royalists determined to increase their garrisons ; a new one was formed at Stoke. Lord Molyneux was ordered to take his regiment to Campden, remain there and garrison it, doing all in his power by sortie, foray,

---

and any other way to intercept and cut off the Parliament convoys.

Massey had not force enough to "beat up" Molyneux at Campden, but what Massey could not do others could. Some of the few attacks on Worcestershire from the east were now made. Warwick Castle had always during the war been held for the Parliament. Sergeant-Major Bridges, who was now in command there, was an active officer. From Warwick Castle he had been carrying on a system of warfare much resembling what Massey had been doing at Gloucester. Bridges determined to make Lord Molyneux move from Campden. He set off one night with a strong force from Warwick, marched the 17 miles so as to reach Campden early in the morning, and at once attacked the garrison. The attack was quite successful; Lord Molyneux was surprised, driven out, a number of prisoners and 100 horses taken. This was, however, only a temporary success. Campden was very soon re-occupied by the Royalists. It was not only that Massey's men had to run the gauntlet of the Royalists in their communications with London; that was a mere inconvenience. The question of supplies was vital. All the autumn Massey's men made sortie after sortie from Gloucester to obtain the supplies that were necessary to sustain the garrison, the chief result of their labours was not merely to procure food, but also to win for themselves, doubtless deservedly, a most evil reputation for being nothing better than a body of robbers.

The autumn showed the use of Bristol to the King. In November about 1000 foot, 100 horse, and 8 guns were landed there from Ireland, under the command of Sir William St. Leger. One of his colonels, Nicholas Mynne, was a man well able to deal with Massey, an officer who had already served under Vavassour. This reinforcement was sent from Bristol to Thornbury and Wootton under Edge. Here they were attacked by a force sent out by Massey to meet them, commanded by a Captain Backhouse. The Parliament troops were repulsed in this attack, with some loss, and the reinforcements proceeded on their way to Cheltenham, Tewkesbury, over Upton Bridge, and so on to Newent, where, much to the disgust of the inhabitants, they were quartered.

Vavassour, being unable to reduce Massey by fair fighting in the open, determined to employ other means. Among Massey's officers was a Captain Robert Backhouse, who was in command of the Parliament cavalry. He had, before he took to soldiering, been an attorney and was well known in the district, and had a large local acquaintance. Among them was a Worcester man, a Roman Catholic, Colonel Edward Stamford, who, on the strength of his acquaintance with Backhouse, wrote the following letter to him from Worcester:—

"19 November, 1643.

" Good Robin,

" It is not unknown to you that once I loved you, and therefore I send this
" to advise you whilst it is in your power to make use of it, and take my word
" I am confident as yet you may not only have your pardon, but raise your-
" self a greater fortune than the condition of those you serve are able to afford
" you.   This you may gain by the delivery ——, you may guess my meaning
" of what place, which is not hard for you to do.   You know the old saying,
" ' Fallere fallenten non est fraus.'   This is the advice of him that, when you
" shall desist the cause, will ever be

" Your loving friend,
" Edward Stamford."*

The person who took the letter told Backhouse that if he
would undertake the business he should have £5000.   Backhouse at once informed Massey, who ordered him to go on with
the affair, as he saw by it a means of helping himself.   The first
result was not an armistice, but such a decrease of vigilance
on the part of Vavassour as enabled Massey to obtain supplies
without difficulty, and relieved the pressure which was
telling so heavily upon the Gloucester garrison.   After several
letters had passed Backhouse required further assurance that
all the promises made to him would be carried out.   To satisfy
him of this, on December 14th, 1643, Lord Digby wrote to
him on the King's behalf,† solemnly engaging his word, both
as a Minister of State and a gentleman, that if Backhouse
performed faithfully what he had promised, then he should
punctually receive immediately after, such a pardon as he
should desire and the sum of £2000, and that as soon as he
sent a definite favourable reply £300, part of it, should be
paid down.   Digby went on to say that the exact way the
surrender was to be carried out should be left to Backhouse
and some one person to settle, and suggested Backhouse
should take his choice of Sir William Vavassour, Commander-
in-Chief of the forces in Gloucestershire ; Colonel Mynne,
Commander of a brigade of English come out of Ireland ; Colonel
Washington, who commanded at Evesham ; or the Governor
of Berkeley Castle.   Backhouse selected Sir William Vavassour
as the man best fitted for the work, and they met on several
occasions, Backhouse succeeding in completely duping
Vavassour, and at each interview obtaining further concessions
for the benefit of the Gloucester garrison.   In fact, but for
these negotiations it is most doubtful if Massey, with the small
and badly-equipped force at his disposal, could have held out
at Gloucester during the winter.

The fighting in the County had to a great extent ceased
towards the end of 1643.   There were continual conflicts, of
which no record has survived, of parties from each side
searching houses for arms : that is plundering, stopping

---

* Rushworth V., p. 295.   † Rushworth V., p. 295.

convoys or messengers, or attacking houses or posts held by opposite sides. A body of troops on the march were always liable to be attacked, and from the different garrisons parties were continually sent out to intercept any of the opposite side who were passing in the neighbourhood, but all these breaches of the peace, although they often involved loss of life, and always damage to property, had little or no real effect on the war.

Fighting was not the only evil the war had brought about. There was a complete cessation of traffic upon the roads, which as a result brought great distress into most of the towns; the markets were ruined, the dealers could not go about the country. At Shrewsbury it was said that

" A want of all commodities, not native with us, will follow the intercourse " between us and London being interdicted."

Merchants were arrested on their journeys and were not infrequently, and perhaps properly, hung as spies. It was dangerous to travel without a pass. On March 8th, 1643, there is an order of the House of Lords :—

" That Mrs. Gerrard, with four small children and two maids, in a hackney " coach, and coachman and two men, should have a pass to go to Malvern, in " Worcestershire, and to have her necessary apparel, and the coach, coach- " man, and one other man to return to London."

But what pressed hardest on the Royalists were two ordinances passed at the beginning of the year. The first, on the 27th March, forbade " tenants to pay rents to delinquents,"* thus practically putting an end to the incomes of most of the County squires. The second, on the 1st April, 1643, was " for sequestrating notorious delinquents' estates."* This ordinance appointed sequestrators in each County, any two of whom were authorised to take and seize into their hands the personal estate and the lands and real estate of

" all persons, ecclesiastical or temporal, as have raised or shall raise arms " against the Parliament, or have been, are, or shall be in actual war against the " same, or have voluntarily contributed or shall voluntarily contribute, not " being under the power of any part of the King's army at the time of such " contributing, any money, horses, plate, arms, munition, or other aid or " assistance for or towards the maintenance of any forces raised against the " Parliament, or for opposing any force or power raised by authority of both " Houses of Parliament."

This practically gave the Commissioners power to take the property and income of anyone they pleased, as they were the sole judges of whether or not the person came within the definition of delinquent. For Worcestershire the Commissioners named were the two County Members, Sergeant Wilde and Humphrey Salway ; the Member for Evesham, Richard Cresswell; Edward Dingley, of Charlton, at whose house Rupert stayed on the first night of his march from White

---

* Rushworth V., 309.

Ladies Aston to Newbury, and doubtless the fact of his being
a sequestrator was not forgotten; Edward Pitts, of Kyre;
Thomas Greves, of King's Norton, whose son commanded the
Parliament troops against Rupert in the fight at Camp Hill ;
and William Jeffreyes, of Earl's Croome, the son of that
Thomas Jeffreyes to whom Butler, the poet, is said to have
acted as justice's clerk. It will be seen that they were selected
from different parts of the County, so that their local knowledge might prove useful.

Worcestershire and Herefordshire had the reputation of
being particularly " malignant counties," so they were specially
treated. In addition to the sequestration, an excise on, among
other articles, cider and perry was imposed—the first excise
that had been levied as a general tax in England.   The
King, by a proclamation from Oxford, dated 7th April, 1643,
after stating that in three months Parliament had raised a sum
exceeding the great subsidy of £400,000, ordered his subjects
not to pay the taxes, nor submit to the sequestration, but to
resist to the utmost of their power all persons who should
oppose the King's orders.*

The people against whom the Parliament were most bitter
were the country clergy. That the clergy were not all that
could be desired is probably true, but the orders framed against
them were usually made on charges of gross misconduct, and
such charges were far too general and wide-spread to be fully
accepted. Worcestershire examples may be cited in the case
of Durrant, the Vicar of Blockley, who was charged with
assaulting the constable ;† and Hollington, the Vicar of Alvechurch, against whom two charges were made : (1) of
misconducting himself with his parishioners ; (2) that in reading
the Remonstrance he left out words,

" so as to obscure from the people the greatness of the danger the House of
" Commons was in, as it is conceived in favour of the other side."‡

To protect the clergy, Charles issued a proclamation on 15th
May, 1643, forbidding them being disturbed or plundered
under illegal ordinances.‖

To show how the sequestration acted one example may be
given. Thomas Savage, of Elmley Castle, had commanded a
troop of horse for the King. For some reason he became
dissatisfied, gave up his command, and went to live quietly
with his mother at Malvern, in the Abbey House. Having
once served the King he came within the definition of a
delinquent in the ordinance, and so was liable to have his
property seized and his rents taken. Elmley was too near
Tewkesbury not to make Savage apprehensive of being

---

* Rushworth V., 313.   † Worcestershire Sessions Records, 1642, No. 59.   ‡ Ib., No. 60.
‖ Rushworth V., 319.

visited.   He accordingly applied to Massey for protection, and
Massey agreed if Savage paid £300 to obtain his discharge
from any sequestration and permission for him to reside at
Malvern.   At that time the Worcestershire sequestrators had
not been appointed, so Massey was the only person to whom
Savage could go.   Relying upon Massey's promise, Savage
paid the money and returned to Malvern.   He was not
long allowed to remain in peace, but was, in spite of Massey's
promise and his payment, arrested and imprisoned by the
sequestrators, who came in the autumn and sat at Tewkesbury,
there being no place in Worcestershire where they were able
to sit.   Massey greatly resented this treatment of Savage, and
wrote to Lord Denbigh remonstrating against it, and asking
for Savage to be released.   After enduring a longish imprisonment Savage was made to pay a fine of £1500 as a composition,
and was set at liberty.

Probably this system of sequestration did more to aid the
Parliament than fighting.   The landowners recognised if they
were not to be ruined they had better submit.   Those who
submitted early got better terms than those who held out.
Those who came in before 1st April, 1644, got off without a
fine; those before the 1st November, 1644, were fined one-
tenth, after that one-third of the value of their estates.   A
letter to Ormonde in October, 1644, shows how this system
worked :

" The poverty of our noble gentry in those shires we possess is so insuffer-
" able that we shall not hold out many months without yielding;   already
" 3000 gentlemen have compounded, and daily more go."*

It is difficult to realise all the exactions that were practised.
The unfortunate Royalists were plundered by the Parliament
for their loyalty to the King.   They were required by the
King to shew their loyalty by their contributions, their faith
by their works.   The case of the Dean and Chapter of
Worcester and others illustrates this.

1st February, 1643.   Resolution of the Dean and Chapter,
agreeing to supply Charles with £1000, to be obtained by the
felling of timber trees out of Cornwood.†   Nor did the
Worcester clergy escape.   They were asked by the King to
make a loan, to be duly and speedily

" repaid with interest of £8 per cent. as soon as these distractions shall be
" somewhat appeased,"‡

but the security offered does not seem to have appealed to
them.   However, in January, 1643, they shewed their loyalty
by their readiness to contribute

"a good sum of money towards the raising of a troop of horse under the
" command of Sir James Hamilton."‡

---

* Carte's Ormonde, III., 352.   † Hist. MSS. Rep., XIV., App. 8, p. 189.
‡ Hist. MSS. Rep., XIV., App. 8, p. 203.

There is also an order from Charles I. to Nathaniel Tomkins, treasurer of the Church of Worcester, signed by the King and Edward Nicholas, to pay to Captain Francis Blunt the sum of £200, or thereabouts, of Church rent due unto us.*

---

* Hist. MSS. Rep., XIV., App. 8, p. 200.

CHAPTER III.

1644.

On the surface it still looked as if all the advantage of the war was on the King's side. At the beginning of 1644, Worcestershire and Herefordshire were still free of Parliament troops. The whole of the Severn Valley, including the port of Bristol, was the King's, with the exception of what Clarendon calls : [*]

"that unfortunately obstinate town of Gloucester, which only kept him from "commanding the whole Severn."

The Royalist troops were thus distributed in Worcestershire at the beginning of the year. On the line from Oxford to Worcester the garrisons were :

Stow-on-the-Wold, Earl of Northampton, 6 colours, 300 foot.
Campden, Lord Molineux.
Stoke.
Evesham, Colonel Knottsford, 150 horse ; Colonel Washington, 400 foot.
Pershore and other places, Sir Walter Pye and others.
Worcester, Colonel Sandys, 300 horse and 1000 foot.

In the north of the County the garrisons were:

Bewdley, Sir Thomas Lyttelton.
Hartlebury Castle, Colonel Sandys.
Dudley Castle, Colonel Leveson.

In the south of the County:

Strensham, Sir William Russell.

And although outside the County border, but forming part of its military system :

Sudeley, Lord Chandos.
Tewkesbury, Sir William Vavassour.

Madresfield does not seem to have become a regular garrison until later.

Webb says that Malvern was then a garrison of Massey's, but this can hardly have been so, the Worcester garrison would not have allowed a hostile post so near them, nor one so close on their line of communications with Herefordshire.

The Parliament does not appear to have had any garrison in the County, but outside, on the east, was Warwick, with Brydges as governor. It did for that part what Massey was doing at Gloucester. In the south and south-west Gloucester, with Massey, on the north-west, in Shropshire, Bridgnorth.

---

* II., 306.

BEWDLEY OLD BRIDGE.

In the early part of the year a new garrison was formed in the north at Edgbaston, later on another at Stourton Castle, near Stourbridge, and one at Hawkesley, between Bromsgrove and Northfield. Neither party possessed any field army for any hostilities, each had to rely upon troops drawn from the garrisons.

Outside Worcestershire the Royalists had again occupied Reading. In January Rupert took Towcester, which enabled the line of communications between Gloucester and London to be threatened.

One great advantage Parliament gained early this year was the advance of the Scotch army into England. This, if it did nothing else, altered the state of things in the north, and indirectly affected the position of matters in the Midlands. Recruits were the great difficulty that the King was beginning to feel, and to find that all, and more than all, his present men would be engaged in the north, was a serious matter. All that need be said here as to the war in the north is that the Marquis of Newcastle, who commanded there, was engaged in putting York into a state of defence, while the Parliament were endeavouring to cut the King's communications with the north by trying to occupy Newark, which they were besieging, but Newark was holding out well, and one of the things the Royalists had to do was to relieve it.

One act of Charles at the beginning of the year was most unpopular. On the 25th January, 1644, he created Prince Rupert, as a reward for his services, Earl of Holderness and Duke of Cumberland. Parliamentarians were never tired of scoffing at " Prince Robber, Duke of Plunderland."

In the first part of 1644 there was comparatively little fighting in the County. In the south and west Massey was still employed in deluding Vavassour about the surrender of Gloucester, and this had a very serious effect on the war, as it prevented the Royalists gaining Gloucester by force and wasted the first two months of the year.

Digby's letter, already mentioned, made the Royalists quite sure of success, and Vavassour's head was completely turned by Backhouse's choice of him. He was ready to agree to any terms or conditions, so certain did he feel of the faith of Backhouse. To further put Vavassour off his guard, Massey had allowed him to occupy Tewkesbury, and he had there about 700 infantry, while Mynne was at Newent with 1000 foot and some Irish horse.

On the 8th January, 1644, matters · had got so far that Backhouse and Sandford met at Corse Lawn to settle the plan for the surrender of Gloucester. Sandford paid Backhouse the £300 on account, and gave him a discharge for a bond for £50 that Backhouse owed a Papist named Font. It was agreed that on February 15th, Gloucester Fair day, the Royalist troops should come to the west gate of Gloucester, and Backhouse should let them in, or arrange for them to be let in, having previously sent them the pass-word to enable them to go by the sentries and pickets. Matters seemed so favourable and so certain that Rupert himself came from Oxford to Newent to settle what should be done, and to make arrangements for what action should be taken on the surrender. Two of Vavassour's officers, Sir Walter Pye, whose regiment was quartered at Tewkesbury, and Colonel Wroughton, who commanded a regiment of horse there, were now instructed by Vavassour to hold themselves in readiness to carry out the scheme.

Massey, feeling he had got Vavassour under his power, directed Backhouse to raise his terms. As a proof of his sincerity, Vavassour was required to order Berkeley Castle to be evacuated, and to march his garrison out of Tewkesbury and station them at Pershore. Strange to say, Vavassour agreed even to these terms. As a furthur display of confidence Massey sent Vavassour a lamprey pie. He also wrote him a letter, expressing how much he felt grieved that an officer so distinguished as Vavassour, who had fought so well against Papists in Ireland, should actually be found serving with them in England. In return for the pie Vavassour sent Massey a butt of Metheglin, and wrote, saying

"if Massey could convince him he was fighting against the Protestant
"religion he would never draw his sword again on the Royalist side."

It is impossible to say to what extent Vavassour would have been humbugged. His officers, however, began to feel uncomfortable, and would not do what he proposed. Instead of marching his men from Tewkesbury to Pershore, Sir Walter Pye went to Oxford and lodged a formal charge of treason and treachery against Vavassour. The Governor of Berkeley Castle flatly refused to evacuate it at Vavassour's orders, Wroughton refused to march his men out of Tewkesbury, and worst of all Mynne was so utterly disgusted with the whole affair that he went to Oxford and begged he might be relieved of his command at Newent and sent back to Ireland. Nothing could, however, shake Vavassour's belief that Backhouse would deliver up the place, so he got ready the men to send to Gloucester to take it over.

On the 14th February, Vavassour, having received a message from Backhouse that the pass-word for the night was "Bristol," sent off his troops, armed with this word, to occupy the place. It was essential, to carry out their plan, that they should arrive in the early morning before it was light. On their doing so, and giving the word at the gates, they were to be admitted. In the evening of the 14th Massey called a council of war and disclosed to them the whole affair, and how he intended it should be dealt with. An hour before daybreak the garrison were to stand to arms. The Royalists would be allowed to cross the Over Bridge, which was then a suspension bridge ; as soon as they had passed the bridge pickets were to cut the cables of the bridge so as to let it down into the river and cut off the Royalist retreat. Then having the Royalists trapped on the long causeway, on an island from which there was no exit, between the fire of the troops at the bridge and the fire of the garrison from the town, they could either be shot down at leisure or made to surrender, as was considered best. Massey's plan was approved, the bridge guard strengthened, and Massey and his men waited with anxious expectation to see the Royalists walk into the trap set for them.

But it was not to be. From two accidents the Royalists escaped the snare. Backhouse's messenger with the pass-word did not reach the Royalists till far later than he should have done, so that had they set off at once on receiving it they would hardly have got to Gloucester before daybreak. When it did arrive Vavassour's officers were so strongly of opinion that there was treachery that they flatly refused to stir. At last, with difficulty, Vavassour got over their scruples and induced them to march, but too much time had been taken up ; as they marched over Lassington Hill, within a mile of Gloucester, the day was breaking, so it was useless going on. They halted, looking down on Gloucester, the Over Bridge, and the trap set for them. Probably the number of the troops at the bridge confirmed their suspicions of the reception prepared for them. They faced about and marched back to Newent. Backhouse made another appointment with Vavassour for the Royalists to come, Vavassour still retained his childlike faith, but the men would not move. So at last, with an impudence one cannot fail to admire, Backhouse, to gain credit from the Parliament, now there was no more to be got out of Vavassour, published a full account of the affair, under the title of "A True Relation of a Wicked Plot." Glorying in his shame, Backhouse boasts how he deceived, and nearly deceived to his ruin, Vavassour and his men.

Having, by the plot, got what he wanted in the way of supplies, Massey resumed the offensive. He kept the Royalists continually on the alert, ever appearing when least expected, raiding and plundering the country for a distance of 30 miles round Gloucester. He was far more than a match for Vavassour both in war and in diplomacy. 'Mynne with his garrison at Newent, his outposts at Highleadon and Taynton, kept that side of Gloucester fairly quiet. But if one side was closed Massey raided the other. He prepared a vessel of sufficient size to carry enough men for a raid or beating up quarters, and took his men up to Upton with the tide or down to Aust. Landing on either bank of the river, when least expected, he carried off what spoils he pleased, and in this way kept his men well supplied. Dropping down the river to the Wye mouth, he ran up to Chepstow, which was garrisoned by a regiment of horse Lord Herbert was engaged in forming. They were utterly surprised by Massey's appearance; some were killed, some were taken. The Chepstow register records the surprise. There is an entry:

"Captain Carvine, who was killed in his chamber in the George Inn by "certain soldiers which came from Gloucester, was buried 20th January."

In addition to dispersing the garrison, Massey's men made a more valuable capture. A Bristol ship was lying there laden with supplies for the Worcester garrison. This turned out a prize of great value, the cargo being sack, tobacco, and ammunition.*

Massey made his name a terror. So much was this the case that when on one occasion Vavassour's men were attacking Boddington House, near Cheltenham, with good prospect of taking it, a rumour was circulated that Massey was on his way from Gloucester to relieve it. Without waiting to see if the report was true or false, Vavassour's men made off and abandoned the attack. It must have caused the Royalist officers much mortification to see the position to which they were reduced. Vavassour had more troops than Massey, and probably better troops; men who, if only decently led and handled, could and would have routed Massey over and over again, but the fear and the dread of the Governor of Gloucester had so entered into the soul of Vavassour as to render him powerless to contend against him. At last even the headquarters' staff at Oxford became disgusted that nothing effective was done, and considered that the time had come for a change. On the 2nd April, 1644, an order was issued from Oxford, directing Vavassour to draw out of Gloucestershire the forces under his command, leaving sufficient in Tewkesbury and the Forest of Dean, but not to remove the garrison of Sudeley Castle, to which Lord Chandos, who was then quartered in Worcestershire, was to march. An iron piece, carrying a 9lb. bullet, was to be sent from Ludlow for its defence, and Mr. Foley was to send 100 shots.†

As has been stated, the advance of the Scots changed the position of affairs in the North of England. To prevent the Parliament troops isolating the north Rupert was ordered to do his best to provide for the security of Shrewsbury, Chester, and North Wales, and to raise the siege of Newark.

---

* Webb, I., 362.   † Harl MSS., 6802, 88.

Rupert's men left Oxford on Tuesday, 5th February, and marched to Chipping Norton. On the 6th he joined them, on the 7th they reached Pershore, and on the 8th Worcester. From Worcester he went to Bewdley; here there appears to have been a meeting of the leading Royalist officers, possibly they brought such men to reinforce Rupert as they could spare from the garrisons. Sir William Russell, Colonel Sandys (the Governor of Hartlebury), Sir Gilbert Gerrard (the Governor of Worcester), Colonel Washington (the Governor of Evesham), were all present; so were Mr. Townshend, of Elmley Lovett (a leading Royalist, whose journal gives interesting details of the war), and a Major Savage. Their presence at Bewdley is shewn by the borough accounts, and it would seem that their deliberations required a supply of drink at the cost of the borough.*

On Rupert's arrival the bells were rung.

	£	s.	d.
" Pd. for ringing at Prince Rupert's coming	0	1	6

Then come the accounts for refreshments :—

	£	s.	d.
" For a hogshead of claret wine for Prince Rupert	4	10	0
" For a pottle of sack and a pottle of claret for the Lord Herbert	0	3	4
" For a quart of sack and a quart of claret for Colonel Sandys	0	2	8
" For a pottle of sack for Sir William Russell	0	2	0
" For a pottle of sack for Sir Gilbert Gerrard	0	2	0
" For a pottle of sack for Major Savage	0	2	0
" For wine for Colonel Washington	0	2	4
" For wine for Mr. Townshend	0	7	4

Lord Herbert lived at Ribbesford, close to Bewdley, and possibly did some entertaining himself.

It is a little remarkable that there is no mention of the Governor of Bewdley (Sir Thomas Lyttelton) during all this feasting.

On Friday, February 15th, Rupert moved on to Bridgnorth, where he stayed four days. On the 19th he went to Shrewsbury, and for the rest of the month devoted himself to clearing Shropshire of the Parliament troops, winding up with defeating Mitton and Fairfax at Market Drayton on the 4th March. An expedition into Wales to Chirk Castle occupied the next week. On Thursday, March 14th, he was back at Shrewsbury; on the 15th at Bridgnorth, on the Saturday at Wolverhampton, on the Sunday at Lichfield, on Monday, 18th, at Ashby-de-la-Zouch. On the 21st he attacked and routed Meldrum, and raised the siege of Newark, thus carrying out the programme laid down for him. It is difficult to say which one admires most, the wonderful completeness with which the work was done, or the wonderful activity in doing it.

The Spring of 1644 produced a new Parliamentary leader in Worcestershire and one who is a most characteristic product

---

* Burton's Bewdley, App., p. xxxii.

of the times, John Fox. After Rupert's sack of the place
in April, 1643, the Birmingham men had again rallied to the
Parliament. A party of them, headed by Fox, had seized and
garrisoned Edgbaston Hall, then the residence of the Goughs,
and from it had made forays all over the district of north Worcestershire. Fox was one of the most active of the Birmingham
men. According to the Royalists he had been a tinker, but it
seems more likely he was one of the many small makers of
sword blades and knives in north Worcestershire. Whatever
he was nature designed him to be a leader of men, for he was
able, by his presence and influence, to keep in order and to
retain in his service a body of unmitigated scoundrels. Fox
was bold, reckless, enthusiastic, able to impart his enthusiasm to others, religious according to the religion of reciting
texts, always ready to ascribe acts of plunder, however felo-
nious, as acts of zeal for the Lord. He was a typical example
of the Puritan military instrument. To the Parliament such
a man was invaluable. In March, 1644, Lord Denbigh gave
him a commission as colonel of a regiment of horse which he
was engaged in raising. It was to consist of six troops and two
troops of dragoons, some 800 men in all, and as their pay was as
doubtful as their piety, they probably formed a most formidable
body of thieves. A commission as major in the regiment was
given to one Russell Fox, who is said to have been the colonel's
son. Fox's influence over his men is best shown by a letter he
wrote to Lord Denbigh, in reply to an order from that nobleman, under whose command he was, to attend him.

"I cannot," says Fox, "leave my men to wait on your Lordship, for fear
"of mutiny and general departure."

Fox very soon proceeded to justify his appointment. He was
a most constant correspondent with his chief. On the 15th
March, 1644, he writes* representing

"the many complaints of the country, by reason of Lord Denbigh's new
"garrisons exacting provisions, pillaging, and issuing warrants (one of which
"he encloses) for money in Lord Denbigh's name, and in places obedient to
"his impositions and under his protection."

On the 18th March he writes giving an account of Rupert's
march from Wolverhampton to Lichfield,

"Yesterday, about 12 of the clock, at Bloxwich, about 4 miles on the way
"from Wolverhampton to Lichfield, was Prince Rupert's rendezvous, being
"not above 900 horse and foot in the outside of his strength. The greater
"part were horse, though but weak, except some 2 or 3 troops that were reason-
"ably good; his foot very poor and ragged, very many no arms but swords.
"The last night his force were at Lichfield, where he himself was the night
"before, as it is believed. Colonel Baggott sent forth warrants to his neigh-
"bouring parishioners to bring in provisions for 4000 of his soldiers. It is
"credibly thought they are bound for Newark."†

---

* IV. Rep., Hist. MSS. Com., p. 264.   † Ib., p 264.

Fox had not been content with Edgbaston. He had been instrumental in carrying out Lord Denbigh's policy of establishing new garrisons and had set one up at Stourton Castle, near Stourbridge. For this purpose he sent his brother with 300 men to occupy Stourton Castle, and turn it into a garrison for the Parliament. This was done successfully, and Stourton became rather a thorn in the side of the north Worcestershire Royalists. Major Hervey applied to Sir Gilbert Gerrard, the governor of Worcester, for help to take Stourton Castle. Fox heard of this; he wrote to Lord Denbigh, on the 24th March, pointing out the advantage of Stourton Castle from its strength and situation, and that it was necessary its garrison should be at once reinforced. As no reply, or no satisfactory reply, was received Fox did his best to drive off Gerrard, who had attacked it with some guns and troops of horse. Fox met Gerrard on Stourbridge Heath, just inside the Worcestershire border. Gerrard seems to have been far too strong for the Tinker, the Royalists' account says that they piteously banged Fox, charged and routed him and his men, pursued them for three miles and slew many.

"The first running rebel being the jovial Tinker himself, whose example was "well followed by all his worthy trayne."

Fox, Richard Turton, and Captain Thomas Hunt write to Lord Denbigh as to this fight on Stourbridge Heath. They state that they were outnumbered and so failed in their attempt to relieve Stourton, ask for reinforcements, "as it would be a great pity to lose such a place."* The reinforcements were not forthcoming and as the Tinker could not go to its relief Stourton surrendered. Fox wrote to Denbigh to say it had been surrendered on honourable conditions. Things could not have been so bad with Fox as the Royalist writers represented, for on the 31st March he wrote proposing an exchange of prisoners. He was, however, under considerable apprehension as to what Rupert might do, and obviously dreaded a possible visit at Edgbaston. Having defeated Meldrum and raised the siege of Newark, Rupert left there on the 27th March on his return to Shrewsbury. On the 31st he was at Lichfield, and Edgbaston was not much out of his road. Fox had a close watch kept on him and thus writes† on the 5th April to Lord Denbigh :

"Intelligence of Prince Rupert, that yesterday he kept his rendezvous at "Shireoaks, and last night quartered at Hampton Brewood. His soldiers "talk of Stafford and some other garrisons as though they meant to besiege "them, but this day's march will discover more certainly which way he "bends."

Fox was needlessly alarmed. It was quite true that Rupert

had a garrison in his mind, but it was not Edgbaston, but Longford House, near Newport, in Shropshire. It was taken by composition. Rupert stayed that night at Newport, and the next day went back to Shrewsbury, which was for the time his head-quarters.

Being freed from fear of Rupert for the time, Fox, on the 5th April, writes to Denbigh, calling attention to his own condition. He

" complains of the want of money and necessaries for the subsistence of his
" soldiers. This garrison needs no enemy to destroy it, for if money be not
" supplied it will destroy itself."*

Somehow the difficulties at Edgbaston were got over, and it remained for some time one of the chief centres of Parliamentary activity in the north of the County. It is likely this development of fighting in the north of the County may be due to the zeal and activity of the Tinker.

It was not only Edgbaston that the people of the north were called upon to supply with provisions. There is an order from Thomas Norreys, whoever he was, to the constable at Hagley, ordering him at once to bring in the supply of provisions for the Worcester garrison.†

Fox was in April preparing his great exploit, one that reads far more like an incident out of "The Three Musketeers," or some other of Dumas' novels, than an actual event. Unfortunately, the accounts are not so detailed as could be wished. Bewdley was a Royal garrison, of which Sir Thomas Lyttelton was governor. The exact strength of the garrison at that date does not appear, but it must have been at least 120 men. These, or the greater number of them, were quartered in the town. The governor lived out of the town in the Royal Lodge, or Palace of Tickenhill, in the Forest of Wyre, and had certainly some, but it is not clear what number of troopers, with him. Lyttelton was the most prominent of the Worcestershire Royalists, high in Charles' favour, and it would be a great achievement to make him prisoner, if it could be done. The difficulties were great, but Fox resolved to try.

Bewdley lies on the west of the Severn. At ordinary times the river is fordable. There was a bridge, but the then bridge had a gatehouse in the middle, which would be kept closed at night, and there would have been a bridge guard. Bewdley consists of one short main street ; at the top a road to the left leads to Tickenhill. It was necessary to cross the river, surprise and overpower the garrison in the town, prevent any word being carried to Tickenhill, and having got the town and garrison in their hands to surprise Tickenhill. As

---

* IV. Rep., Hist. MSS. Com., p. 265.   † Ib., p. 265.

stated, it seemed an almost impossible task, yet it was a task Fox resolved to try.

Fox had a 24-mile ride before him from Edgbaston to Bewdley. Starting off in the afternoon he managed to get there after dark. He selected some 60 of his troopers as the party for the business. Rupert had gone from Shrewsbury to Oxford, and it was very probable he would be followed from time to time by detachments or stragglers of his regiment, and Bewdley would be on their road. Fox determined to pretend that he and his men were a detachment of Rupert's regiment. Coming to the gate on the bridge he ordered the guard to open it and admit men of the Prince's regiment, who wanted quarters for the night. It was dark, no enemy was supposed to be within 20 miles, and the bridge guard, probably sleepy, possibly drunk, obeyed mechanically the peremptory orders that they were used to receive from Rupert's officers, and allowed Fox's party to pass the bridge without question. Boldly riding on, Fox came to the main guard in the town. A chain drawn across the street prevented anyone passing. Again Fox demanded admission and quarters for the night, and again it was granted. Fox then halted his men, sent some forward as he had arranged, some to seize the sentinels, others to guard the doors of the houses where the officers and men were billeted, with orders to cut down anyone that tried to come out into the street. Some five or six of the sentinels had to be killed to prevent them giving an alarm, then Fox went to each house, making the officers and men surrender, placing a guard over each. Without the loss of a man his plan so far succeeded. He overpowered the garrison, was master of the town, and, what was more important, not the smallest note of warning had reached Ticknell. Securing his prisoners and leaving a guard over them, Fox with the rest of his men marched to Ticknell. All were in bed—the surprise was complete. Lyttelton and some other gentlemen were made prisoners without difficulty, the garrison was overpowered and surrendered. Then Fox turned his attention to what could be carried off. He took " Four brave Flanders mares, great store of provisions, and 40 gallant horses of the King's." Leaving such of the prisoners as were not worth taking bound, so they should not give an immediate alarm, Fox, with Sir Thomas Lyttelton, set off at once, not to Edgbaston, where he would have been followed, but into Warwickshire to Coventry. This ruse was successful. Pushing on, he reached there with his prisoner in safety. As soon as the Ticknell garrison got free they roused their neighbours and sent word to Bewdley. This took time. Thinking Fox would go back to his quarters led them astray, and took up more time, and when at last they got upon

Fox's trail and pursued with the intention of rescuing the prisoner they found he had got too much start. Fox had reached Coventry, or, as he put it, " Blessed be God, they came a day after the fair."

It was certainly a brilliant bit of impudence, and deserved success, and it is difficult to avoid feeling sorry for Fox, as he reaped no substantial advantage from his bravery. Lyttelton was too great a catch for an irregular colonel to be allowed to reap a ransom. Parliament at once appropriated him and sent him to the Tower. Essex, however, who knew Lyttelton, offered to become his bail, and on this he was soon afterwards released, but in the autumn, for some reason, he was re-arrested and again sent to the Tower, where he remained for some time. He subsequently regained his liberty. He died, however, soon after, in 1650, and is buried in Worcester Cathedral.

Fox still was active. It was probably owing to him that at the end of May Lord Denbigh undertook the siege of Dudley Castle. Fox appears to have assisted at the siege, but it is not quite clear if he took part in the fight with Wilmot when he tried to raise it in June.

Fox is said to have been instrumental in planting another garrison in the County, Hawkesley, the house of the Middlemores, strong Royalists, strong Catholics, and consequently strong malignants. A party from Edgbaston, it is not quite certain when, turned the Middlemores out, and converted the place into a garrison for the Parliament. Symonds says* : " The rogue, Fox, pulled down the church to make the works." But, whatever sins Fox may have been guilty of, it does not seem that he was guilty of this, as there is no church anywhere near Hawkesley.

Fox also appears to have been governor of another garrison known as Rushin Hall, said by Symonds to be in Warwickshire, but it seems more likely to be the Rushall Hall, near Dudley, that was taken during the siege of the castle.

Fox made himself so active and so objectionable that it was determined to make a serious attempt to get rid of him. On 5th October, 1644,

" Forces went out from Worcester and joined with others from Dudley Castle, " to recover Edgbaston House from the rebels. Returned without doing " anything.†

As has been stated, early in April Vavassour ceased to be the commander in the south-west of the County. A little time elapsed before a new appointment was made, and Massey took advantage of this to get some supplies from London. They had to come round by Warwick and over the Cotswold Hills. The difficulties attending the transit are well shown in

---

* Diary, 190.   † Noake, Notes and Queries for Worcestershire, p. 329.

a letter from E. M. (Edward Massey) to Brydges, the governor of Warwick Castle.

"Desiring to know your resolution of March, and the word signal, and the "way by which you mean to march. The enemy is reported to be very strong "about Stow, Broadway, Campden, Evesham, Upton, and Tewkesbury, and "if he be not drawn off by His Excellency's other forces, your party will be "too slender I am afraid. Yet if I have your timely and certain notice I shall "endeavour to divert the enemy in these parts, and keep them on the other "side of the river."*

Massey did his best to carry out his promise. A Dutchman named Behr, who commanded the cavalry that escorted the convoy, seems to have been a very skilful officer. Although Rupert knew of the convoy, and did his best to intercept it, yet Behr was too wary. He took his convoy in safety past the Royalist's posts, between Warwick and Gloucester, and thus furnished Massey with sufficient supplies and ammunition to take the offensive. This greatly delighted the Parliament. The *Perfect Diurnal* states †

"Part of the ammunition is arrived safe at Gloucester, whereby the garrison. "is settled in so good a condition. Colonel Massey will venture abroad, and "be in action suddenly."

On Vavassour being deprived of the command the King consulted Rupert on the selection of a successor. Rupert at once suggested Mynne, and Mynne was accordingly appointed. No sooner was this done than he let Massey know that he had now a very different class of man to deal with to Vavassour. Mynne's head-quarters were at Newent, but he had no idea of confining himself to Newent or the neighbourhood; he at once assumed the offensive. Posting men from the Vineyard Hill or Maisemore he broke down the bridge and waited for Massey to move. Massey was very weak in cavalry, and thus was handicapped to a great extent. He, however, thought his chance had come. Behr, with the cavalry, which had escorted the convoy, was still at Gloucester and might be utilised. With some difficulty he got the Dutchman to agree to help in an attack on Newent. Mynne was equal to the occasion. In the early morning Behr attacked the place, for three hours making assault after assault, each of which Mynne successfully repulsed. Massey then retired having lost a number of men in killed and wounded, and leaving behind him two guns probably the guns with which the church tower of Newent was so battered that the marks of the balls were visible on it for years after, until the days of modern restoration. If Mynne had only had a sufficient force of cavalry, things would have gone badly with Behr and Massey, but as it was the pursuit had to be stopped. Behr was therefore able to get his wounded away in carts and make good his.

---

* Hist. MSS. Com., IV. Rep., 264.   † Apri 1—8, 1644.

retreat to Gloucester. To prevent the repetition of such exploits Essex peremptorily ordered Behr at once to return from Gloucester, but did not leave Massey without help. Colonel Purefoy, a Warwickshire man, from Westow, near Tamworth, was sent with his regiment of cavalry to Gloucester to assist Massey, who was once more able to take the offensive. For some reason which does not appear, but, in all probability, to carry out a scheme in conjunction with Rupert, to draw Massey out of Gloucester and cut off his retreat, Mynne decided to concentrate his force on the west side of Gloucester, leaving the Leadon Valley and the Worcestershire border undefended. Taking advantage of this Massey advanced up the Leadon Valley and occupied Ledbury. Massey was acting in concert with Lord Denbigh, who proposed to advance on Worcester from the Warwickshire side, and if he did not attack it he would at least prevent any force being sent out to oppose Massey. This caused great alarm at Worcester. Sir Gilbert Gerrard, the governor, wrote on 1st May, 1644, to Rupert, complaining of the state of things, adding that at Worcester many of the town were "very base," and that if he was not sent help, "with some considerable force, the County would be ruinated." Gerrard was right, the whole of southwest Worcestershire was now at Massey's mercy. Purefoy's cavalry, having a new and comparatively unplundered district in which to forage, certainly made the most of it. The cavalry working the district between the Severn and the Malvern Hills caused the greatest alarm at Worcester. It was fortunate for the city that Massey had Mynne, not Vavassour, to deal with, for he deemed it better, under existing circumstances, to keep his front rather than his rear towards the enemy. Massey accordingly devoted himself to the country towards Hereford rather than the country towards Worcester. He resolved to fortify Ledbury and make it a base for future operations; but he was not allowed to remain in a position in which he could select his own base. Rupert considered Gerrard's complaint required attention. Setting off from Shrewsbury on Easter Monday, 22nd April, he marched to Ludlow and the next day to Evesham, his plan being to march to Upton, join hands with Mynne, and thus cut Massey off from Gloucester. Had he marched the next day he might have succeeded, but on the 24th April (Wednesday), Rupert was summoned to Oxford, and was detained there until 5th May (Sunday), when he got back to Evesham it was too late to carry out his scheme. Massey's scouts had heard of it and warned him of his danger; he abandoned Ledbury and fell back on Gloucester. For a time south Worcestershire was freed from Massey, who devoted his attention to the Forest of Dean. Rupert, on his return to

Evesham, accordingly found that there was no need for him to cross the Severn. So on Monday, 6th May, he marched to Worcester, on the 7th to Ludlow, and on the 8th back to Shrewsbury.

Mynne placed a garrison in Tewkesbury, and directed that the place should be fortified and held for the King. Massey was desirous to retake Tewkesbury, so determined to carry it by storm. Everything was ready for a night attack by the troops, but they did not arrive till after daybreak, when they were seen, the garrison at once became on the alert. Massey, therefore, departed for a season and tried the south-east of Gloucestershire.

Massey had, however, not given up, but only postponed his plan for taking Tewkesbury. He put it off until the beginning of June, when he again came there. A garrison of 700 men, under Major Mynne, held it. Massey determined to attack at once. Taking with him 120 horse and 30 dragoons, under Major Hammond, and 300 foot, he sent the cavalry on in advance of the infantry. About a mile from Tewkesbury, on the Gloucester side, the cavalry halted, and, believing their approach had not been noticed, determined to try a surprise. Three men were sent on ahead to see if the drawbridge was down. Six more followed them, the " Forlorn Hope," and then came the main body. They advanced on the town, found the bridge down, the guard slender, the enemy without intelligence, and supremely negligent. The three selected men did well, they rushed the bridge, killed the sentinels, a pikeman, and a musketeer, who could not get his match lighted, and so could not fire his musket. They were closely followed by the " Forlorn Hope," who, supported by the horse and dragoons, pressed forward, fell on the bridge guard before the alarm was given, dashed up the street to the main guard, upsetting the guns. They charged on up the street as far as the Avon bridge, some even crossing the Avon and going on up the Worcester road. Here they took the governor, Major Mynne, prisoner. So utterly surprised were the garrison that many threw down their arms and surrendered, others made off and escaped up the Bredon road. In the first charge Colonel Godfrey, the Quarter-master General, and a Lieutenant were killed. The men at the main guard were at first too astonished to do anything, but after the first rush, when the Parliament dragoons dismounted and the Royalists realised the real state of things, especially that the Parliament men had left the Swillgate Bridge without any guard, they rallied, charged, and drove them out of the town. At this moment Massey came up with a few of his horse. He ordered the dragoons to fire on the Royalists on the Gloucester road who were defending the Swillgate Bridge. He worked round to the north of the

town, trying to enter it by the Bredon road. It had, however,
become dark, and Massey hardly liked to attempt it. He
sent on a few men, and to his surprise and joy they
returned, reporting that the garrison had fled over the
Avon Bridge towards Worcester, having utterly abandoned
the place.* Besides the place itself, Massey took two drakes,
18 barrels of powder, and some stores.

The loss of Tewkesbury was a great disappointment to
Mynne. On the very day that Massey took it he was on
his way there from Hereford to take steps to make it
more secure. Massey's exploit again earned him the thanks of
Parliament, and this time a more tangible proof of their
gratitude than thanks. They ordered the Gloucestershire
Committee, who were dealing with delinquents' lands, to settle
out of those of Papists and delinquents upon Massey an estate
of inheritance of the yearly amount of at least £1000. Reinforcements were ordered to be raised and sent him. Massey
requested Parliament to send him instead what he required
far more, money. He had nothing wherewith to pay the men
he had with him. If he had only money he could enlist as
many men as he pleased, men who were fit for any fighting,
against any odds.

Massey's fame as a successful soldier had become so great
that it attracted men from all sides, as they felt sure of
securing tangible advantages from serving under him. If the
accounts are true, recruits came in so numerously that Massey
had to refuse over 1000 applicants, men who had served on
both sides ; soldiers of fortune, men who desired to share the
profits and gain the honours which fell to Massey's men. The
recruits the Parliament enlisted in London were of a wholly
different kind. There the refuse of the unemployed came
forward to be enlisted, men who, if they had not previously
deserted, would bolt at the sound of the first shot.

The Royalists found great difficulty in getting men. As a
rule their generals had not been successful, and the consequent
attractions to their side were but few. They had, therefore, to
resort to impressment to keep up their forces, which rendered
them even more unpopular. Sir Gilbert Gerrard, as Governor
of Worcester, Sir William Mynne, as Governor of Hereford,
were both authorised to impress men and horses to fill up the
gaps in the regiments, to assess and levy contributions for their
payment, billet and quarter them according to their convenience, and punish all disorders by martial law. The sheriffs
and all other officers were ordered to assist and obey them in
executing their commissions.

About the middle of May Parliament resolved to resume the

---

* Corbet's Military Government of Gloucester.

offensive, their idea being still the one of the year before: either to shut up the King at Oxford and force him to surrender, or compel him to leave Oxford, fight a general action in the open, when they hoped to destroy his army and compel him either to surrender or take to flight. It was only by one or other of these ways that, in their opinion, there was any possibility of ending the war, as all attempts at accommodation were at an end. They therefore ordered Essex and Waller both to march on Oxford from opposite sides, drive in the Royalist forces, blockade the town, and compel a surrender.

The plan was at once put in operation and was all but successful, so nearly so that some of the King's advisers actually proposed to him to surrender to Essex.* The King would not hear of it. So nothing remained for him but to leave Oxford at the earliest possible date. On Monday, 3rd June, at 9 p.m., he left, escaping between Waller's and Essex's armies, reaching Handborough in the early morning, he did not consider it safe to halt there, so pushed on to Burford. At night he again set out and marched to Bourton-on-the-Water. So secretly was all this done that Essex would not believe Charles had quitted Oxford, so made no haste to follow him up. Waller was better served by his spies; they told him the King had really gone, so he set out after him. So rapidly did he march that at Burford he fell in with some of the stragglers of the Royal army. Hearing Waller was on his track Charles pressed on, and the next day reached Evesham, then held for him by Colonel Knottsford. He was here met by fugitives from Tewkesbury, who gave different versions of the storm and capture of that place by Massey on the previous day. Both Waller and Essex were now following after the King; Essex had got as far as Chipping Norton, Waller as Broadway. Here, hearing that Charles was safe over the Avon at Evesham, Waller did not pursue any further. Charles did not feel safe at Evesham, both his flanks were open to the enemy. Massey could move up from Tewkesbury, Denbigh march down from Warwickshire, and if one or both got between him and Worcester, encumbered as he was by women and baggage, he had with him 30 coaches of ladies with their belongings, his position would be very critical. Evesham was also very disaffected. Charles ordered the bridge across the Avon to be destroyed—probably Twyford Bridge on the old London road. Knottsford was ordered to remain till he saw the enemy approach, then to demolish the fortifications. Charles, passing through Bengeworth, Charlton, and Cropthorne, reached Pershore, breaking down the bridge over the Avon behind him.

---

* Clarendon, II, 377.

This work was done in such a hurry that all the troops failed to get safely over. Major Bridge, two or three officers, and 26 privates were drowned, as well as some 80 countrymen, whose hats were picked up floating down the river. Charles accordingly left Pershore and pushed on to Worcester; reaching there on June 12th. Here he stayed nearly a week, and knighted the mayor, Sir Daniel Tyas. By blandishments, or more forcible means, Charles induced the city to advance him £1000. He was lodged in the Bishop's Palace, his troops, some 6000, were quartered in the town. Stockings, boots, and general supplies for them came in, so that at the end of the week Charles was at last in a position to shew some resistance to the enemy.

He really owed his safety to a dispute between Waller and Essex. A council of war was held at Burford, at which it was decided

" that Waller, who had the lighter ordnance and the less carriage, should
" have sent an addition of force as Massey, the Governor of Gloucester, could
" give him, and should pursue and follow the King wherever he should go,
" while Essex, with the greater ordnance and heavier carriages, should reduce
" the west to the obedience of Parliament."*

Against this decision Waller protested, stating that " Worcestershire was not a fortunate County for him." His previous service there with Massey had not redounded to his credit. Waller wanted to go to the west, leaving Essex to deal with the King, but this did not suit the Lord-General. He gave Waller his positive orders to march according to the advice of the council of war.† This Waller was obliged to obey, but he sent a strong complaint to Parliament about Essex's conduct. They wrote Essex a very angry and imperious letter, censuring him for not submitting to the directions they had given him, and requiring him to let Waller go to the west. To this Essex replied that their directions were contrary to the discipline of war and to reason, and continued his march westward.

Waller was right, Worcestershire was not a lucky district for him, but he had nothing to do but to obey his general's orders. Taking advantage of Massey's capture of Tewkesbury he marched to Winchcombe, compelled Sir William Morton, the Governor of Sudeley Castle, to surrender, with 250 soldiers, three guns, ammunition, horses, and 100 quarters of grain. Waller then marched the nine miles to Evesham, and found the inhabitants had repaired the bridge, so as to facilitate his crossing the Avon. Here he remained on the 11th and 12th June.

Lord Denbigh did not, as Charles expected, attack him at Evesham. He had settled on another plan of operations. Dudley Castle had always been a thorn in the Parliamentary

---

* Clarendon, II., 378.　　† Clarendon, II., 378.

side. Aided and exhorted by Tinker Fox, Denbigh considered the present a good opportunity to take it. So while Charles was at Evesham he, supported by men under Colonel Mytton, the Parliament Governor of Wem, and Sir Thomas Middleton, set out to attack it. Leveson, the Governor, refused to surrender when summoned, and made a stout defence. Charles determined he should be relieved. On the 11th June he sent Lord Wilmot from Worcester, with the Earl of Northampton's and Lord Cleveland's horse and 1000 foot, to raise the siege. Crossing the Severn they marched up the west bank of the river to Bewdley. Here they recrossed, marched through Kidderminster and Stourbridge to Dudley. Denbigh was informed of Wilmot's approach, and ordered Colonel Mytton to hold Wilmot in check with his brigade. What actually took place is a matter of some uncertainty. There was a sharp fight, Wilmot attacked Mytton, charged his men so furiously that they were not only routed but their retreat was cut off. On Denbigh's men seeing this they became so alarmed that they begged him to retire and leave Mytton to his fate. Denbigh flatly refused to do anything of the kind, and at once charged Wilmot with all his available force. This very unexpected attack disconcerted Wilmot, compelled him to abandon his pursuit of Mytton and face about to meet Denbigh. Wilmot's men were in their turn very hard pressed by Denbigh's horse. Here it is that the accounts differ. The Royalists say that Denbigh's charge having secured Mytton's retreat was not pressed further. The Parliament writers say that Denbigh's charge caused an utter rout of Wilmot's force. Two things both sides agree upon : that Wilmot did not at once raise the siege ; but retired, taking some prisoners with him.

The Royalist account is :—

"Our men, following close upon them, beat them from the ground where "they made a stand, and forced them to retreat again in so great disorder "that it was no better than a plain and downright routing, and in the action "(which was performed with the loss of scarce 20 men, and not one officer at "all) His Majesty's forces took two colours of horse, two majors of foot, two "captains, three lieutenants, and 50 common soldiers prisoners and killed, "many of them in the fight, as these letters testify."

The account given in the *Perfect Diurnal*,* the Parliamentary paper, says :—

" In this fight the enemy lost about 100, and amongst the rest one person "of special note killed, for whom they made great lamentation, and it is "conceived to be the Lord Wilmot, a great incendiary of these wars. There "were also 17 persons of quality taken prisoners, besides other soldiers, "horses, and arms. And of the Earl of Denbigh's only 7 men killed and some "wounded, and about 10 that were too busy pillaging the enemy in the time "of the fight surprised by a strong party. Some report that the King was "himself in person in the fight. What men were killed or taken prisoners in

---

* 10—17 June, 1644.

" the pursuit at present we hear not.   Lately it was further certified that Sir
" William Waller, being with his force about the Vale of Evesham, and under-
" standing that the Earl of Denbigh was engaged with a party of the King's
" Horse, immediately sent away 2000 horse to his relief, who, notwithstanding
" that the enemy were beaten off from the siege about two hours before they
" came (as some report), they may undoubtedly do good service in the
" pursuit."

This account abounds in inaccuracies.   Wilmot was not
touched, no officer of note on the King's side was hurt,
Charles was not nearer the battle than Worcester, nor Waller
than Evesham.   The following private letter gives a better
account of the affair :—

" Truly if God had not fought for us we were all lost men, for they were, by
" the confession of those prisoners we took, between 4 and 5000 and we not 2000.
" They fell upon our rear before we could begin to march, only our forlorn
" advanced.   They assaulted us a quarter of a mile this side the leaguer with such
" fury that had not our men behaved themselves very gallantly we had been
" utterly defeated, but they were encountered so sharply that they were fain to
" retreat towards the castle, and were so handsomely beaten that they had no
" mind to come on again.   We slew about 30 of their men, whereof some of note,
" and one they wished His Majesty had been killed rather than he (you may
" perceive by this their love to His Majesty), and very many ill wounded and
" dangerously.   All the flower and the greatest part of the King's forces were in
" this body.   There was the King's General of Horse (Lord Wilmot) and the
" Earl of Cleveland.   The King and the poor remainder of his forces is at
" Worcester, where Sir William Waller is advancing.   Sir William, hearing of
" the enemy coming to raise our siege, sent 2000 horse to our relief which came
" not till the next morning.   Had they come in time by God's help we had
" given the enemy a great defeat, but not knowing of their coming we durst
" not pursue them we being so inconsiderable in strength, the place affording
" the enemy many advantages."*

There was no pursuit, Wilmot drew off in good order with
his prisoners towards Bewdley.   A day or two after the siege
was raised and the Parliament force drew off to Stafford.
Symonds, who was present with the King at Worcester, says
in his diary :

" Monday, June 10th.   The Lord Wilmot, with his horse, went from
" Worcester on that side of Severn next Hereford, so to Bewdley, and relieved
" the Castle of Dudley, which was besieged by the Earl of Denbigh ;   took
" some prisoners."†

Wilmot may have failed to relieve the castle but his attempt
was far from a failure.   Waller had been doing his utmost to
get Denbigh to raise the siege, join forces with him and attack
the King.   This Denbigh was unwilling to do before Wilmot's
attack, although he was thinking of raising the siege and
returning to Stafford.   In the fight Wilmot had so crippled
Mytton's Brigade as to make it non-effective.   Denbigh
did not care to risk Brereton's, the only other cavalry he
had, leaving himself with only infantry to resist, as he retired,
an attack of Royalist horse.   Whatever else Wilmot did, or
failed to do, he had hampered Waller's movements by

---

* Hist. MSS. Com., XIV. Rep., app., pt. IV., p. 63.   † Symonds' Diary, p. 13.

depriving him of all aid from Denbigh's forces, and thus prevented him from taking the offensive against the King.

On the 12th June Charles left Worcester and marched north. His idea is said to have been to have pushed on to Shrewsbury and then across country into Yorkshire, and having joined his men with Rupert's, with this very considerable force marching back to crush first Waller and then Essex It is doubtful if this was the King's real plan, for if it had been there was nothing to prevent him carrying it out. His march is thus described :

" Wednesday, the 12th June, 1644, His Majesty marched out of Worcester " on that side of the Severn next Hereford, by the Parish of [Hallow], where " is a park where Sir Walter Devereux lives, two myles on the right hand on " the way from Worcester. Then by Shrawley, a parish. At last to Bewdley, " ten miles from Worcester, where the King lay that night, at the Manor of " Ticknell, on the top of the hill near the town, a house belonging to the " Prince of Wales, now farmed out to Sir Ralfe Clare, a fine, hilly park about " the house. The church is a myle from the town ; in the town is only a " chapel-of-ease, two myles from Kidderminster. This is an enclosed country, " small pastures and corn fields, a narrow way, most part of it stony, the " quarry of stone of a brickish colour."*

Outwardly the inhabitants of Bewdley received the King with pleasure. The accounts say:

" Pd. for ringinge at the King's coming to town and going forth   o 2 o
" For pulling down the Bailiff's seat and setting up again when
    the King was here   o o 4
" For paving, which the Reformadoes broke up   o 6 10"†

One thing made the King's stay in Bewdley memorable. It was while here that he sent his orders to Rupert to fight in Yorkshire, the consequences of which was the defeat of Marston Moor.

Waller must have heard of Charles' march from Worcester. The next day, 13th, he left Evesham and marched to Bromsgrove, sending his horse on to Kidderminster, with orders to watch the Bridgnorth road and intercept the King if he tried to march northwards. The two armies were therefore now within striking distance. Some of Waller's horse, probably those sent on to Dudley when Wilmot went there, were posted at Stourbridge. Waller went there himself in order, as he says, to interpose between the King and Prince Rupert in case the King offered to advance from that side to Shrewsbury. Although the two armies were nearly equal in number, all the advantages from arms, equipment, and discipline were on Waller's side, still he did not consider himself strong enough to attack the Royalists.

Things could not have been pleasant for the people living in the district. A letter from a Colonel Frazer, dated 6th June, 1644, contains an offer

---

* Symonds, p. 13.   † Burton's " Bewdley," App., XXXII.

"to march between Worcester and Evesham, where there is no other way for
"His Majesty to pass to Prince Rupert but through Worcester and so to
"Shrewsbury. No intelligence yet, but last night there appeared at Kidder-
"minster, at 12 of the clock at night, a party of 120 horse, which threatened
"the inhabitants to ruin them if they sent any prisoners to your Lordship's-
"army."*

With Waller's cavalry wandering about the inhabitants were
not safe from being plundered, and those who desired to make
themselves secure had to get protection from the Parliament
generals. Among Lord Denbigh's papers is the following :

"7th June, 1644. Order to all commanders in the service of the King
"and Parliament to forbear to plunder the cloth in the fulling mills in
"Kidderminster and Hartlebury, belonging to Robert Willmott, Treasurer
"for the Committee for the County of Stafford."†

Charles only stayed two days at Bewdley—Thursday, 13th
June, and Friday, 14th. He had made up his mind what
to do. On Saturday, 15th, he ordered some of his cavalry to
march up the Severn towards Bridgnorth. While thus throwing Waller off his guard, the infantry, guns, and baggage were
put on board boats and sent off down stream to Worcester.
Having despatched them the cavalry were ordered to fall
back to Bewdley, when they and those who were there
set off and marched to Worcester, where they arrived on
Saturday evening. Waller had sent his cavalry forward towards Bridgnorth to intercept Charles, but the King completely deceived him and was falling back on Worcester
without Waller's knowledge.

On Sunday, 16th June, Charles attended service at the
Cathedral, and about noon set off for Evesham. Reaching it
in the evening he only halted an hour or so, but long enough
to compel the town to pay a fine of £200 on account of their
disloyalty in enabling Waller to pass the river by repairing the-
bridge—which he again broke down. The town was also
called upon to provide the army with 1000 pairs of boots.
Having thus punished disloyalty the King marched the
same evening to Broadway where he slept at Mr. Savage's
house. From Broadway, by Charles' order, Digby wrote to
Rupert saying:

"They were raised to comfortable hopes from a state almost of desperation.
"The truth of it is had Essex or Waller jointly either pursued us or attacked
"Oxford we had been lost. In the one course Oxford had been yielded up to
"them, having not a fortnight's provisions, and no hope of relief. In the
"other, Worcester had been lost and the King forced to retreat to your
"Highness."‡

Charles was once more safe. From Broadway he went
by Campden, Stow-on-the-Wold, to Burford, sleeping there
at the "George." Here he was joined by a reinforcement of

---

* 4th Rep. Hist. MSS. Com., p. 267.   † 4th Rep. Hist. MSS. Com., p. 267.
‡ Webb, II., 44.

4000 men from Oxford and some guns. Essex was at Salisbury, so it was safe to take some troops out of the Oxford garrison, who
"with their pikes and colours, for before there was none, marched with the
"King this March, and the trayne also."*

Charles was now in a .position to resume the offensive. He had been absent from 31st May to the 18th June, just under three weeks, and instead of being a hunted fugitive was now at the head of a formidable army.

Waller had been left behind. He was at Kidderminster on the 15th, watching the King, on the 16th he was at Stourbridge. He left on the Monday, the 17th.

"As soon as I received assurance of His Majesty, I rose, and leaving my
"foot to march gently after with two regiments of horse to cover them, I
"advanced, with the rest of my horse and dragoons after me, to Evesham, 22
"miles distant, but when I came thither I found that His Majesty had gained
"above 20 miles before me, so that I conceived I should ruin my horse to
"pursue him further."

This is Waller's own account of his movements. It does not quite agree with those of others. Waller was at Kidderminster on the 14th, on the 15th he was at Wordsley, near Stourbridge, and his men occupied Bewdley. Mrs. Conningsby writes, on the 17th June, to her husband,

"I hear that Waller's forces, some of them, came into Bewdley last night,
"and forced the townsmen to make up the bridge."†

From Stourbridge Waller marched on the 17th to Droitwich. On the 18th he marched, or is said to have done so, from Droitwich to Worcester, but did not try his luck against it. Clarendon says :‡

"He first shewed his army all the walls of Worcester to terrify that city,
"which had contemned his power a year before, when it was not so well able
"to resist it, but he quickly discerned 'They could do no good there.' Waller
"then marched on to Pershore, where Rushworth says he met with an
"accident like that which befell the Royalists. The great stone bridge being
"pulled down by the inhabitants, after they had demolished the arches the
"rest suddenly tumbled down, whereby about 60 of the workmen were
"knocked on the head or drowned."

In the evening of the 18th Waller was at Evesham; he wrote from there a letter to the Earl of Leven, General of the Scotch army, and Lord Fairfax, who was commanding the Parliament troops in Yorkshire, explaining that he stayed at Stourbridge to intercept the King going north to join Prince Rupert, adding that the King had broken down the Evesham bridge, and also had had broken down the Bidford bridge. From Evesham, the next day, the 19th, he marched to Tewkesbury, and sent on to Gloucester, ordering Massey to send him some reinforcements. Being, it was said, a creature of Essex, Massey refused. But Rushworth says Waller got 270

---

musketeers, a company of dragoons, and 100 musketeers from Malmesbury. With these troops he marched to Stow-on-the-Wold, on the 24th to Shipston-on-Stour, and on to near Edgehill. Here he received from Coventry and Warwick 11 guns and more reinforcements. Waller now considered himself strong enough to meet the King. The two armies met at Cropredy bridge on the 29th June, and again Wilmot shewed himself a superior general to Waller.

After Cropredy bridge, once more the King returned to Worcestershire. He marched by Farthinghoe, Aynhoe, Dedington, to Moreton-in-the-Marsh.

" From thence His Majesty, with his whole army, marched over the
" Cotswold Hills, with colours flying, on to Broadway, thence to Evesham
" that night, where he lay. His troops were quartered at Fladbury."*

Charles staved at Evesham nine days—from the 4th to the 13th July. He lodged at a house on the north side of Bridge Street, then occupied by Alderman Martin, belonging to the Langston family, one of whom had been Member for Evesham. From " our court at Evesham, the 4th day of July, 1644,"† the King sent a message for peace to the Lords and Commons of Parliament, assembled at Westminster, to which no answer was returned.

" Tinker " Fox had his eye on the King. He wrote from Edgbaston at 10 p.m., on the 8th July, that the King was moving from Evesham towards Dudley Castle ; quite a false bit of information Charles' attention was directed to quite a different quarter. A force of Royalists were stationed near Bredon, whose object was to retake Tewkesbury. On the 13th Charles left Evesham and joined them. They were within a mile of the town and all was ready for an assault. Massey did not intend again to lose Tewkesbury. He sent up a reinforcement of 200 musketeers from Gloucester, who were to cross Upton Bridge, come down to Tewkesbury on the Ripple side. A force was sent from Worcester, with orders to advance down the west bank of the Severn, secure the bridge at Upton so that Charles, when Tewkesbury was taken, could with his men march over Upton Bridge into Hereford-shire, and so on into Wales. Once again Massey was too nimble for the Royalists. He waited on the west bank of the Severn for the force sent from Worcester. They did not merely secure the bridge at Upton, but tried to secure, or rather sweep, the country round from the enemy. Massey waited for them in Eldersfield, at Corse Lawn. A sharp fight took place, and Massey taught the Worcester men a lesson by completely defeating them.

On July 9th the Parliamentary journal‡ says :—

---

* Symonds, 25.   † Rushworth, V., 687.   ‡ *Perfect Occurrences*, July 5—12, 1644.

"By letters it was certified to the Committee that the King had faced "Tewkesbury, and was gone towards Gloucester, it was supposed for "Bristol."

The result of the fight at Corse Lawn was that instead of the bridge at Upton being in the hands of the Royalists it was in those of Massey. Crossing over the Severn by it he was able to bring up his men to relieve Tewkesbury on the north side, and to seriously threaten the Royalist position. Charles and his advisers saw that the confines of Tewkesbury were no place for him. It was therefore resolved to raise the siege. The King returned to Evesham, marched to Broadway, over the Cotswolds near Sudeley Castle, "from where," says Symonds, "the rebels gave us two great shot. That night, at one of the clock, the King got to his quarters at Cubberley, and so on by Sapperton, Dagleworth, Badmington, to Bath."*

Massey profited by his victory and by the King's retreat; he sent out troops of horse into the country round Tewkesbury on the Royalist line of march. He attacked the rearguard, cut off all stragglers, and took some 50 or 60 prisoners.

Mynne thought that Massey's absence at Tewkesbury gave him a chance that he was not slow to use. He was determined to take Gloucester, and his system of continued fighting had greatly reduced both Massey's forces and his resources. To keep up his supplies Massey had to make constant forays, most of which were successful. From Tewkesbury Massey sent his pickets all over south Worcestershire, and his men came on forays to within four miles of Worcester, causing the greatest consternation to the inhabitants. They carried off Sir Humphrey Tracy and two other officers as prisoners. It was felt to be necessary to do something to abate this nuisance. Mynne accordingly made his plans to assemble at Eldersfield all the forces he could, including a party from Worcester, march on Gloucester, laying waste to all the country through which they passed, so that it could not, even if willing, furnish supplies to Massey. Mynne had learnt in Ireland that the most effective way to dishearten a garrison was to destroy the standing crops. He determined to try this in England.

On the 26th July Mynne, taking with him such men as he could muster, advanced to Hartpury, on the way to Gloucester. Massey saw the move was dangerous and should be stopped at once. Collecting all his available men, calling in some part of the Tewkesbury garrison, he got together what he thought a sufficient force. He had some difficulty in retaining his men owing to a quarrel between two of his officers, which set them all by the ears. At last, late in the evening, he arranged matters, marched out and surprised an outpost of Mynne's at

---

* Symonds, 28 and 30.

High Leadon, driving off some and taking others prisoners. Mynne had meanwhile fallen back on Redmarley with his main body, waiting for the Worcester men to join him before he attacked. After wandering about for some time in the dark, and marching by and missing the Royalists, Massey halted his men at Eldersfield, the forces being about two miles apart.

In the early morning Mynne's drummers, by beating the *reveillé*, disclosed the position of his force to Massey. Mynne had drawn up his men, 850 infantry and 160 cavalry, in some enclosures, lining the hedges with his musketeers, waiting for the Worcester men to come, who, but for the fog, should have arrived and taken up ground to Mynne's left, after crossing the open common. But Mynne soon found he was not to be allowed to wait for the Worcester men. On the fog lifting Massey advanced his men in two bodies in order of battle. Colonel Hurley led the van with three troops of horse, supported by that Captain Backhouse who had so deluded Stamford and Vavassour, with three more troops. On the flank of the horse were a body of infantry. The rear was brought up by another troop of horse and infantry. The reserves were stationed in the village of Redmarley.

Massey at once began to attack the right flank and front, drove the Royalists out of the enclosures and from the hedges, put the horse to flight, broke into the foot and shattered the whole body. Mynne, with 130 of his men, fell fighting, and 30 officers, 1 sergeant, and 200 soldiers surrendered; the remainder made off at their top speed to Ledbury. At the moment when Massey had routed Mynne, Colonel Passey, the commander of the Worcester troop, rode up asking for orders. He was wounded and left for dead. His men, however, continued to advance until they saw on their right the bulk of Mynne's horse fleeing in disorder, then they halted. They were not long left in uncertainty. Massey retired quickly, while the Worcester men, having lost their leader, and not knowing what to do, remained halted and allowed Massey, with his prisoners, to escape.

Such was the battle of Redmarley. Had the Worcester men arrived a little earlier, Massey himself admitted he must have been destroyed. The fog and the Worcester men losing their road alone saved him from destruction, but he was saved, and not only saved, but freed from one who had done more than anyone else to render his efforts as governor of Gloucester unavailing.

Massey conveyed Mynne's body to Gloucester and had it buried there; the precise place of burial is not known. It does not matter, for Mynne could not have had a better monument or a more eloquent epitaph than one sentence of contemporary testimony:

" He was missed by his friends, honoured by his foes, who gave him a
" stately burial in testimony of his worth and value, being ıhe fairest and
" shrewdest enemy in Christendom."

Matters were not going smoothly in the north of the County.
Fox appears to have been jealous of Lord Denbigh and tried
to oust him from his authority. A Mr. W. Crowne, of London,
writes to Lord Denbigh, on July 16th, saying :

" he had had an interview with the Committee of both Kingdoms, and had
" heard of an ordinance put in by one Mr. Guest and some friends of Colonel
" Fox, to give to a committee of six in Worcestershire power to appoint com-
" manders and raise money, which would be destructive of Lord Denbigh's·
" power."*

The letter goes on to detail the steps he, Mr. Crowne, had
taken to preserve that power to him.

On July 19th Crowne wrote again to Lord Denbigh :

" I think I have stopped the ordinance of Parliament concerning Worcester-
" shire until your Lordship cometh, and for the order of the Commons·
" concerning Sir F. Middleton for my Lord Newport and his son's estate, I
" believe I have stayed that.'†

This design of taking away power from the person who had
exercised it, and handing it over to a body of fanatics would,
if it had been agreed upon, have caused a great injusticè in the
County.

At the end of July there was a skirmish somewhere in the
County. It is an instance where the name of the place has
been allowed to sink into oblivion. The matter is contained
in a letter dated 27th July :

"Although the enemy's loss hath been great, yet their cowardice is worst,
" running through so many of their owne contributory towns. Their com-
" manders were very nimble, and I persuade myself they looked not back till
" they came into Worcester, where they and the residue of their forces are
" taking breath."‡

Lord Denbigh kept on working in the east of the County,
and his officers seem to have given the Royalists considerable
trouble. On August 16th, a Colonel Archer, of Alcester, writes:

" Hearing of a convention of the Commissioners of Array for Worcestershire,
" which was to be held at Ombersley, the Parliamentary troops marched in
" pursuit of them, but the Commissioners, being warned from Droitwich,
" escaped across the Severn and fled to Hartlebury Castle, not daring to make
" Worcester their sanctuary. Since this action the County, seeing how unable, at
" least how slow, their Worcester friends have been in protecting them, come
" daily to us, and we doubt not but by their assistance, had your Lordship two
" regiments of foot and one more of horse, in short time to take in that
" garrison."§

The writer had not much local knowledge. Hartlebury
Castle, Ombersley, and Droitwich are all the same side of the
river. It does not appear to whom this letter was addressed.
It seems to show that some attempt on the garrison, possibly
Worcester, was meant.

---

* 4th Rep. Hist. MSS. Com., p. 269.   † Ib., p. 269.   ‡ Ib., p. 269.
§ Hist. MSS., Com., 4th Rep., p. 270.

The defeat of the Royalists at Marston Moor enhanced the part the Scotch army played in the war. It was no longer a fight between the two great English parties, it was a fight between the English Royalists and the Puritan party, whether that party was English or Scotch. The importance of the Scotch help will be seen when it is said that their army, when it entered England under Lord Leven, consisted of 18,000 foot, 3000 horse, and 5000 or 6000 dragoons. The Scotch had not much to do directly with the fighting in Worcestershire until 1645; but indirectly, by setting free more Parliamentary troops, and so allowing the different garrisons to be reinforced, they had considerable effect, especially as it was just the time when the Royalists were feeling the greatest difficulty in keeping up their numbers. The Scotch were intensely unpopular with both sides. A Scotch army was represented as being all that was bad, and the combined effect of this teaching with the practical experience the Scots gave the country of their greediness for supplies went far to justify their unpopularity. So strongly was this felt that Charles, in August, gave secret instructions to a Mr. Harding, directing him to go with the Marquis of Hertford's son (Earl Beauchamp) to Essex, as secretly as possible, deliver the King's letter, and inform him that

" the evidence therein relates to himself, and if possible to induce the Earl to " join the King with his forces in order to effect a general pacification."

Another memorandum directed Harding to endeavour to induce Essex

" to try to preserve the country from the common danger of a conquest by the " Scots, and directed him to avoid suspicion of any other design than that of " accompanying Lord Beauchamp."

The Royalists, naturally, did their best to stir up every prejudice against the Scots. They were successful, and they had their reward, for when, seven years later, another Scotch army came to England to fight for the King the hatred which the Royalists in 1644 and 1645 had roused against the Scotch still continued, so that there was not the slightest sympathy and enthusiasm for them. It is indeed more than probable than the chilling reception Charles II. met with in 1651 was in a great measure due to the prejudices and dislikes which the Royalists had excited against the Scotch in the first Civil War.

The introduction of the Scots seems also to have had a considerable effect in inducing both parties to arrive at an accommodation. Certainly the people of Worcestershire were becoming tired of the war. In August,

"divers of Worcestershire offered to raise forces for the Parliament, and an " ordinance was passed to enable them to do so."*

---

* Whitlock, p. 96.

A petition was sent from divers Worcestershire gentlemen to the House of Commons, dated September 4th, on behalf of themselves and others of the said County, stating that they

" have for the last two years been under the power of the enemy, who have
" exacted large sums of money from the County, besides seizing cattle and
" horses without payment. Your petitioners have, besides, suffered at the
" hands of the Parliament forces, who in their inroads and requisitions make no
" distinction between the ill-affected and well-affected. There is now a great
" opportunity for reducing the County entirely, and your petitioners desire that
" there may be no delay in passing the ordinance for that purpose sent up by
" the House of Commons, and now before your Lordships."

It was this and similar complaints that persons in the County were plundered alike by both sides—by the Royalists and by the Parliament equally—that led to the formation of the Clubmen, and the associations that were formed for mutual protection of life and property, which afterwards gave so much trouble.

The fighting in the north of the County during the autumn of 1644 degenerated, to a great extent, into plundering raids. Two instances will give an idea of what the plundering was. The first is a passport for a clergyman, who it is true was a pluralist, as he held the livings of Halesowen and Suckley, and would, therefore, if he visited both, have to do a good deal of travelling. It says a good deal for the insecurity of the district that this clergyman should require a pass. It is as follows :—

" To all officers and soldiers of the Parliament, or under Lord Denbigh's
" command. Forbear to molest, disturb, or seize up n the person, goods, or
" chattels of Thomas Littleton, Parson of Suckley and Vicar of Halesowen, a
" laborious, painful minister, well-affected to the Parliament."*

The other is a letter from George Varney to William Wilmot,† written in 1644:—

" I had eleven horses taken away by the King's soldiers, and four of the
" 11 were well worth £40. I rode after the 11 horses and bought 9 of them
" again and brought them home ; then, riding after the other two, while I
" was abroad the King's soldiers took the other 9 away again, and could never
" have them more. Since, again, the last winter, going to market with a load
" of corn, the Earl of Manchester's soldiers met with my men and took away
" my whole team of horses, letting my cart stand in the field 4 miles from
" home ; never had them more. . . . Besides all this, when the King's
" soldiers come to me they call me ' Roundhead,' ' Rogue,' and say I pay rent
" to the Parliament garrisons, and they will take it away from me. And, like-
" wise, when the Parliament soldiers they reckon with me, and tell me I pay
" rent to Worcester and Winchester, therefore the Parliament soldiers say they
" will have the rest."

William Bathe, of Amblecote, collier, writes to Lord Denbigh, complaining that

" certain soldiers had arrested him while he was drinking with a friend, and
" took from him his purse, money, and writings, which he prays may be
" restored to him, and that he may be set at liberty."‡

---

* IV. Rep. Hist. MSS. Com., p. 265 ; possibly Suckley is a mistake for Lutley, which is near Halesowen. † Hist. MSS. Com., XI. Rep., app. VII., p. 217.
‡ IV. Rep. Hist. MSS. Com., p. 272.

If the following is true, it explains a good deal of the plundering and misconduct of Denbigh's men. His officers and soldiers petition, representing their destitute condition in respect of money and clothes, and recalling their great service at Dudley and other places. When the existence of an ill-disciplined, starving soldiery, destitute of money and clothes, in a country which could be pillaged with success, is borne in mind, bad as are some of the stories that have survived of the pillage of some of the Worcestershire people, it seems fairly certain that we do not know the full measure of the iniquity.

In the south of the County the fighting during the autumn of 1644 still centres round Massey, who was at last receiving recognition for his bravery and perseverance. At the end of August, 1644, he went to London, waiting for the orders of the Parliament. During his stay there he was highly honoured, as he deserved to be. His return to Gloucester is described in the following terms :—

"We met with Colonel Massey on the last Saturday night, so late, and the "night so dark, that we knew him only by the lustre of his valour, which "honoured and overcame the darkness. He was then returning to his govern-"ment of Gloucester, and made haste by the privilege of night to get a day "upon his enemies."*

Parliament had become fully alive to the great importance of Massey's work. An ordinance was passed directing £10,000 a month to be raised for the County of Gloucester for the relief of the garrison and soldiers. To give them value for their money, Massey extended the area of his operations to the south as far as Bath, where he tried to put an end to Rupert's efforts to recruit; eastwards to Banbury, to help the besiegers there; and northwards, through Herefordshire and Shropshire into North Wales, to scour out the scattered horse and fugitives after the battle of Montgomery. It need hardly be wondered that, consequent on all this activity, at the end of September Massey had to write to Parliament complaining of his need for horses and men. But Parliament were unable to supply his wants. In October he again wrote that all he wanted was an addition of 2000 foot and 500 horse to conquer all South Wales. A report was circulated that Massey was following up Charles so closely with 4000 horse and foot that the King's army were so distracted that

"they knew not whither to go, nor what to do, and that the King himself, who now "by this vigilant and active Colonel Massey is now pursued, is fearful to lodge to "any town or garrison, but hath lain several nights in the field. Thus we have "our report, but afterwards it is said Colonel Massey hath no strength of thou-"sands, as we heard it reported he desires but 1500. I would he had them, for "his strength is so small, and his artillery so great, that whilst he took 600 "horse from Gerrard's rear, Sir John Winter hath taken Monmouth from him.

* *London Post*, No. 3, 27th August, 1644.

" N.B.—Monmouth was not taken, only a house Massey had fortified, five " miles from Monmouth."*

Most of this was mere idle boasting, but in September Massey inflicted a severe loss on the Royalists. Lieutenant-Colonel Kyrle, a person of some influence in the district, was induced by Massey on the 26th September, to hand Monmouth over to him.† The loss of the place caused the Royalists great inconvenience. It was called, and rightly, the key of South Wales, as it lay on the direct line of the Royalist communications, not only with Wales but what was, perhaps, even more important, with Raglan and Lord Worcester.

To counteract this loss an attempt was made to fortify Beachley, and thus obtain an alternative route into Wales. But Massey frustrated this. He attacked the Royalist works at the passage, took them and " slighted " them, as destroying them was then termed.

Massey was now ordered to march into Oxfordshire to intercept some Welsh reinforcements which Gerrard, the governor of Worcester, was bringing up to join the King. It was a race between Gerrard and Massey, who could first get across the Cotswolds. Massey, with his own regiment, marched from Monmouth for Evesham. The fortifications had been destroyed during Waller's visit in June, and not been renewed, nor the garrison replaced. Gerrard had a shorter distance to march, so when Massey got near Evesham he found the place occupied by Gerrard, with his Welsh, and his march a failure. This was not the worst, no sooner had Massey left Monmouth than the Royalists attacked and retook it.

During the autumn of 1644 a spy mania seems to have broken out among both sides. That there was a good deal of espionage going on is true, but each side appear to have run to absurdities with regard to it. In October, 1644, Francis Pitt, of Wolverhampton,‡ was tried before a court-martial at Wolverhampton, as being a spy of Colonel Leveson, the governor of Dudley Castle. Pitt was one of the governor's tenants, and had been employed by him to take a letter to Governor Captain Grethill, of Rushall Hall, near Dudley, a Parliament garrison. The letter offered Grethill £2000 if he would surrender the garrison to the King. Grethill pretended to consent, and Pitt went backwards and forwards on several occasions to arrange terms, Grethill insisting that certain men who had formed part of his garrison, and who had been made prisoners by Leveson, should be released. Leveson agreed and to shew his good faith released the men. He then sent a party, in accordance with the arrangement, to take over Rushall Hall. Grethill changed his mind, refused to surrender,

---

* *Perfect Occurrences*, 25th October, 1644.   † Rushworth, V., 742.
‡ Rushworth, V., 727.

arrested Pitt, and fired on the party, killing some of them.
Pitt was handed over to a court-martial, tried as a spy, convicted, and executed.[*]

The other case was that of a girl of from 16 to 17 years of
age, who

"disguised as a boy, offered herself as a recruit for the Guard at Hyde Park.
"She was a native of Gloucestershire, and was put to a master for an appren-
"tice for six weeks upon trial, but fled upon the eve of the day she was to be
"bound. She was taken up, and thought by some to be a spy to discover
"the state of London, but her age and her sex seemed to destroy this
"opinion."

The account, which is a French one, continues :

"Neanmoins la malice du sexe feminin, est bien grand elle va bien souvent
"au dela de l'age."[†]

A good deal of time during the autumn was spent in nego-
tiating what was called the Treaty of Uxbridge. Like all other
attempts at negotiation it failed. The interesting point in it
with regard to Worcestershire is that the Parliament proposed
to make a number of the more active Royalists, as a punishment for their loyalty, incapable of holding office or of coming
to Court. These persons were selected from all over England.
In Worcestershire, "that loyal county" as it was said to be,
Parliament only proposed to except one man, Sir William
Russell, of Strensham [‡]

There was a good deal of desultory fighting during the
winter, of which little or no trace has survived. For instance,
Major Robert Harley, writing to his brother, Colonel Edward
Harley, on the 28th November, 1644, says : "I mentioned
Worcester in my last, which design miscarried." What the
design here referred to was there is no record.

During the autumn two rather important Worcestershire
Royalists were taken prisoners by the Parliament. Both had
been Commissioners of Array, and both had done what they
could, but in different ways, to help the Royal cause. The one,
Sherrington Talbot, of Salwarpe, one of the Shrewsbury family,
was a magistrate and deputy-lieutenant, and had at the outbreak of the war been very active for the King, especially in
raising men. He was a Commissioner of Array in 1642, had
been arrested at the instance of Sergeant Wilde, and sent to
London in custody. He obtained his release, but still showing
his Royalist views, was again arrested and sent to the
Tower. The other was Richard Dowdeswell, also a Commissioner of Array, who carried out a successful plot to get
Tewkesbury surrendered to the Royalists, and an unsuccessful
plot to get Gloucester surrendered. He was also arrested and
sent up to London.[§]

---

* Whitelock, 101.   † *Le Mercure Anglois*, No. 16, Oct. 3—10, 1644.
       ‡ Rushworth, V., 798.   § Whitelock, 130.

The rest of the year was taken up in small local raids and fights. A lull came over both parties, possibly from mutual exhaustion. The Parliament recognised the necessity of doing something to infuse new vigour into their army, and took steps for that end. Probably the Royalists also recognised it, but it was hardly possible for them to reform their forces under existing circumstances. The best idea of how matters stood at the close of 1644 can perhaps be gained from a local account, which may fitly close the narrative of the war for the year.

The letter is dated Tewkesbury, December 16th, 1644.*

"For news in these parts we have this, that the Worcestershire Committee "are come safe to our town of Tewkesbury with 240 horse and men, well "appointed, and Colonel Rous is raising a regiment of foot, I hope to good "purpose, which, with those horse belonging to our governor, Colonel Massey, "may do well, for he is still abroad and in action.

"We have a front quarter hereabouts with the enemy by reason of the loss of "Monmouth. The Welsh are still hearkening for our governor's absence; and then "on the Forest of Dean side we never want constant alarm, especially when he is "towards Stroud or Cirencester, so that we have a hellish life unless we could "divide our forces, and that cannot be until these horse do join with us. Sir, I "can inform you of a successful passage of late, that was acted by Captain "Gainsford, who keeps one of our garrisons on the forest side. He had "intelligence that Sir John Winter's forces were gone abroad to plunder the "country, and taking about 40 men with him he met with the plunderers, "killed 21 of them, and took 14 of them prisoners, together with 4 waynes and "the drivers of them and 16 oxen. It was a brave defence, I will assure you. I "could certify you of some other passages, but it would be too tedious. One is "of our Governor's Captain-Lieutenant, who, with a party, met with a party of "the King's horse, killed 12 of them, took 4 prisoners, and one captain of "great note, and a scarf worth £10 at the least. Captain Robert Massey was "at the same time near taken in his quarters, but his trumpet sounding unto "horse the enemy fled, though they were within a stone's cast of him. I "think we could fright them with Rams' horns. There was lately a mutiny "at Sudeley Castle by the base abuse of unruly soldiers being but one day "behind of their pay. Captain George Massey, the Governor thereof, was "gone to borrow money to pay them accordingly, and hearing of it came "home, and demanding who was the mutineers, one of them answered that "what was done was done but in jest, but he understanding that he who made "the answer was chiefest stickler, he did prick him in the thigh with his "sword, whereof he died. But all is well again in that Castle, which is of "great consequence. Some unruly knaves will be do what a man can. "We have now three brothers, all honest men—our Governor Massey, Captain "George Massey, and Captain Robert Massey, of London, who is coming on "with a good troop of horse. He is a valliant man, as well as the rest. Other "slight businesses have been done, but those I omit till further proceedings be "to satisfie you at large. To conclude, if some of your great forces do not "come forward to suppress the enemies sallying out so near us, here will be "no resting in quiet; they do so follow us on three or four sides. Thus for the "time I take leave and rest,

"Your Friend."

From this description of things at Sudeley, life in "Ein kleine garrison," in 1644, must have been quite as unpleasant as life in a similar place at the present day in a foreign army, but possibly not for the same reasons.

---

* *London Post*, January 18th, 1645.

CHAPTER IV.

1645.

At the beginning of 1645 the garrisons in Worcestershire remained nearly the same as before. Colonel Sandys had succeeded Gerrard as Governor of Worcester; Evesham had had its fortifications destoyed in the summer when the King and Waller were there, and it remained for a time without fortifications and without a garrison, but both were restored, if not at the beginning, early in 1645. Major Robert Legge, a major of horse in Prince Maurice's regiment, was made the Governor. Symonds* puts down Droitwich as a Royal garrison, but gives no governor's name. Except this statement there appears to be no authority for saying that it was so.

Symonds does not mention Bewdley among the garrisons, and it does not appear that any governor was appointed after Sir Thomas Lyttelton. There were constantly troops at Bewdley, but there is no evidence of a regular garrison being kept there after 1644.

At Hartlebury, Sir Samuel Sandys was governor, with his kinsman under him. For some reason, during the year the defences of Hartlebury were greatly strengthened. To do this men were impressed from the different places in the neighbourhood, and made to work on the castle and its defences. Among other places directed to send a contingent for this work was Bewdley, the Bewdley people objected to going, and if possible to get them off gave one of those in authority a drink to get excused. The Bewdley accounts† have this entry :—

"Pd. for wine for Mr. Turton, to get off our men from going to work "at the Castle   0 01 0."

It is not recorded what effect the wine had.

Dudley still continued to hold out for the King. Sometime in the autumn of 1645 Madresfield was made into a Royal garrison, but neither the date when it was made, nor the reason for making it appear. It was before October, for in that month it was besieged. Chipping Campden remained an important Royalist post, and also the latest garrison, Stoke, the command of which had been given to Captain Henry Baird, who, unless much belied by report, appears to have been one of the most lawless of the Cavaliers of that day, which is saying much.

---

* Diary, p. 167.   † Burton's Bewdley, App., XXXIII.

In 1645,* Parliament is credited with two garrisons by Symonds, Hawkesley House, two miles from Bromsgrove, four miles from Edgbaston (the distances are, in fact, much greater), and Strensham House, belonging to Sir William Russell. Strensham House was so near Tewkesbury that any party who held that town would possess itself of Strensham. It might, in fact, be regarded as an outpost of Tewkesbury, on the high ground up the Avon. It must have changed hands some time in 1645, for in 1646 it was one of the Royalist garrisons, and was as such included in the articles for the surrender of Worcester.

In the beginning of January, 1645, the King appointed Prince Maurice General of Worcester, Hereford, and Salop. It is not quite clear whether there was a vacancy, or if this superseded the former appointment. In the summer of 1642 Lord Capel had been appointed to this, or to some similar appointment, and it does not appear that Capel had resigned. Maurice was certainly a good deal more in the County for the next 18 months, and spent a considerable portion of his time at Worcester. Curiously enough, though tradition points out numberless places where Charles lodged in Worcester and Worcestershire, and some few places where Rupert is said to have stayed, yet both record and tradition are wholly unacquainted with Maurice, and there is no house or place even said to have been his residence in Worcester or Worcestershire while he commanded here.

One of the first steps that Maurice took was to increase the importance of the Campden garrison by fortifying Campden House,† the residence of Sir Baptist Hickes, a house which is said to have cost £30,000 in beautifying and decorating, and was then one of the marvels of the district.

Major-General Brydges, the Parliamentary Governor of Warwick, did not regard this increase of strength at Campden with favour, as it threatened still more his line of communication with Gloucester. So he determined to take some steps to turn the Royalists out of Campden.‡ To put them off their guard, two or three companies were sent out to plunder, or, as it was called, "gather supplies." This was so usual that it attracted no notice, but Brydges gave them further orders that they were to go on gathering contributions, and not to return to Warwick until sent for. Brydges then went himself to meet them, taking with him 80 foot and 70 horse. Marching all night he found himself next morning at Stoke House by daybreak, a place the Royalists were engaged in strengthening. Brydges gave the order to storm it. The house was strong and strongly defended, but after an hour's fighting Brydges, as he reported, forced his way in without the loss of a man,

notwithstanding that the stormers were without shelter and
the bullets and stones flew thick about them. As soon as the
Royalists heard of the attack, the troops forming the two garrisons of Evesham and Campden came in hot haste to the rescue
of their friends. But Brydges, who had suspected they would
come, on taking the place at once fired the house,
collected all the plunder he could, and made off for Warwick.
He says that Stoke was only a fort of Papists, and that he
carried off with him five Papist captains, 30 other Papist officers
and gentlemen, besides the common soldiers.

The destruction of this garrison was only another of the
acts that were driving the persons on both sides who had
anything to lose to take steps to defend their property,
wholly irrespective of party. The state of the County was going
from bad to worse. Not only did levy follow levy in frequent
succession, but there was no safety for life or property.
Royalists plundered, Parliamentarians plundered. When
either party was collecting supplies the question was not if the
owner of the property about to be taken was on the side of the
King or of the Parliament, but had he any property worth taking ;
if so, it was seized, if the owner was on the plunderers' side
because it was his duty to support them ; if he was not because
it was their duty to prevent him supporting their opponents.
In all Counties this plundering was felt, but in Worcestershire
more than in all others, as there were more plunderers Every
detachment of troops that passed or repassed along the County
roads wanted something, and they took it. The unfortunate
inhabitants were left almost destitute. Whitelock* says
Parliament received petitions complaining of the " insults to
the women and the murdering of men," to redress which evils a
committee was appointed to consider:—

" These fruits of civil war ; robberies, and innumerable wicked actions
" committed by the barbarous soldiers, to the unspeakable misery of the
" poor country."

In some Counties the movement was made mainly against
one party, notably the Cavaliers. As in Dorsetshire, where it
was said † there were 4000 men, armed, who threatened to
plunder all who did not join them to extirpate the Cavaliers.
But the usual thing, and the one that prevailed in Worcestershire, was an alliance of both parties against all who plundered,
to whatever side they said they belonged.

In Worcestershire some 2000 persons got together and put
out a declaration of their intentions against the Popish party,
that they should preserve the King's rights and the privileges
of Parliament. Their numbers kept increasing so fast that
Rupert became alarmed, and tried and tried in vain to pacify

---

* Whitelock, p. 120.   † Ib., p. 130.

them. The chief difficulty was that the constables would not bring in the names of those who took part in these assemblies.

In March, 1645, the symptoms of popular risings became accentuated, both in Worcestershire and Shropshire, while in Herefordshire there was an actual rising. "Oppression was their plea, neutrality their cry." These bands of farmers and peasants called themselves "Clubmen," a name for which two derivations are given; one that they were armed with clubs, the other that they were members of a club or association. The latter appears to be the most likely. They displayed banners, on which were inscribed—

> "If you offer to plunder, or take our cattle,
> "Rest assured we will give you battle."

In Herefordshire the storm first burst, mainly from the acts of some Royalist soldiers, probably some of the Anglo-Irish whom Mynne had brought over to fight Massey, and who, when discipline became lax after Mynne's death, became little removed from banditti. A body of peasants resisted some of the plunderers, this led to an encounter between them and some troops of Scudamore's, the Governor of Hereford. The Clubmen appeared before Hereford, demanded redress of their wrongs, and in default threatened to take vengeance. Scudamore, at first, treated them and their grievances with contempt, but he soon found the matter was serious. Massey, on hearing of it, thought it might be turned to the advantage of the Parliament, so set out from Gloucester and marched to Ledbury to meet the Clubmen.* He soon found that they disliked him every bit as much as they disliked his opponents. Their only object was to stop plundering, and as he had to live by it there was no greater plunderer than Massey. Parliament were determined to put the Clubmen down at once, and sent peremptory orders that all plundering should forthwith cease. For the Royalists Scudamore took prompt action. He denounced their conduct, called on all loyal persons to come to his help, mentioned the ringleaders by name, and ordered their arrest.

Massey sent the following letter to Sir Samuel Luke.†

"Sir,

　"Major Harley's hasty departure here meeting with my extraordinary "occasions was such that he overran my intention and letter purposed by him "unto yourself, for the paying of that tribute which I acknowledge to owe, and "you may justly claim from me. Sir, this post can relate the Hereford "business ; the whole County being now in arms in a confused manner, and "before the City of Hereford, and some of the Worcestershire side have joined "with them. They keep the soldiers in the garrison, and are resolved to "have the governor and soldiers out of it before they leave it, there being "together since Tuesday last 15 or 1600, and amongst them, as is reported, "at least 6 or 7000 muskets and other fire arms. I have sent you a copy of "their articles and demands from the Governor of Hereford.

---

* Birch's Memoirs, 112.　　† Birch, 216.

"Sir, upon this noise, I advanced upon Wednesday last to Ledbury, with
"500 foot and 150 horse, being as many as I could spare or make at present,
"and demanded their resolution, and desired them to join with me in observ-
"ing the Parliament's commands. They would fain have me assist them (for
"they dare trust me), but they will not as yet declare themselves for the
"Parliament, but they conceive themselves able to keep off both the Parliament
"forces and the King's also from contribution and quarter in their Country.
"That is their main hope, and upon that ground I understand they have taken
"up that resolution.
"Sir, it is an opportunity offered to the Parliament, if they lay hold of this
"occasion and send me speedy force, to gain them all to the Parliament; if
"not the loss will not be small to us. Be it how it will, I have used all the
"best arguments I can to move them to declare themselves for the Parliament,
"then they may have protection and authority for what they do. Now their
"act is a perfect act of rebellion, to be justified by no law or statute, and their
"confusion will be certain. My humble request to you is to furnish this my
"post with a horse to London, that my letter, sent by him to the Committee
"of both Kingdoms on this behalf, and to His Excellency, may find a speedy
"resolution and return, whilst I hold fair way with the County.
                                      "Sir, I am,
                              "Your affectionate and ever obedient servant,
"Gloucester, 22nd March, 1645.   Edward Massey."

Parliament do not seem to have realised the meaning of the
movement, or its importance. Neutrality was to them punish-
able—the sin of the Laodicean Christians. Sir Samuel Luke
wrote to Lord Essex that as he had property of his own in
Herefordshire he had better come down and deal with the
matter himself. Scudamore seems to have felt the necessity for
something more than correspondence. He arrested and hung
the ringleaders, and having shewn the conciliation of severity,
brought the others to terms and thus got out of the present
difficulty. But the relief was merely temporary, the evil was
too deeply spread to be easily cured. The Clubmen had a real
grievance, and a grievance intensified by the fact that their
action led the soldiers of both sides to greater and greater
atrocities.

"The soldier," says a Parliamentary account,* "hath of late assumed great
"power and presumption (or, rather, indiscretion and disobedience), to him-
"self, as is too manifest by this last mutinous imprisonment and murders."

There was reason for this complaint. If property was inse-
cure, life was more so. Colonel Robert Sandys is said to have
stabbed Colonel Price, the member for Radnorshire, in the
streets of Presteign. Sherrington Talbot, whose arrest has
been mentioned, is said to have been seen in the streets of
Worcester, his sword in his hand, dripping with blood, boasting he had just killed an unarmed rebel, a poor prisoner, who
was being brought into Worcester. Parliament ordered that
all Irishmen in the King's service, who might be taken in
arms, should be put to death; in obedience to this order,
Brereton, after the battle of Nantwich, hung his so-called Irish

---

* *Perfect Diurnal*, 17th March, 1645.

prisoners merely because they were said to be Irish. Baxter
tells a gruesome story. Grenville ordered several men to be
hung. The rope suspending one broke. A second rope was
produced, that also broke. A third rope was produced, that
also broke. The executioner then refused to go on. Symonds,
in his journal, states* that at Durweston, Sir Richard Grenville
"hanged the High Constable and then asked the Prince."
Possibly the best instance is contained in Rupert's letter to
Essex :—

"If any prisoner under my command shall be taken, executed and murdered
"in cold blood, under what senseless and unjust pretences whatsoever, for every
"officer and soldier so causelessly and barbarously murdered I will cause so
"many of the prisoners remaining in my power to be put to death in the same
"manner. . . . The war is like to be so managed that the English
"nation is in danger of destroying one another (or, which is a kind of
"extirpation), of degenerating into such an animosity and cruelty, that all
"elements of charity, compassion, and brotherly affection shall be extin-
"guished.'

There is a letter from the Staffordshire Committee, dated 5th
August, 1642, to Speaker Lenthall, that puts matters very
plainly :—

"The Governor of Dudley Castle has lately executed one, and the Governor
"of Hartlebury Castle threatens to execute another, of Colonel Fox's soldiers.
"We have, therefore, delivered to Colonel Fox two Irish soldiers which, upon
"this occasion we purposed to have put to death by the ordinance of October
"24th last, but as they were not put to death on their taking but so long
"forborne, we desire the pleasure of Parliament."†

Such was the state of things as to life. As to property it was
worse. Colonel Baird, a leading Royalist, who was created a
baronet for his services, was an active, able soldier, but nothing
less than a professional robber. He had been governor of the
garrison of Stoke, and when that was destroyed by Brydges was
made governor of the garrison in Campden House. In this
place he plundered the neighbourhood in the most approved
style. The officers did not, it would be more correct to say
could not, get in the monthly contributions. Baird would
listen to no excuses. To secure compliance with his demands
he issued the following notice :—

"Know you that unless you bring unto me (at a day and hour in Worcester)
"the monthly contribution for six months, you are to expect an unsanctified
"troop of horse among you, from whom if you hide yourselves they shall fire
"your houses without mercy, hang up your bodies wherever they find them,
"and scare your ghosts."

The constables complained to Parliament of the insolence of
Baird.

Some persons endeavoured to avoid being plundered, and
to preserve some of their property paid a sum as a protection, but it was useless to pay it to one side if it was not also
paid to the other. Hornyold, of Blackmore Park, paid £12 a

* P. 127.   † Hist. MSS. Com., XII Rep., app. I., p. 238.

month to each of the garrisons of Worcester, Gloucester, and Madresfield. Henry Townsend, of Elmley Lovett, paid the Committees of both Worcestershire and Staffordshire.

Among other persons who suffered was Sir William Russell. A garrison from Tewkesbury took his fortified house at Strensham and occupied it. It was said they found in it plate and money to the value of £4000. This is doubtful, considering how completely Nehemiah Wharton and his friends had cleaned out the house in October, 1642. This state of insecurity for property caused a condition of things of which tradition still lingers, the concealing of plate and money by the owners to avoid plundering. There is hardly a family who possessed a landed estate at the time of the Civil War that have not some legend of concealed treasure. For instance, the Berkeleys, of Spetchley, say their butler to save the family plate hid it under one of the elms in the avenue. The butler was wounded, and tried with his last breath to confide to a member of the family his secret, but could get no further than " plate," " elm," " avenue," and died, so that the plate remains hidden to this day.

To allay the prevailing discontent, Maurice was sent to Worcester. Not only did he utterly fail to do this, but actually aggravated it, as he required the County to make him an allowance of £100 a month for his own personal expenses. What was worse, he was a friend of Baird's, and so hated was Baird that this alone would have ruined Maurice's popularity if there had been nothing else. Baird's last act may be mentioned. He joined the King in May, 1645, on his Leicester march. Abandoning Campden House, he burnt it to the ground, an act, according to Clarendon,* that was quite needless. He says:—

> " It had brought no other benefit to the public than the enabling the
> "licentious governor thereof (Baird), who exercised an unlimited tyranny
> "over the whole country, and took his leave of it in wantonly burning the
> " noble structure which he had too long inhabited, and which, not many years
> " before, had cost £30,000 the building."

Rupert determined to put an end to the Clubmen and their organisation. Based on the idea of the Solemn League and Covenant, he drew up a protestation, which he required all commanders, soldiers, gentry, citizens, and freeholders, within the County and City of Worcester, to make when tendered to them by the High Sheriff and Commissioners of the County, and ordered that a schedule of the names of those who refused to make it should be delivered unto Sir William Bellenden, the Commissary General.

Another act of 1645 had an important result on the war, the new modelling of the Parliamentary army. For

---

* II., 503.

some time the jealousies and differences between the different leaders had been becoming acute; to get rid of these the army was reformed on a new model or basis. The "self-denying ordinance" was the main part of the scheme. It was based on this resolution :—

> "That no member of either House of Parliament shall, during the war, "enjoy or execute any office or command, military or civil, and that an "ordinance be brought in for that purpose."*

The new army was to consist† of 21,000 men—6000 horse, 1000 dragoons, and 14,000 foot. The horse to be divided into 10 regiments, the dragoons into 10 single companies. Each regiment of foot to consist of at least 1200 men, and the whole charge to be £44,955 a month, to be raised by an assessment proportionately throughout the kingdom. Sir Thomas Fairfax was appointed General, Skippon Major-General; Fairfax to nominate all the officers. The colonels of horse were : Middleton, Sidney, Graves, Sheffield, Vermuden, Whaley, Sir Michael Livesey, Fleetwood, Rossiter, and Sir Robert Pye. The colonels of foot : Crayford, Berkeley, Aldridge, Holborn, Fortescue, Ingoldsby, Montague, Pickering, Welden, Rainsborough.‡

The consequences of the ordinance had a marked effect on Worcestershire. It got rid of one of the most active of the Parliamentary leaders, Denbigh. He, as a member of the House of Lords, had to give up his command, as had also Essex and Manchester.

While the Parliament were re-organising and strengthening their forces the Royalists were becoming more and more disorganised. Maurice was most unpopular with the people, one reason being that in his eyes a soldier could do no wrong. If he did not actually support, he did not restrain his men in their plundering. The worst feature was the increase of lawless outcasts. Men had left their homes to avoid paying Maurice's taxes enforced by Maurice's soldiers, and taken to the woods. Shrawley Wood was said to swarm with them, 50 men out of one parish being among the outlaws there. Some notion of Maurice's ideas of discipline and good government can be obtained from one instance. In April, 1645, Maurice sent out a party of 600 horse to take a convoy of powder and ammunition going from Warwick to Gloucester. On reaching the place where they had resolved to intercept the convoy, Maurice's men found it had been too quick for them and had passed on its way to Gloucester Disappointed of the convoy, they determined not to return empty-handed. They collected a good deal of plunder from the farms and houses on their route. Riding into Stratford-on-Avon they put the town to

---

* Rushworth, VI., p. 4.   † Rushworth, VI., p. 7.   ‡ Rushworth, VI., p. 13.

ransom, asking in the first place £800, but after a time·
agreeing to take £10.   The Warwickshire Committee
assembled some men to cut off the plunderers' retreat to·
Worcester, when, if they could do nothing else, they might at
least recapture some of the plunder.   The Warwick men waited·
till Maurice's troops reached a narrow part of the road, then
charged and completely overthrew them.   Several of the
officers were taken prisoners, all the plunder retaken, all
Maurice's men dispersed to Evesham, Droitwich and Worcester.
Whitelock* thus describes it :—

"Warwick horse, and some from Newport, in all about 160, fell upon a
"party of about 300 of Worcester horse, who had much plundered the county,
"and routed them, killed about 10, wounded many, and took 60 prisoners,
"170 horses and arms, one colour, and recovered all the plunder."

The fighting this year began by the Scots joining Sir
William Brereton.   On this Rupert marched from Oxford to
Worcester, and thence to Ludlow.   Here he heard of Sir
Marmaduke Langdale's victory over the Scots at Pontefract.
Rupert then marched across to Bridgnorth, joined Langdale,
moved on to Wenlock, Market Drayton, and Whitchurch.
Collecting such troops as he could from his Worcestershire
garrisons, Maurice marched out and joined them on the
19th April, when they raised the siege of Beeston Castle,
which had lasted for 17 weeks.   Here Rupert halted, as
Brereton and the Scots advanced against him.   Considering
himself too weak to fight them, Rupert retired to Whitchurch,
Market Drayton, High Ercall, and Newport.   While here
he heard of the proceedings of the Worcestershire and
Herefordshire Associations and Clubmen, these he at once
determined to put down.   Setting off from Newport he
marched to Bewdley.   Here he halted.   Marching west to·
Bromyard he was told of a meeting of Clubmen in a
village near.   Turning aside he went to the village,
suppressed the meeting, marched all night, reached Hereford in the morning; thence he proceeded to Monmouth and
Bristol.   He returned rapidly to Hereford, where he was
met by Astley with the news that Massey had marched out of
Gloucester and had occupied Ledbury.

If Rupert was active Massey was more so.   From
Gloucester he scoured the country in all directions.   In.
March one of his bands went to Pershore and destroyed
the house adjoining the Abbey Church, it being rumoured
that the Royalists were going to plant a garrison there.
Subsequently Massey had received reinforcements, and
desirous of doing what he could to harass the Royalists
set out for Ledbury.   On reaching it he intended to make

---

* Memorials, p. 138.

it a base for further forays. Rupert hearing that Massey was there determined he should be at once dislodged. Collecting what troops he could, and setting out at night, he marched the 16 miles from Hereford to Ledbury; at dawn the next day he was in front of the place. Ledbury is a large open village, consisting of two cross roads, the one from Gloucester to Hereford intersecting the one from Worcester to Ross. Rupert's approach was not even suspected. He sent some men round the village to the Gloucester and Ross side of the town, ordering them to occupy those roads to cut off Massey's retreat. Having done this he gave the order to attack the town from the Hereford side. Bursting into it with his horse he drove Massey's men back on to the troops he had placed on the Gloucester side. The following is the Royalist account of what followed : *

"On Tuesday last Master Massey was sent, broken and bruised, to " Gloucester by His Highness Prince Rupert. For Master Massey last week, " taking opportunity of the increase of his horse by the addition of a convoy " to Gloucester, drew out and marched to Ledbury, with intention, as is con-"ceived, to fall on a new garrison of His Majesty's at Canon Frome, where "he stayed, thinking to draw Prince Rupert after him, and upon His " Highness' retreat to creep away again towards Hereford, to have gained " time and disturb the Prince, and not to fight with him, though the man "talked high on purpose to revive his Forresters of Dean. But His Highness "having intelligence of his quarters, numbers, and security (for Massey was "then busy at a court of war to hang up one of Prince Rupert's soldiers), "advanced presently and came near Ledbury on Tuesday morning last, at "whose approach the rebel horse drew to arms, having barricadoed the streets "with carts, &c. The Lord Astley's foot were ordered to fall on first, and "were seconded by Colonel Washington's and some others. Their horse "kept out His Highness' foot for a while, but within half an hour the "barricadoe was opened, and then the way was made for His Highness' horse "to charge. The first charge was committed to the Lord Loughborough, "with command if he could to make a through charge, who, like himself, did "it most gallantly, and that without any hurt to himself, though shot five "times through his clothes and upon his arms. He was seconded from His "Highness several ways, so that Massey's horse, beaten out of the town "(while the foot fell into the woods and enclosures), were pursued up a very "steep hill, which yet could not hinder the rebels from galloping. The "pursuit was committed to Colonel Thomas Sandys, who, after he had chased "the rebels four miles, came to a village barricadoed by the rebels [?" "Dymock], though this also could not hinder the chase, which was continued "through the town or further, even up to the rebels' garrison, the rebels "having galloped their horses into lard, till they were able but to trot. There "were killed in the town and pursuit 120 rebels (besides many hiding their "wounds in the woods). More had been slain, but that His Highness rode up "and down and commanded to give quarter. Among the dead there were one "major (conceived to be Kyrle, who betrayed Monmouth) ; near 400 "prisoners, whereof 27 officers—majors, captains, and lieutenants. One of "those is Major Backhouse, that betrayed His Majesty in the delivering up of "Gloucester. Many hundreds of arms, all their baggage and ammunition, "with Master Massey's own rumpster. And all this with the loss of five "common soldiers (but not one officer), only Colonel Lingham is shot in the

* " Mercurius Aulicus," April 25th, 1645.

" leg, and some few other gentlemen had hurts, whose names as yet we have
" not.   His Highness' horse did most gallantly, leaping hedge after hedge to
" come at the rebels, so as the foot acknowledge themselves much indebted to
" the horse for disengaging them at the barricadoes, and vow (when time
" serves) to make a fair requital.   Massey himself was observed to charge
" well in the fight, and to draw off his foot in the rear to make them run
" faster away;   which, yet, could not serve him, but that at last he was
" glad to slip off towards Tewkesbury, and with 80 horse spur home to
" Gloucester."

Massey's despatch to the Speaker is as follows :

" Sir,
    " On Tuesday last, the 21st of the instant, April, Prince Rupert, marching
" all that night, came the next morning, Wednesday, the 22nd, before
" Ledbury, where I then was, but the enemy intercepting our scouts we had
" no intelligence until they were near at hand.   The enemy advanced and
" charged into the town upon us, and myself (with divers gentlemen, viz. :
' Major Horton, Lieutenant-Colonel Kyrle, Major Bacchus, Captain Gifford,
" Captain Moore, and Captain Bailey, with some others), and some common
" soldiers, with the assistance of 200 musketeers out of the country force,
" received them.   And as soon as we received the alarm we drew out upon
" them, and marching close up to them fell upon them, beat them to a
" retreat, and made it good against them so long till my foot might retreat a
" secure way to Gloucester.   After the foot were marched off and out of the
" town we had two or three hot charges upon them, when we slew near 40 of
" the enemies' men, and many of them that were killed were officers, at which
" charge, as it seems, the Lord Hastings, with some others of quality, were
" slain.   On our part we had very few killed, not above 6 or 7, but I was
" enforced myself to charge at the head of all my troops to encourage all the
" Warwick and Northampton horse ; I and my officers bearing the heat of the
" day.   At length, intending to retreat to our place of advantage (some horse
" of those sent to me not standing to it as they should have done), the enemy
" got in amongst our foot, but we redeemed that again, and so marched off
" into the field.
    " The enemy have sent us a list of the prisoners they took from us.   The
" number of their own list is 110 prisoners, but above 80 of these were none
" of my men, only such country people as they swept away with them in their
" retreat that did never bear arms, only they carried them away and caused
" them, by money or making friends for exchange, to redeem themselves.   My
" major (Sergeant-Major Bacchus) is desperately wounded in the head, and
" was carried away prisoner by the enemy to Hereford.   Major Horton had a
" slight wound in the head and another in the arm, but came bravely off.
" Captain Bailey and Captain Foster, with some other common men of ours,
" are taken prisoners by them.   I have sent for their freedom by exchange
" of some of those prisoners I took from them, many of them being of
" quality, enough to redeem them all if they were thrice as many.   Prince
" Rupert sent me word by my trumpeter that I sent, that in the fight he
" sought me out, but knew me not till after, no more than I knew him, but it
" seems we charged each other, and he shot my horse under me and I did as
" much for him.   At that charge many commanders of theirs fell.
    " Prince Rupert, I hear, is very much enraged to undertake so great and
" toilsome a march and so much to miss his end.   I had, by God's blessing,
" my intendment, and stopped his present march northward.   To God be
" the glory.   Prince Rupert's army, by the report of the country, is noised
" about to be 6 or 7000 horse and foot, who are now upon their march again
" towards Ludlow, and so, as I hear, intend for Salop, if they be not prevented
" again, which must be by a more considerable strength than I have.
    " The forces that were with me in all about 5000 foot and 350 horse ; nor
" were these all with me at Ledbury, for my guards were not come.
    " The enemy brag little of their getting, but lament much.   The names of

" the commanders and officers that were slain by us I shall send you by
" the next.

" Your humble servant,
" April 25th, 1645.   E. Massey."

Massey admits a defeat. But it was something more than a defeat, it was a rout. Rupert says*

" Massey was soundly beaten yesterday, his foot quite lost, and his horse
" beaten and pursued within six miles of [Gloucester?]. He himself and
" some of his officers made a handsome retreat."

Massey ordered his foot to retire, and did his best with his horse and his officers to check Rupert while the foot retreated. On the whole he succeeded, but at one place Rupert's horse broke through or round the foot, fell on Massey's rear-guard, and took nearly 200 prisoners, amongst whom were two captains, and Sergeant-Major Bacchus, who died soon after of his wounds.

Rupert lost some commanders and many common soldiers. Although successful in driving Massey out of Ledbury, he failed in his plan, which was so to cripple Massey that he would make no more sorties. Not having done this, Rupert did not care to advance to the north and leave Massey in force and on the offensive in his rear. As Massey was still able to fight, Rupert returned the same day to Hereford. Here he remained, recruiting his force to fill up the vacancies caused by the late fighting. Charles, who was then in Oxford, sent a party of about 2000 horse to Rupert's help, so as to enable him to pass to Oxford if he wanted to do so. Parliament heard this force was about to march, and sent word to Fairfax to intercept all reinforcements going to Rupert. This, however, they were not able to do. Rupert, with his men, marched without any interruption from Hereford to Worcester. At Worcester he joined with Maurice, and was now so strong that Cromwell, who had been instructed to intercept them, fell back from want of troops to do so.

On May 1st, Rupert and Maurice, with all their forces, marched to Evesham and continued their march to Oxford; making no stay at Evesham they reached Oxford in safety.

They did not stay there long. On the 7th May, Charles began that march, the " Leicester march," which was to be so very fatal to his fortunes and to himself.

When they left Oxford, on the 7th of May, the army with the King and Rupert consisted of about 8000 horse and foot. On the 8th the King was at Stow-on-the-Wold, on the 9th at Evesham. Here he was joined by Lord Astley's foot, 3000 strong. The King's own troops were quartered at Childs Wickham, between Broadway and Evesham. With the King

---

* Warburton, II., 408.

came Sir Henry Baird and the Campden garrison, the house having been burnt. Rupert stayed at Bretforton, between Campden and Evesham, with Mr. Canning. On Saturday, 10th, the King went to Inkberrow, Rupert to Alcester. It is said that at the Vicarage at Inkberrow, about 50 years ago, there was still a book of maps of England and Wales,

"with every shire and the small towns in every one of them, on six maps, "portable for every man's pocket, useful for all commanders for quartering of "soldiers, and all sorts of persons that would be informed where the armies "be. Never so commodiously drawn before this, 1644."

This was the King's copy, and he is said to have left it behind him on the visit to Inkberrow.* It is locally said that Charles stayed at Thorn Farm, near Inkberrow. On Sunday, May 11th, the King, with his own regiment of foot and horse, marched to Droitwich, where he stayed till Wednesday, May 14th. Two letters which the King wrote while staying here are extant. One to Lord Jermyn, complaining that he had sent him no news of the Queen.

"Only take a little more in writing to me concerning my wife's "health."

The other to the Queen herself, in which he says he

"could not brag for stores of money," and continues : "So farewell, sweet-"heart, and God send me good news of thee."

Both these letters were intercepted by Parliament, and are now in the House of Lords. On the 14th the King went to Cofton Hackett. Rupert's baggage, "his family" as it is termed, was sent to Bromsgrove. He, however, went on beyond Bromsgrove towards Northfield, where there stood, and still stands, the remains of an old house known as Hawkesley, the property of the Middlemores, a strong Catholic family, most zealous cavaliers. Fox had turned them out of the house and converted it into a Parliamentary garrison, under a Captain Gray. Rupert desired to check the "Tinker's" activity, and determined to take it. On the night of Tuesday, 13th, Rupert quartered before the house. It was not strong enough to resist for long this force brought against it. About 2 p.m. on Wednesday it surrendered, just as the King came up. It was agreed that the officers should be freed from the insolence of the common soldiers. A month's provision and ammunition was found in the house, but the soldiers declined to fight. The garrison consisted of 60 foot and 40 horse. These were made prisoners and were handed over to Lord Astley, as was also the plunder of the place. When Lord Astley's men had finished plundering, the house was set on fire and burnt. The King returned to Cofton Hackett, to Mr. Jolliffe's, where he held a meeting of the governors

---

* Noake, Notes and Queries for Worcestershire, 321.

of the different Royalist garrisons. Colonel Scudamore, of
Hereford; Colonel Leveson, of Dudley; Colonel Woodhouse,
of Ludlow. At 4 a.m. next morning the King started for
Himley, Lord Ward's house, near Dudley. The Prince and
soldiers stayed behind to "slight" the Hawkesley works.
Having done this Rupert marched towards Wolverhampton.
It is believed that it was on this march on the 15th May,
that Rupert, passing by Frankley, the home of the Lyttelton's,
had the house burnt so that it might not be occupied as a
garrison as Hawkesley had been, and thus undo all the results
he had gained by his march, by setting up a new garrison at
Frankley. Whatever was the motive, Frankley was burnt
down by the Cavaliers.

Charles and Rupert now quitted Worcestershire. It will
not be necessary to describe their movements outside the
County. They marched about Staffordshire and Leicestershire,
and on the 31st May took Leicester by storm.

So far all had been in the King's favour, he was now about
to enter on a series of reverses. The first that happened took
place in his rear. Massey, recovered from his Ledbury
defeat, was desirous to let the Royalists see what he could
do. Charles left Evesham on the 10th May. Massey conceived the idea that he could greatly obstruct Charles by
occupying Evesham. He had been reinforced from London,
and considered himself ready to take the offensive, so on
May the 23rd he left Gloucester at night. Marching by
Tewkesbury to Evesham he reached there on May 25th.
Colonel Legge, the governor, had but a scanty force with which
to defend it, but, notwithstanding the greatly superior strength
of Massey, when summoned

" to make a speedy surrender of the garrison, with all persons, arms, ammuni-
" tion, and provisions, or upon refusal to expect such justice as fire and sword
" would inflict,"

Legge replied :

" You are hereby answered, in the name of His Majesty, that this garrison,
" which I am entrusted to keep, I will defend so long as I can, with the men,
" arms, and ammunition therein, being nothing terrified at your summons."*

On receipt of this reply, Massey determined at once to
storm the town.

Evesham is situated in a horse-shoe, formed by the river
Avon. On the Gloucester side is a suburb known as Bengeworth, which was connected with the town by an old bridge.
Massey selected this bridge which leads into the heart of the
town as one of the points to be attacked. The road from London to Worcester crossed the river above, a little to the east of
where the railway now goes. But parallel to it, between the
old road and the railway, some fortifications, consisting of a

---

* Corbet's Military Government of Gloucester.

breastwork, surmounted by palisades, with a ditch on the outer side, had been thrown up. Massey conveyed the bulk of his men from the Bengeworth to the Evesham side of the river, probably at Twyford Bridge, a spot now marked by the ferry, known as Offenham Boat. Why he was allowed to do so is not clear. Possibly Legge's garrison was so weak that he could not spare the men to oppose it. In order to prevent any relief coming from Worcester, Massey sent his horse as far as Fladbury, to guard the Worcester road. Five separate points in the breastwork were selected for attack, and dividing his men for the purpose Massey ordered that these five points, and the bridge at Bengeworth, should be simultaneously assaulted, obviously thinking that with so small a garrison no effective resistance could be made against such numerous onsets.

At daybreak, on the 26th, the signal was given to storm. Massey himself led one party up to the ditch. They carried faggots with which to fill the ditch and enable them to rush the breastwork. Throwing the faggots into the ditch they crossed over on them, swarmed up the breastwork, tore down the palisades, and effected a lodgment on the rampart. Legge was not yet beaten. Pouring in a heavy fire from his musketeers, Massey's men, unable to stand against it, gave way, abandoned the rampart, and sought the shelter of the ditch. Massey reformed his men and led them again to the ramparts, and this time they stood firm, in spite of the fire, charging down into the town. Here they were again repulsed and driven back. But the men who had gained the rampart, in their turn, opened a fire on the town, and Legge's garrison was too weak to dislodge them. Massey ordered his men to make a passage through the breastwork as soon as possible, so that his horse could enter, and his men, working hard at this, were again attacked by Legge, and began to give way. They were slowly driven back over the ramparts, Massey contesting the ground, foot by foot, with Legge's soldiers. Matters were becoming serious, when suddenly Massey heard a cheer and saw his horse on his right flank, charging down into the town. A passage had been made practicable for cavalry through the breastwork away from the fighting, and through this Massey's horse streamed. Taking Massey's assailants in flank they drove them back into the town with considerable loss. Legge, however, again rallied his men, and was leading them on to another attack on Massey's force, when a cheer was heard in the town. On looking round they saw the Parliament horse making their way up the town to attack them in the rear. Massey's men had carried the bridge at Bengeworth, pushed up Bridge Street, and had now got Legge between two fires, in front and in rear. There was no escape. Legge's men had fought well but their courage was not enough

to resist this double attack.   Massey's troops kept pouring
in over the earthworks.   Resistance was hopeless, the assailants
tumbled

" over the works on all sides, and charged up both horse and foot with equal
" gallantry, bore down the enemy and mastered the garrison after a fiery con-
" flict, maintained for almost an hour with much resolution by the enemy."*

This was the end.   Further fighting was useless.   Surrender
was the only course open to Legge.

So fell Evesham, and fell by the valour of Massey's men.

" The gentlemen and officers who charged with Massey acted their parts
" with courage, and spurred on the valour of their soldiers, the reserve of
" foot divided into three bodies to second.   The assailants performed as became
" resolved men, and the whole action was complete according to the idea and
" platform of the design."*

It was a brilliant feat of arms, and every credit is due to
Massey for it.   550 prisoners, 70 of whom were officers, were
the result of the fight.   Massey even deserved the somewhat
high-flown praise of one of his admirers.

" Who was he that went out from the command at Gloucester in such a
" blaze to add glory unto conquest, and crown his actions with a never-dying
" honour, when he took the strong-garrisoned Evesham in a storm of fire and
" leaden hail, the loss whereof did make a King shed tears?   Was it not
" Massey ? "†

Massey's despatch to Lenthall was as follows :

" Evesham, 27th May, 1645.
" Evesham was yesterday morning assaulted by storm and took, in which
" we took the Governor (Colonel Robert Legge), Colonel Foster, and Colonel
" Bellingham, Major Tresillian, 13 captains, 13 lieutenants, and other officers
" and soldiers to the number of about 545.   Of ours was only slain about 7 or
" 8, and of the enemy about 12.   The assault was hot, and the defence not to be
" disparaged.   I desire that the government of the place be settled by
" Parliament with all speed, to enable me to march to the west, where
" Parliament has commanded me.   And also that there may be taken further
" settlement of Gloucester."‡

Parliament felt their obligation to Massey.   Evesham was
stormed on the 26th May, the news reached them on the 29th
May.   They at once ordered the Speaker to send Massey a
letter of thanks, acknowledging his great services.§

Gloucester was most unwilling to part with Massey.   They
sent a petition to Parliament praying he might be allowed to
stay there,

" as by his valour, through God's blessing, they had been so defended against
" continual fears of the enemy."

What Massey's brothers were has already been stated.   A
glimpse in one of these papers is given of his sister.

" She has lately come from Gloucester to London, in which place she left
" behind her many admirable examples of piety and discretion, and in that
" county, made wild and desolate by war, she appeared like another nature,

---

* Corbet's Military Government of Gloucester.
† Virtue and Valour Vindicated.   London, 1647.
‡ Hist. MSS. Com., XIII. Report, App., p. 235,   Duke of Portland, I.
§ C. J. I., 156.

" and was as great a housewife as the earth itself, which turneth all things into
" nourishment and beauty."*

As Massey had requested, measures were taken for the defence of Evesham. Six guns and 500 muskets were ordered to be at once sent out of the public stores to the garrison newly reduced. On the 18th July, Colonel Rouse was appointed governor of the town, and upon his death, which took place in 1647, Major William Dingley became his successor.†

On the 25th July 500 muskets and bandoliers were sent to the garrison at Evesham. On August 1st the committee of the army was desired to lend the committee of Worcestershire 500 muskets for the service of the garrison of Evesham.

The loss of Evesham was a serious blow to the King. It severed the direct line of communication between Oxford, Worcester and South Wales. For the future all convoys and troops going to the King could be attacked and harried on their way backwards or forwards. Charles' communications were no longer safe.

Thus ended Massey's connection with Worcestershire as far as the first Civil War is concerned. When next he appears it is as the commander of a Scotch division. For three years, in spite of much discouragement and of great difficulties, Massey had been the author and the sustainer of the Parliamentary party in the County. But for him the war would have ended differently; Gloucester would have fallen, and the Parliament been crushed. He and he alone maintained the cause of the Parliament when all else despaired. Possibly the best testimony to his work was the fact of the Gloucestershire Parliamentary Committee calling the attention of Parliament to the danger of that place and County by the removal of Colonel Massey.

Charles, meanwhile, on the 31st May, took Leicester by storm, and things appeared to be going well, but on the 14th June was fought the Battle of Naseby. This marks the beginning of the last part of the first Civil War. It now became clear that the King was beaten, as it was not possible for him to put another army into the field strong enough to defeat the Parliament. The end was therefore in sight. When the end would come was merely a question of time. Naseby was fought on Saturday, June 14th.

" Towards‡ night His Majesty, after the wounded were taken care for in
" Leicester, and the two Princes were come safe to him and had taken order
" with that garrison, and left two regiments of horse there, the Queen's and
" Colonel Carye's, marched that night (for now we had left running) to Ashby
" de la Zouch. On Sunday, June 15th, His Majesty, about 10 a.m , left Ashby
" and went to Lichfield. That night he lay in the Close, the horse were
" quartered in villages round about, some in the city. Here the King left

---

* *Parliament Post*, No. 11, July 15th—23rd, 1645.
† Mercurius' Britanicus. No. XXIII.   ‡ Symonds' Diary, p. 194.

"Colonel Bagot's regiment of horse ; the stout governor left here, wounded in "his right arm. Monday, June 16th, His Majesty marched to Wolverhamp- "ton ; Tuesday, 17th, to Bewdley, the Earl of Lichfield to Nether Arley "(Arley Kings)." Mr. Mucklow lives there.

One incident of the march is given in the Kidderminster register. Probably in the King's train came a poor wounded woman, who was left at Kidderminster to die as the army marched through on its way to Bewdley, for in the Burial register this entry appears :—

"1645, July 1st.—A woman buried, wounded at the battle in Leicester- "shire."

At Bewdley Charles stayed for two days, the 17th and 18th, at the "Angel," in Load Street. While here Charles heard that Lord Loughborough had surrendered Leicester. Charles left a few troops at Bewdley to hold the place and the bridge, and on the 19th (Thursday) marched to Bromyard, where he dined, and then the 16 miles on to Hereford, which he reached the same evening; "a 26-mile march, a very bad way, hilly and woody," says Symonds.* At Hereford Charles stayed for some days, vainly trying to rally his forces.

On the 1st July he marched to Abergavenny, having with him four troops of horse (King's, Queen's, Prince Rupert's Life Guards, and Prince Rupert's regiment of horse). The next day he reached Raglan, which now, for some little time, he made his head-quarters.

But if the Royalist cause was not to be trodden under foot it was necessary to do something. Goring and Rupert had gone to the west, Fairfax had followed them there. Parliament was doing all it could to get the Scotch to move, but this was diffi- cult. At last, on the 1st July, Lord Leven, at Nottingham, wrote to the Earl of Manchester that on the next day, July 2nd, the Scotch would march on Worcester On that day they left Newark. They proceeded by very easy stages. On the 8th they got as far as Alcester. Here, for some reason that is not clear, they reconsidered their policy of marching on Worcester.

The idea of the Scots marching on Worcester greatly dis- turbed the King. On the 5th July he wrote to Rupert :

"I shall not cross your orders by any direction of mine, yet I would have "you consider if both your brother and Washington be drawn out of Wor- "cester if that place will be safe, for I hear that Sam Sandys is at present "highly discontent (having not yet worn his sword since his restraint), and I have "diverse war intelligence that the northern rebels are likely shortly to besiege "that town. I likewise desire your opinion how soon I shall pass the water, "because all the forces which are already levied I believe will be transported "within these five or six days at soonest, before the rest can be at the water "side. Now, I would be loth to stay for these last, because before then it is "likely that there will be some action of moment, and yet I know not whom "to leave behind me to bring up the last recruits, and if I leave none I shall

---

* Diary, p. 195.

"certainly have a very ill account of them.   So desiring your answer as soon
" as you can, I rest, your loving Uncle and most faithful friend,
                                                        " Charles R."

Charles was doubtless right. It would have been the height
of folly, with the Scotch on the march for Worcester to have
withdrawn Maurice and Washington with their men. What
was done does not appear, but from the Scots abandoning
the idea of an attack on Worcester, it seems fair to assume the
garrison was not reduced, or if so only in a very slight degree.
Meanwhile the Scots were not at all in love with their under-
taking.   Lord Leven writes from Alcester, on July 8th,
to the Scotch Commissioners :

" We wrote to you from Birmingham the daily increasing hard condition of
" our army. We think ourselves ill-used. We are called to march, march,
" that a plentiful country is still before us, where nothing will be wanting to
" us, but we find nothing by the way but solitude. Pleasant places, indeed,
" for grass and trees, but for no other refreshment, the country people looking
" upon us as enemies to take from them without paying for it, as others do,
" and so eschewing to bring us any provisions, all which hath been endured
" hitherto with admirable patience by the poor soldiers. . . . We are
" now in this shire. We are desired to march to within a little distance of
" Worcester. . . . We shall be ashamed to be so nigh the enemy and to
" do nothing worthy of the army."

The Scots remained some days at Alcester, and the idea
certainly was that they would march on Worcester.   On 20th
July, H. Verney wrote to Sir R. Verney :

" The Scots are at present with 9 or 10,000 horse and foot before Worcester,
" but I cannot learn what their design may be, to besiege it or not, or to follow
" the King, who is at Raglan Castle a-recruiting."

This, however, is a mistake, the Scots never got to Worcester. After some deliberation they changed their plans and
determined to march on Hereford. To carry this out they
marched from Alcester to Pershore, intending to pass over the
Severn at Upton, but the frequent demolitions of Upton bridge
were said to have rendered it unsafe for the passage of troops.
A reconnaissance from Alcester on Worcester had been met and
routed by Prince Maurice with the Royalist cavalry. The result was that the Scots determined to find some other place to
pass over the river. They accordingly marched to Droitwich,
and after a halt there to Bewdley, where they crossed the
Severn. From Bewdley they marched to Tenbury, through
the Forest of Wyre, and then on to Hereford, deviating a
little from the direct route in order to attack Canon Frome.
It refused to surrender, was attacked, and carried by storm.
Seventy of the garrison were put to the sword, that is, killed
in cold blood, for presuming to attempt to hold an indefensible place.

Parliament was delighted with the Scots' victories. Speaker
Lenthall wrote on the 2nd August, to the Earl of Leven :

" In the name of the House, thanking him   . . for recommending the

" Governor of Canon Frome to the House, and stating that they were sending
" him (Lord Leven) a small remembrance in token of their love."*

The small remembrance was a jewel worth £500, which was
ordered from a goldsmith named Allen, who was a member of
the House.   The governor who Lord Leven recommended
was Colonel Edward Harley, son of Sir Robert Harley.

The Scotch found themselves very short of supplies. Leven,
writing to the Scotch Commission, on the 7th August, 1645,†
says :

" The army is reduced to that extremity for the present service whereon
" they are engaged, that without the pears, apples, and wheat that they gather
" from the ground they are not able to subsist."

Possibly it was the shortness of supplies that led them out of
the direct route, for from Canon Frome they marched to
Ledbury, from Ledbury to Mitcheldean, from there to
Newent, and then to Hereford.   A letter from Sir John
Corbett to Speaker Lenthall describes this‡

" On Wednesday last was sevennight the army marched towards Hereford,
" and on the next morning the foot were drawn up before the town.   The
" general forthwith summoned it, and we, by his advice, sent a letter to the
" Mayor and Corporation.   The trumpeter which was sent could not be
" admitted into the town, but threw his message over the works, and we have
" just cause to believe that our letter came not to the Mayor's hands, because
" we have received no answer thereunto.   Since we came hither we have found
" the country very backward in assisting us. . . .   His Excellency receiv-
" ing certain intelligence of the King being marched to Wolverhampton last
" night with about 6000 horse and dragoons, sent a party consisting of eight
" regiments of horse, one of dragoons, and 500 commandeered musketeers on
" horseback, under the command of Lieut.-General Leslie and General Major
" Middleton, to secure his motion."

The Scots complained to Parliament as to the shortness of
provisions and to the wretched state of the army.   On the 5th
August, 1645, Parliament answered:§

" Orders were given to the High Constables of all the Hundreds in the
" County of Hereford, and also to the Committees of the adjoining counties,
" to bring in £200 per diem in money and provisions, much fruit whereof
" could not be expected in 4 days' time, consideration being had of the
" malignancy of the County. . . .   The horse taking free quarters in those
" parts out of which the daily provision was to be brought for the foot, not
" only before the army sat down before Hereford, but since, plundering of
" houses, taking away goods and cattle of all kinds, and some officers taking
" upon them to send forth warrants for money and provisions of all sorts, hath
" disabled many from providing and bringing in perpetual supplies."

This gives some idea as to the conduct of the Scots.   Can it
be wondered at if living in this way, at free quarters, they
made themselves thoroughly hated in the County?

On the 13th August, 1646,‖ Sir John Corbett writes to
Speaker Lenthall from the Leaguer before Hereford, asking for
" A copy of the orders as have been passed as to the taking free quarters,

* Hist. MSS. Rep. XIII., App. I., p. 222. Duke of Portland, I.   † Ib., p. 238.
‡ Ib., p. 244.   § Ib. p. 248.   ‖ Ib. p. 250.

" and of the rules to be observed about the same. He encloses a copy of the
" orders under which Leslie marched after the King."

This shows how things were going, but a letter from Colonel
Morgan, Massey's successor as governor of Gloucester, written
from Gloucester on the 14th August, 1645, to Speaker
Lenthall,* throws a further light on the matter. He says:

" The burden of the Scotch army quartering for a time in the County upon
" free billet hath much impoverished a great part of it. We are sending the
" 3 of our greatest pieces of ordinance, with a proportionate quantity of ball
" and match, to the Leaguer, near Hereford, besides keeping their sick
" men near our garrison, hath not a little charged and pressed the County to
" cry out for succour and support if they knew how be remedied. As
" though these persons were not sufficient to undo and ruin a County, we are
" charged by the Commissioners residing about Hereford with £20 a day
" towards their maintenance, notwithstanding a great part of the County be
" under the power of the enemy."

If this was the version of one of the Parliamentary Colonels on
the conduct of the Scots, it is not difficult to imagine what the
Royalists would say. Every day the Scots stayed they were
more and more hated.

On the 22nd August, 1845, Sir John Corbett wrote to
Lenthall † from the camp before Hereford, acknowledging the
services of the horse for the despatching a

" party to attend on the motions of the King's forces, declaring on that and
" every other occasion they would do their best to make it evident that the
" common cause, according to the Covenant, was the chief desire of their
" hearts."

The Scots were pressing the siege of Hereford. They did
not consider there was a chance of its relief. This appears
from a letter of Leslie—who had been detached to watch the
King—to the Scotch Commissioners, from Nottingham, on the
26th August, 1645, he says:

" There be few horse left with our foot near Hereford. It were good if
" General Pointz and Colonel Rossiter with other county forces, had orders
" to attend the King's motions, and chiefly to interpose between him and our
" army. Yet I am confident the King cannot much trouble them."

Leslie was wrong. The King proved, in an unexpected way,
that he could rise to the difficulties of his position, and no part
of the Civil War reflects greater credit on him than the action
he took to relieve Hereford.

While at Cardiff, at the end of July, he was told of the
Scotch advance, and that if he could not relieve Hereford in a
month it must fall. At that time he had no regular force.
There were some 2000 men, chiefly horse, between Monmouth
and Raglan, and another 3000 scattered about towards Ludlow,
in the Shropshire garrisons, but this was his whole force. He
at once took steps to collect supplies, ordering pikeheads from
Stourbridge. The Sheriff of Worcestershire was ordered to
call out the *posse comitatus;* the Dudley garrison were to meet

---

* Hist. MSS., XIII. Report, App. I., p. 250.　　　† Ib., 258.

the horse, march to Worcester, join with the force there, and advance to meet him. The King set off collecting troops, marching to Brecon, Radnor, Ludlow, Bridgnorth, Lichfield, Tutbury, and on August 13th to Ashbourn. On his way here a skirmish took place, the King's rear-guard was attacked, but the attack was repulsed, or, as the account says, "the enemy were well received." On the 14th the King reached Chatsworth.

This activity of the King's alarmed the Scotch. On Leven hearing that Charles had reached Wolverhampton, with about 6000 horse and dragoons, he sent Leslie and Middleton to attend his movements. Marching to Bewdley they defeated Lord Molineux, who was in command there, and took most of his men prisoners. Charles, however, was able to get from Chatsworth to Oxford without being attacked. With such forces as he could collect he set off at once to relieve Hereford. Starting on the 28th August, on that night he reached Shipston-on-Stour, on Sunday, August 31st, he arrived at Worcester. His guards were quartered at Claynes, and preparations were made for improving the defences of the city. Maurice had done what he could. He had made outside the walls, on the side that is dry, the north side, or, as is said, the side which goes to Droitwich, the Foregate Street side,

" a low breastwork and a stockade without. The top of the breastwork is not " a foot above the ground on the outside, very necessary to safeguard a dry " ditch and wall."*

The Scots heard of the King's advance and wrote urging Parliament to order Pointz, who was in command of the only Parliament Field Army in those parts, to interpose between the King and Hereford. Pointz was at Nottingham and in no position to move. Writing from there, on the 27th August, 1645, to the committee of both kingdoms, he says : †

" I have been hindered in my intended pursuit of the King by the mutiny " of my whole army, who would not stir without pay."

This saved Charles. He was able, from Pointz's inability to move, to remain two days at Worcester. Leaving on the 3rd September he marched to Bromyard, and on the 4th to Hereford. On arriving before the city he found no enemy. The news of his advance had greatly disconcerted the Scots. On the 2nd September, finding Pointz would not help, and that the King was really marching against them, they resolved to raise the siege and marched off to Fownhope and Highnam, on the way to Gloucester. Writing from Maisemore, near Gloucester, on the 3rd September, 1645, Colonel Purefoy says to Speaker Lenthall:

" In our last, of the 31st August, we again gave an account of our doubtful con-" dition concerning Hereford. Yesterday morning the army rose from before

---

* Symonds' Diary, p. 231.   † Hist. MSS., XIII. Report, p. 263.

" Hereford and were upon their march to Fownhope, 4 miles thence in the road
" towards Gloucester. On Monday last His Excellency informed us of the
" King's coming to Worcester with 4000 horse and dragoons. They said they
" should have been ready to storm the next day if this had not happened. We
" urged them to storm before the King could arrive there, being then 20 long
" miles off. The general said it was too dangerous to be attempted. We
" proposed to continue the siege, and draw off such party of horse and foot as
" might encounter the King, our information being that their horse were weary,
" and not of the number reputed. The general replied it could not possibly
" be done ; they had so few horse, Middleton and Leslie being gone to
" Scotland with all the horse that followed the King. We cannot but inform
" you of the sad and most miserable condition of these parts; it much grieves
" us to see our friends ruined and all left to the fury of a merciless enemy."

On the same day Balmerino wrote to Lenthall : *

" Having certain information that the King's forces are marched towards
" Hereford, that Prince Maurice from Worcester, and Sir Jacob Astley from
" Wales, are making all the preparations they can for their assistance, whereby
" the Scotch army, in the absence of their horse, and those under the command
" of Colonel General Pointz being few and at a great distance, may be brought
" into great distress, we do earnestly desire that you would be pleased to move
" the House to give orders to Sir Thomas Fairfax for sending some force for
" their relief and assistance."

Charles had reason for triumph. With a much inferior
force he had struck terror into the great Scotch army that was
to have done such wonders. He could say with truth, as the
governor of Hereford said for him, at his
" coming the Scottish mist began to disperse, and the next morning vanished
" out of sight."

On the 5th September Colonel Purefoy wrote to Lenthall :†

" In our last of the 3rd we acquainted you with the rising of the Scots army
" before Hereford upon information of the King's approach to Worcester.
" The general and whole army quartered last night at Highnam, and are now
" marching through Gloucester to Cheltenham, 6 miles hence, on the way to
" Warwick."

Scudamore had done more than he had promised. He had
held Hereford for six weeks, having refused to listen to all pro-
posals of surrender. He had scorned alike the menaces of his
foes and the importunities of his friends urging him to give up
the place. He had been hard pressed. Symonds ‡ says:
" The Parliamentarians had got near the town, and had made two breaches,
" but were repulsed. Two mines and drained the ditch."

Charles was naturally as jubilant as the Scots were furious.
They complained, and not without reason, that the Parliament
had not given them the support they had a right to expect.
Possibly this is true. Parliament had ordered Pointz to
follow up the King, but he refused to do so, declaring that he
was both outnumbered and outmatched. In addition, the successes of Montrose in Scotland had alarmed the Scots army.
They alleged that they had no horse, and so could not fight,
Leven having sent all the horse away with Leslie and Middleton.

---

* Hist. MSS. Com., XIII. Report, p. 264.   † Ib., p. 265.   ‡ Diary, p. 232.

Parliament, they alleged, had promised to keep them supplied
with provisions, but had failed to carry out their promise.
They had been obliged to live as best they could, and this was
by plunder. Even to our own day stories have survived of
what the Scots did during their occupation of Herefordshire.
No story of their acts was too absurd to be believed. A
letter from Tewkesbury, gives some account of their retreat.

"On Wednesday, the 3rd September, they marched to Newent, where they
"quartered that night. On Thursday, the 4th, to Isingham [Highnam], 2
"miles short of Gloucester. On Friday they marched all through Gloucester-
"shire, and quartered at Oxendon, 4 miles on this side Gloucester; on
"Saturday to Cleave. On the Lord's Day they all rested, and this night they
"entered their quarters at Wickhamford, 3 miles from Evesham, and so
"onward to the north."

"At this very instant Major-General Pointz is here with the Commissioners,
"and his horse are now passing over Severn in boats on the Worcestershire side,
"and so onwards, intending to be observant of the King's motions, especially
"if he look towards Bristol." *

Another account says:

"From Gloucester it was this day certified that the Scottish army had
"raised the siege of Hereford and were marched this way. That on Thursday
"last the whole army passed their quarters at Highnam, 2 miles of Gloucester.
"That on Friday they marched through Gloucester, intending to quarter that
"night at Cheltenham, and so towards Warwick, and thence homewards.
"Major-General Pointz, with between 3 and 4000 horse, was then within 6
"miles of Gloucester, and was making a bridge near Tewkesbury, over
"Severn, to attend the King's motions, who is now about Monmouth and
"Hereford." †

So ended the siege of Hereford. Great was the gratitude of
the citizens. At St. Peter's Church it is recorded:

"Here is also intended an anniversary sermon for the deliverance this city
"had from your Scots, August 6th (sic), 1645. Mr. Rowland Andrews gives
"£10 per annum therefor."

Clarendon‡ blames the King for not following up the Scots
on his arrival before Hereford. He says:

"If the Scots had only been pursued, there is little doubt very many, if not
"the greater part of that army, had been destroyed."

Charles was, however, in no state to pursue. It was mar-
vellous, little short of miraculous, that he had done what he
had. Even if the Scots had been a beaten, instead of an un-
beaten, force, it was best for Charles to let them pass away
without a fight. Pointz was on the line of march covering
their retreat, and Pointz would have been more than a match
for Charles without paying any heed to the Scots. But Charles
could not afford a battle, still less could he afford a defeat. He
very wisely allowed the Scots to pass away. That this was so
is shown by what followed. From Hereford Charles went to
Raglan, there he heard of the surrender of Bristol. He
returned to Hereford, thence to Worcester, from whence he

---

* *Perfect Occurences*, September 5—12, 1645.   † *Perfect Diurnal*, September 8—15, 1645.
‡ II., 535.

proposed to retire to Oxford. But he could not do so as.
Pointz was on his line of march to Oxford, Evesham being in
his hands. So Charles gave up the idea of Oxford. Charles
therefore undertook to raise another siege, that of Chester.
He marched from Worcester to Ludlow. Here he heard that
a body of Royalist Horse had been defeated between Leominster and Bromyard, so he returned to Ludlow and passed on
from there to Newtown in Montgomeryshire. Pointz now began to follow the King up closely. At last Charles reached
Chester. On the next day his hopes and his army were alike
crushed, hopelessly crushed, at Rowton Heath.* Charles' wan-
derings are now very difficult to follow. On October 1st he
was at Bridgnorth. He ordered a quantity of brimstone and
saltpetre to be sent to him at Oxford through Worcester.
Maurice, who had been with the King, was sent back to
Worcester.

There had been some fighting before Dudley, and in this
the Parliament claimed to have been successful. On the 3rd
September, 1645, a letter to Lenthall from Shrewsbury says:
"Since our last success before Willenhall and Dudley." What
this fight was is not clear, possibly only a skirmish.

There had also been some fighting in or near Kidderminster.
Colonel Jones, a Parliamentary Colonel, claimed to have
attacked and dispersed a Royalist force near Kidderminster.
Shortly after another Royalist force was sent to Kidderminster
They occupied Trimpley and it seems made a fort there. Sir
Thomas Aston was the officer who was in command there. It
appears from the Kidderminster register that during the
winter of 1645 there were several soldiers buried at Kidderminster. At the beginning of November the troops who
occupied the post at Trimpley had to fight a battle. The
account is given in a letter dated Stafford, 10th November,
1645, written by Edward Leigh to Lenthall:

" Upon Thursday last we sent out Captain Stone's troop to Wrottesley
" House, a garrison which we have lately erected near Dudley Castle. That
" night they understood by the scouts where Sir Thomas Aston quartered,
" who was then upon his march towards Worcester, and upon Friday morning
" Captain Stone's and Captain Backhouse's troops from Wrottesley marched
" towards Sir Thomas Aston, whom they overtook between Bridgnorth and
" Kidderminster, and found him drawn up in a place of advantage, with about
" an equal number of horse to those ready to fight with them. Our troops
' made the first charge, and were stoutly received, but at last they routed Sir
" Thomas Aston's party and put them to flight, in which Sir Thomas Aston
" often rallied with such as he could procure to stand, and engaged for the
" safety of his men, until our troops slew about 20 of his men upon the place,
" whereof Captain Aston, son of Sir Arthur Aston, and Captain Moor were,
" and took prisoners Sir Thomas Aston himself, his lieutenant, cornet, quarter-
" master, and corporals, one Captain George of Worcester, 40 troopers, and 80
" horses, which they brought to the garrison. . . . There do remain yet

---

* Rushworth, VI., 117.

"in the County three strong garrisons of the enemy, Lichfield, Tutbury, and
"Dudley Castle, which command a large contribution weekly from a great
"part thereof. And in the absence of our greatest part of our force, now at
"Chester leaguer, where we have according to command 600 horse and
"foot, the enemy from the garrisons do much oppress the country near them."

From the Kidderminster register it appears that the
Trimpley fight took place on the 8th November, 1645. One
of the soldiers killed on that date was buried. A few days
after two soldiers under Captain Denham were killed in the
town.

It was not only the Parliament that felt the pressure of
Chester. Sir William Vaughan wrote to the Governor of
Dudley Castle :—

"Having received His Majesty's commands for to attempt the relief of
"Chester, desiring to know of you what horse and foot can be conveniently
"spared for the present expedition. I, being here, now waiting for further
"orders from His Majesty, being willing to do you any lawful favour, but for
"the present cannot spare any."*

One post which more than another harassed the Royalists
during the autumn was Canon Frome. The Parliament
garrison here was in the direct line of their communication
between Hereford and Worcester. Harley, the governor,
resigned about the end of September. Morgan wrote from
Gloucester on the 3rd October, 1645, to Lenthall,† recommending Lieut.-Colonel Kyrle to be governor of Canon Frome
in the place of Colonel Harley. The recommendation was not
carried out; a Scotch officer, Major Archbold, being appointed.
He proved so active and so daring an officer that it was
determined to try and retake the place. Maurice was now
back in Worcester. Writing from Derby, on 4th October,
1645, Sir John Gill tells Lenthall that

"there is no other commander of note with the King, Prince Maurice being
"gone to Worcester, but hath left his regiment with His Majesty."

This must have crippled Maurice to some extent, but
Archbold had become so very objectionable that Maurice
determined to spare such men as he could to join with
Scudamore in an attempt to retake the place. Parties both
from Hereford and Worcester summoned the place but without
effect, so the Hereford men resolved it should be taken. For
this purpose they prepared a "sow," a wooden tower on
wheels, drawn by oxen. It had inside platforms, loopholed
for musketry, and bullet proof, one above the other, the top
platform being high enough to overlook the besieged works.
Taking the sow with him, Scudamore set off from Hereford to
take Canon Frome. A reinforcement from Worcester was to
meet his men at Malvern. Scudamore left the sow well
guarded near Canon Frome, and marched on to meet the
Worcester men.

---

* Hist. MSS. Com., XIII. Rep., p. 325.   † Hist. MSS. Com., XIII. Rep., p. 280.

Archbold sent word to Morgan at Gloucester of the state of things and begged for help. Morgan at once marched with some of his own men to relieve Canon Frome. He got some more men from Corse Lawn. Scudamore retreated to Malvern, but left a force at Ledbury. Archbold, sallying out from Canon Frome, attacked them. Taking them completely by surprise, he routed them, captured the sow, and the Canon Frome expedition thus proved a failure.

Another fight in the same district is almost too romantic to be true. On the 17th November a report was sent to the House of Commons,* that 60 of the King's troops came to Ledbury to take up their quarters there. They were met by 15 of Mr. Hopton's men, who had taken the great plunderer of those parts. The 15 charged right through the 60, killing two and taking four prisoners, and were making their way back to Gloucester when they met another party of Royalists, who were carrying off to their garrison some 200 cattle they had collected. The brave 15, notwithstanding they were encumbered with four prisoners, attacked the Royalists, rescued the cattle, and, if the account is to be believed, instead of driving them into Gloucester restored them to their owners and, it is said, went on their way rejoicing.

The Worcester garrison appears at times during the autumn to have been very hard pressed, and to have found it necessary to scour the County for supplies. Their constant demands and plundering drove even some of the Royalists over to the Parliament, and led to greater activity by the Clubmen. It was reported that, on the 25th November, 1645, Mr. Dineley and divers of Worcestershire had declared for the Parliament, complaining of the insolence and injuries of the garrison of Worcester. The effect of this process of plunder was seen on the 1st November, when a great meeting of Clubmen was held on Bredon Hill. It is said that they were 3000 strong. Whatever their number, they met there to choose officers in order to be able to take armed action to protect themselves. Sir Edward Dineley, of Charlton, near Fladbury, was selected as leader, aud other officers were chosen to serve under him. They declared for Parliament, and demanded to be supplied with arms. Dineley was desirous of shewing what the Clubmen could do. Early in December Rupert and Maurice, with a slight escort, were on their way from Worcester to Oxford. It was determined to intercept them, and had these two arch plunderers fallen into the hands of the Clubmen their fate might have been doubtful. But Dineley with his Clubmen, whatever their advantage in numbers, were no match for Rupert. Dineley placed his men in the way to obstruct the passage of the Princes, and, if possible, to take them. Rupert and his escort charged, cut their way through the mob of peasants, and went on to Oxford without further interruption.

The two places as to which most interest was felt at the end of 1645 were Chester, the key of North Wales, and Hereford. Chester, where Byron commanded, was holding out gallantly, and the Royalists were doing all they could for its relief. The Parliament were trying to cut off all attempts to collect the scattered forces for the purpose. 2000 men were advancing from Oxford, they were met on Broadway Hill and driven back to Oxford. The Parliament held the bridges and fords of the Avon with so tight a grip that no one could pass that way. All the Parliament efforts were directed to prevent the small parties of Royalists uniting. Vaughan collected a party from the different garrisons and marched to Ludlow. Their route, it is stated, was marked by their plundering, for it was only by plunder they could exist. They were said to be so ragged and ravenous that the Governor of Ludlow refused to admit them into the place. Sir Gilbert Gerrard led another party to Stourbridge and Kidderminster, who are described by a Parliamentary writer as being "the most rude, ravenous, and ill-governed horse that I believe ever trod upon the earth." They hoped to be reinforced, but some men under Morgan from Gloucester defeated Washington, who was coming to their help, near Abberley, and when they proposed to march on Worcester, Parliament troops occupied Ombersley in force and prevented them. On the 17th December Captain Pickering left Worcester for Kidderminster. On the 12th December, 1645,[*] Christopher Hales wrote from Coventry to Sir William Brereton :—

"We have even now received intelligence that the King's forces are upon "their march towards Evesham, and then, as we are informed, towards "Chester. They are about 1500, rather more. We have given notice hereof "to Colonel General Pointz to the end that he may do what he can to inter- "cept their passage."

Sir Thomas Rous wrote from Evesham the same day to Sir William Brereton :—

"A body of horse and foot, they say themselves 2000, but others which "viewed them 1000 or 1500, came in yesterday at 11 to Stow-on-the-Wold, "some 10 miles from this garrison. There and thereabouts they quartered "last night. They talk of making for Worcester, which is not improbable, "and the rather because Sir William Vaughan and those horse which stay "formerly about Worcester are not yet advanced. It may be they intend to "join and so pass on towards the relief of Chester. We have sent to Colonel "Morgan, with whom most of our horse are at present, to advertise him of "this body. The Lord Northampton commands the party from Oxford."

Another skirmish took place at Malvern. A party of

---

[*] Hist. MSS. Com., XIII. Rep., p. 320.

Parliamentarians from Herefordshire crossed the hill and came upon a body of some 50 troopers. Completely surprised, they were not able to offer any great resistance, and 50 horses and 28 prisoners were taken.

Various of the Royalist garrisons were also captured and "slighted," one near Tenbury, but in Shopshire, Burford (Sir George Cornwall's) being thus treated.

In the middle of December the Parliament had a great success by the capture of Hereford. Morgan very cleverly surprised it and took it almost without resistance, thus doing with a handful of troops what the great Scotch army had failed to do. It was a crushing blow, and, what was worse, so utterly unexpected. Scudamore, the Governor, who desired to make his way to Oxford and explain matters at head-quarters, was arrested at Worcester on his way there and put in prison, and there remained until the city surrendered in the following summer.

On all sides things were going against the King. He had no longer an army, and very little chance of being able to raise sufficient men to be able to meet the Parliament forces in the field. Naseby and Rowton Heath had made the King's defeat certain. The only question that remained was how long could his garrisons hold out, and the most important of these (Chester) was now in dire distress.

CHAPTER V.

1646.

The year 1646 began badly for the King. On no side was there the smallest break in the gloom that surrounded him. He had no army, and there was but small chance of his being able to raise one. All his resources were exhausted. Without money, without arms, without supplies, his fate was clear. But what was still worse, if possible, was the disunion among the Royalists. Charles' quarrel with his nephews, although patched up, might break out again at any minute. It was obvious to all, Royalists or Parliamentarians, that whatever the rights or wrongs of the struggle might originally have been its continuance could do no good to either party, and only aggravated the prevailing discontent.

Lord Astley, in the early part of 1646, was the most prominent Royalist leader in Worcestershire. He left Oxford on December 22nd, 1645, to go round the different garrisons in the Midlands, trying to raise an army. His task was a difficult one, and not the less so by his extreme want of money. Had Astley had a good supply of this he might have raised a fairly formidable force, without it he could do nothing with the drunken dissolute bands of robbers who formed the bulk of the soldiers in the Royalist garrisons. Astley arrived at Worcester early in 1646. One of his first acts was to march out to Madresfield. The Royalist garrison here had been besieged since October, by men from the Gloucester and Evesham garrisons, but it had held out bravely, and Astley was now able, with a party from the Worcester garrison, to drive off the besiegers and raise the siege.

Astley went from Worcester to Ludlow, intending to unite with Vaughan, but not only the Parliament troops but the floods, in consequence of the breaking up of the great frost and the thaw made movements impossible, and prevented Astley attempting anything. He fell back towards Bewdley. On the 5th February Chester surrendered. Byron had held out to the last and had to yield to want of fuel and want of food. Horses, dogs, and cats had been eaten, and Byron was unable to do more. He had held the place for 16 weeks, and there was no hope of relief.

The fall of Chester was a serious blow to the King, in that it set free a large force who would now operate upon the other Royalist garrisons. Astley, finding that it was useless to look towards Chester, set to work to collect men to go to the relief of the King at Oxford. But he was too late. In the Cotswolds, barring his way, was Morgan, the governor of the Gloucester garrison, with a formidable force. On his right flank was Birch, the governor of Hereford, with a force more than equal to any that Astley could bring into the field, while in his rear, pushing him onwards towards Morgan and Birch, was Brereton, his army now able to act as Chester had fallen. The wonder is, that with all these forces arrayed against him, Astley was able to make so good a fight as he did.

Astley had visited Stafford and other garrisons to collect his force. He had tried to relieve High Ercall, which was being besieged, but had failed. At last he perceived that if he was to join the King the time had come to do so, therefore, in the beginning of March, he gave orders for all the men from the different garrisons who would join him, to rendezvous at Bridgnorth; here he collected some 3000 men. It may be imagined to what straits the Royalists were reduced when it is said that out of these more than half were "reformado" officers, that is, officers of regiments that had either ceased to exist, from being destroyed or disbanded, or become so reduced in numbers there was no need for such officers. They formed a desperate band of broken men, who had all to gain by plunder and everything to lose by peace. Astley was in dire need of money, so much so that he had to borrow from the corporation of Bridgnorth to pay his personal expenses there. Having collected his men Astley advanced from Bridgnorth to Kidderminster. Some sort of a post, probably a look-out post, to watch any movement of men, was kept at Trimpley. Some sort of skirmish took place near Kidderminster, as the registers show that Captain Charles Dungham and one of his soldiers were killed and buried. From Kidderminster Astley marched to Worcester, here he halted for a few days, and here his troubles began. He was aware that Morgan and Birch were waiting for him at Broadway, and Brereton was moving up in his rear and pressing him forward. Astley's task was a difficult one. Evesham had a Parliamentary garrison and the Avon could not be crossed there. In the hills, on his road to Oxford, were Morgan and Birch, waiting for the first sight of his men to unite and fall on him; while still nearer Oxford, if he got past these forces, Fleetwood was waiting between Stow and Oxford to intercept any Royalist attempt to relieve Astley, or to cut off any of Astley's men who got past Morgan.

Astley's first move quite deceived his opponents. He sent some of his men forward towards Evesham, but with the main body he marched back to Droitwich, thus leading Brereton to think he was about to attack him. Then making across country by Feckenham and Inkberrow to Bidford and Cleve

Prior, he crossed the Avon, and pushed down the Buckle Street road to Honeybourne, leaving Morgan at Broadway on his right, he marched past his flank to Campden, Blockley, Bourton-on-the-Hill, for Stow.   Morgan, finding that Astley had out-manœuvred him, made a series of attacks on his rear-guard, harassing and delaying their march, so as to give time for Birch to come up in front and Brereton to advance in the rear.   Astley, by pushing on, had reached Donnington, a village seven miles from Stow-on-the-Wold, just outside the Worcestershire boundary.   Brereton having now come up, Morgan attacked the wearied Royalists in the dark, two hours before dawn, on the 21st March.   Birch in front, and Morgan in the rear tried to surround the Royalists.   Morgan charged Astley's rear with 200 firelocks and 400 horse.   He was repulsed twice, and Astley nearly succeeded in breaking through the ring that was surrounding him.   But as Astley pressed through Morgan's men in the rear, Birch pressed his charges home in the front.   Still Astley shewed a stubborn resistance, Birch's horse was shot under him, his regiment had 32 men killed.   In spite of all the Royalist efforts the ring gradually tightened round Astley.   At last, seeing a possible way of escape, some of the Royalists broke and fled; through their broken ranks Birch's horse rode in; there was nothing then left but to surrender.   This was done, and the last Royalist field army ceased to exist.   Lord Astley, Sir Charles Lucas, Colonel Corbet, Colonel Gerrard, Colonel Molesworth, Lieut.-Colonel Broughton, and Major Billingsley were among the prisoners.   Out of the 3000 men Astley had with him Morgan returned 1600 prisoners.   Many were killed, more were wounded, the rest dispersed.   Those who had broken through were possibly the worst off; they were overtaken, cut down and killed by Fleetwood's dragoons.   All the Royalist arms and ammunition were taken.   The rout was complete; Astley's force, which he had collected with so much care, and manœuvred with so much skill was destroyed.   Astley fully recognised this.   Worn out with his marches, his manœuvres, his fight, he sat down on a drum and, addressing Morgan's men, said:—

" You have now done your work and may go to play, unless you will fall out
" among yourselves."

So ended the last Royalist field army   The King could not hope to bring any further force into the field, as Clarendon says:—*

" There remained from that time no possibility for the King to draw any
" other troops into the field."

All was over.   Charles had fought from August, 1642, to March, 1646, with the result that the Parliament only had to

---

reduce the few strongholds as still held out for him.   When
this was done their victory would be completed.

Morgan, as soon as possible after the Royalist defeat, sent
his prisoners to Gloucester, and marched his force towards
Worcester, accompanied by Birch and Brereton.   They arrived
in front of the city on 26th March and summoned it to surrender.   Washington, the Governor, refused.   The generals,
stating they had not a force sufficient to undertake the siege,
drew off to Droitwich, but gave Washington notice that they
only did this to give him full opportunity to learn his hopeless
condition.   Some sort of skirmish ensued, and Birch had a horse
shot under him.   For a time Worcester was not attacked, and
that time was employed by Washington in making plundering
expeditions in order to get in supplies.   One of the forays
went as far as Evesham; this probably led Morgan to appoint
Major William Dingley Governor of that place.   Washington
knew that a siege was certain; the date when it would begin
was the only uncertainty.   Accordingly, on the 30th March,
he began clearing the ground outside the walls to prevent any
buildings giving shelter to a hostile attack.   St. Oswald's
Hospital was pulled down, but Mr. Somers' house at the White
Ladies, a large stone house, capable of accommodating 500
men, was for some reason spared.   With the timber from the
houses a store of fuel was laid up, and 1000 loads of firewood
were obtained from Shrawley Wood.

The three Parliament generals after summoning Worcester
broke up their joint forces.   Morgan went to Raglan, Birch
to Ludlow, and Brereton to Lichfield.

The Royalist garrisons in the County that were still holding
out were Dudley, Hartlebury, Madresfield, Strensham, and
Worcester.   No regular operations against any of them were
begun for some little time, but there were continual skirmishes
in the County; parties of Parliament men moving about,
parties of Royalists collecting supplies.   On the 19th April,
1646, there was a skirmish in front of Worcester, the record of
which appears in the Kidderminster register, where the burial
of a soldier is mentioned, under that date:

" John Jones, a Parliament soldier, slain at the skirmish at Worcester." *

On the 27th April, about mid-night, Charles left Oxford for
the last time, in company of Dr. Hudson and Mr. John
Ashburnham.†   Charles was disguised as Ashburnham's servant
in a cloak with a bag behind him.   They went to Henley,
Brentford, Harrow, St. Albans, Market Harborough, where
they expected to meet a French agent, who did not appear;
then to Stamford, Downham (in Norfolk), and Southam.
From here, on the 5th May, Charles went to Leslie's quarters

---

* Burton's Kidderminster, p. 217.   † Rushworth, VI., p. 267.

at Kellam and surrendered himself to the Scots, thus parting with his liberty, which he never regained.

Parliament were completely deceived. They imagined Charles had gone to London, and issued orders that he was at once to be given up, upon pain of anyone concealing him forfeiting his estate and dying without mercy as a traitor to the Commonwealth. On the 6th May the Scots wrote to the Parliament* from Southwell :—

" That the King had come to them yesterday in so private a way that after
" they had made search for him, upon summons of some persons who pretended
" to know his face, yet they could not find him out in sundry houses."

On the King's arrival, Leven insisted that he should at once order Newark to be surrendered to the Parliament. Charles did so, sending an order to the governor, Lord Bellasis, to that effect. On 8th May it was given up, the officers and soldiers marched home,

" and the place,† with the guns, including a very great piece of ordnance,
" called ' Sweetlips,' 2 mortars, divers drakes and small pieces, 4000 arms, 40
" barrels of powder, great store of bullets, matches, and ammunition "

handed over to Parliament.

On the next day, the 9th May, the Scots marched northward, taking the King with them. In four days (on the 13th) they reached Newcastle-on-Tyne, where they halted and remained. On the 10th June, 1646, Charles issued the following warrant :—‡

" To our trusty and well-beloved Sir Thomas Glenham, Sir Thomas
" Tildesley, Colonel H. Washington, Colonel Thomas Blagge, Governors of our
" cities and towns of Oxford, Litchfield, Worcester, and Wallingford, and all
" other commanders of any town, castle, and fort in our Kingdom of England.
" Charles R.
" Having resolved to comply with the desires of our Parliament in everything
" which may be for the good of our subjects, and leave no means unessayed for
" the removing of all differences amongst us, therefore we have thought fit, the
" more to evidence the reality of our intentions of settling a happy and firm
" peace, to require you upon honourable terms to quit those towns, castles, and
" forts entrusted to you by us, and to disband all the forces under your several
" commands.
" Newcastle, 10th June, 1646."

The Parliamentary commanders had not waited for this order. On the 1st May, 1646, Fairfax, with the aid of Skippon, who had recovered from his wounds at Naseby, began his operations against Oxford. It may have been designed for effect that Skippon returned to his command on the 1st May, the anniversary of the new-modelled army taking the field. Before doing more at Oxford than driving in the outposts, Banbury was attacked, and surrendered on 6th May. Fairfax now sent off as many horse as he could spare to Worcester, under the command of Colonel Whalley, to straiten the

---

* Rushworth, VI., p. 268.   † Ib., 271.   ‡ Rushworth, VI., p. 276.

garrison until such time as the army were at liberty to advance against it.*

On the 13th May, 1646, the Worcester garrison wrote to the King asking for his special instructions. On the 16th May Fairfax wrote from Heddington, near Oxford, to Washington, the Governor of Worcester, requiring him to surrender the place. Washington replied :—

"It is acknowledged by your books and by report out of your own quarters,
"that the King is in some of your armies. That granted, it may be easy for
"you to procure His Majesty's commands for the disposal of this garrison, till
"then I shall make good the trust reposed in me. As for conditions, if I shall
"be necessitated I shall make the best I can. The worst I know and fear not.
"If I had, the profession of a soldier had not been begun, or so long continued,.
"by your excellencie's humble servant.

"Henry Washington."

This answer, as might have been foreseen, was at once followed by the arrival of some Parliament troops under Whalley. On the 21st May they encamped on Wheeler's Hill, near Elbury Wood, and built huts. Washington at once made a sally with a small body of horse. This was repulsed by a large force which, following up the besieged, came under the fire of the town guns and suffered some loss.

While steps were being taken as to Worcester two of the other garrisons were disposed of. The first was Dudley. At the beginning of May, Brereton moved up to attack Dudley. This place had long been an eyesore to the Parliament, Leveson having defended it successfully for the King during the whole war. Its turn was now come. Leveson, expecting an attack, had prepared for it by clearing away all the buildings round the Castle that could shelter the enemy. A note in the parish register shews this :—

"Note. The church of St. Edmund being demolished by Colonel Leveson,
"in 1646, both parishes did meet in that of St. Thomas, and became as one in
"all administrations, and so in their officers, within a few years after, so that
"the register book became one also from thenceforth."

No details of the final struggle appear, but it could not have lasted long as the castle was surrendered on the 10th May, and the terms approved by Parliament on May 13th.† The articles of surrender are given in a tract, printed in London, 14th May, 1646.

"Sir Thomas Fairfax his summons sent into Oxford, &c., and the copy of the
"articles for the surrender of Dudley Castle to Sir William Brereton, with all
"ordinance, armies, and ammunition, bag and baggage."

"Articles agreed upon the 10th day of May, 1646, between Lieut.-Colonel
"Beaumont, Major Christopher Henningham, and Major John Gifford, de-
"puted on the behalf of Colonel Leveson, governor of the Castle of Dudley,
"and Colonel Skipkins, Lieut.-Colonel Hunt and Captain Stone, commis-
"sioners appointed by Sir William Brereton, commander-in-chief of the forces,
"employed for reducing of the said castle, touching the surrender thereof.

---

* Rushworth, VI., p. 285.   † Whitelock, p. 210.

" 1. That all gentlemen, with their servants, and all officers in commission,
" shall march away with their horses and arms so that they exceed not the
" number of 30, and all common soldiers that will march to any of the King's
" garrisons unbesieged, without their arms, and all such as will live at their
" own houses, to have protections, submitting themselves to all ordinances of
" Parliament, and all gentlemen soldiers and others to carry with them their
" own proper goods and no more.

" 2. That they shall have two months' time to consider whether they will
" live at home or depart the kingdom, without molestation or arrest for any
" hostile act or debt, so far as in our power, and to have passes for that pur-
" pose, provided in the meantime they do nothing prejudicial to the Parliament.

" 3. That at the end of two months all that will live at their houses shall
" enjoy their goods and estates without plunder or molestation, submitting to
" all ordinances of Parliament ; and such as will go beyond seas to have passes
" accordingly, and convenient time allowed them to travel to any port towne to
" take shipping, with passes accordingly.

" 4. That no oath shall be imposed on any officers or soldiers that shall
" choose to go to the said garrisons during the time of their march.

" 5. That a sufficient convoy be appointed for such as will march away, and
" carriages provided for their goods, and not to be forced to march above 10
" miles a day, and to have free quarters in their march and care taken that no
" abuse be offered to their persons, or any of their proper goods diminished.

" 6. That all prisoners in this County belonging to this garrison shall be
" released, and likewise all countrymen and soldiers in the castle set at
" liberty.

" 7. That the governor shall on Wednesday next, by 12 of the clock,
" deliver up the said castle, with all ordnance, arms, and ammunition, victuals,
" provisions, goods, bedding, and all other accommodation necessary and
" belonging to the said castle, except what is allowed by the aforesaid articles,
" and all those safe and unspoiled unto the said Sir William Brereton, or whom
" he shall appoint for service of the Parliament.

" 8. That (the Parliament giving order) the works, walls, and tower of
" the said castle shall be sleighted, and made incapable of a garrison.

" 9. That all goods in the castle that can lawfully be claimed and owned by
" any of the County shall be restored.

" 10. That all wounded soldiers shall have liberty to remain in the town
" until they are cured, and then have passes according to the articles.

" Commissioners for the King.   Commissioners for the Parliament.
    " John Beaumont,   ⎫   ⎧ " Robert Skipkins,
    " Christopher Henningham,   ⎬   ⎨ " Robert Hunt,
    " John Gifford.   ⎭   ⎩ " Henry Stone."

These terms were as good as could be expected, so good that
the Royalists said that the governor had been guilty of
treachery. Insinuations were made that he was bribed. But
no evidence is forthcoming to support either charge. The
Royalist cause was hopeless ; there was no prospect whatever
of relief, and those who surrendered first got the best terms.
In this Leveson shewed his wisdom.

In August the Staffordshire Committee proposed that under
the 8th article of the surrender, Dudley Castle should be
dismantled. The proposal was not adopted, but on the 2nd
March, 1647, the House of Commons resolved it should forthwith be made untenable, and it was referred to the Staffordshire
Committee to carry this out. Still nothing was done. On the
19th July, 1647, the question was again before Parliament, and
they resolved to adhere to their former vote that the castle be

made untenable. Whether this is the same as "slighted" is not easy to say.

Hartlebury was the next Worcestershire garrison to be dealt with. Morgan advanced with a strong force against it, arriving before it on the 9th May, he summoned it to surrender, stating in his summons that it might well do so as far stronger castles, such as Newark and Banbury, had already capitulated. The governor, Colonel William Sandys, replied,* admitting that

"if Newark was really taken he could not possibly expect relief, and desiring "that he might have so much time as might be' sufficient to inform himself of "the certainty thereof, and if he should find it accordingly he would forthwith "treat."

Sandys' request appears to have been granted, at all events to some extent, for it was not until nearly a week later, on May 14th, that the place surrendered. The surrender was made on terms, but there were secret articles, one of which was that Morgan pledged himself to Sandys to use his best endeavours to secure that the sequestration

"of the Sandys' estate at Ombersley might be taken off without any fine or "composition."

On January 7th, 1648, Morgan petitioned the House of Lords

"that this might be done, so as to be tender of his honour and grant a per- "formance of his promise."

Here again the allegations of treachery and bribery were made on account of the surrender, but it is difficult to see what else could have been done. It must be admitted that in this case Sandys' bargain with Morgan has a very nasty look and makes a doubt arise if the best possible terms were obtained.

When Hartlebury surrendered Morgan got a number of prisoners, nearly all the Sandys' family. Nash gives a paper from the Townshend MSS: †

"Names of those gentlemen who were in Hartlebury Castle at the surrender "thereof, 14th May, 1646:—
"Lord Windsor, Hewell Grange.
"Colonel Samuel Sandys, late Governor of Worcester.
"Mr. Anderson, his brother, Lady Sandys, 120 foot, and 40 horse.
"Captain William Sandys, Governor of Hartlebury Castle.
"Captain Martin Sandys."

The surrender of Hartlebury left only three Royalist garrisons in the County, Worcester, Madresfield, and Strensham. As to the last it is not clear when the Parliament took it. In the articles of the surrender of Worcester it is provided that it be disgarrisoned, but it does not state it was then in Royalists' hands, if it had been probably more would have been said about it.

---

* Hist. MSS. Com. Duke of Portland, I., 359. † Nash, II., cv.

The siege of Worcester had been carried on for some time before anything was done about Madresfield.   The Governor (Captain Aston) had been present at a council of war, at which he had stated that he could hold the place against all force for three months at least if mortar pieces were not brought against him.   On the 17th June Captain Aston sent a messenger (Captain Blinkow) to Colonel Washington, telling him he had been summoned that morning to deliver up the house, and asking his pleasure.   Washington sent word back recalling Aston's promises, and told him that without any treaty he expected him to hold out for a month, promising that if in the meantime Worcester should be treated for Madresfield should be included in the treaty.   On the 19th June horse and foot were sent from St. John's to besiege Madresfield.   On the 20th news came from Madresfield

"that Captain Aston, notwithstanding his charge to the contrary, had "treated and delivered up the house to Colonel Whalley, most basely, and "contrary to his faith, the enemy only coming before it, having no cannon "with them, and, as it is said, sold the same to Colonel Lygon, who was the "owner of the house and one of the enemy's colonels.   His condition was to "march outway with his arms, and to be paid £200 in money; his troops were "to have 30s. in hand per man, and foot soldiers 10s., and to leave all his "ammunition and provisions behind him."*

If the terms are correctly stated, Madresfield has even a more uncomfortable look than Hartlebury.   It does seem as if, in these two garrisons, some private reasons had weighed in settling the surrender.   Such was the opinion of that day, for the writer of the Townshend MS. goes on :—*

" There were never four such governors as Sir Michael Woodhouse, of Ludlow; "Colonel Lucen [Leveson], of Dudley ; Captain William Sandys, of Hartle-"bury ;   and Captain Edward Aston, of Madresfield ; which delivered up "traitorously, cowardly, and basely four such strongholds, the weakest whereof "could withstand an army, as themselves asserted, for a quarter of a year, and "three of them for an age, if victuals and ammunition could have lasted.   But 'the golden hook was supposed to have been swallowed, and so the loyal city "of Worcester was surrounded by the united forces of Shropshire, Hereford-"shire, and Gloucestershire, and Colonel Whalley, from Banbury, notwith-"standing, it held out longer than Oxford and the Close, at Litchfield, and "was the last that surrendered."

It remains to give an account of the siege of Worcester, the last of the Royal garrisons in the County.

As has already been stated, while Fairfax was besieging Oxford he sent Whalley to reduce Worcester.   Whalley arrived on the 21st May, encamped on Wheeler's Hill, near Elbury Wood, and made huts for his men.   Nothing was done on the 22nd and 23rd May.   On the 24th the besieged made a sally, fell on the Parliament foot about Roger's Hill, killing and wounding at least 40.

On 25th May a summons to surrender was sent in to the

---

* Nash, II., xcix.

Mayor, Aldermen, and Common Council of the city.   The next day an answer refusing was returned.

The besiegers, on receipt of this, began to make a line of forts between Roger's Hill and Wheeler's Hill, for security to lodge in and to enclose the city.   Soldiers and townsmen complained of want of provisions.

On the 27th May Colonel Whalley and the committee sent in a reply to the Mayor's answer.

On the 28th May an accidental fire burnt the besiegers' huts.

On the 29th May the garrison had a review.   They found that their total strength was 1507, beside gentlemen and the city bands.   They computed the besiegers to be 5000 strong.

On the same day a parley took place, but without any satisfactory result.   The governor sent out a foraging party to Astley.   They returned, having taken six horses and two men.

On 31st May Whalley crossed the river and occupied Hallow, placing there, in Mr. Fleet's house, 140 foot and two troops of horse.

On the 1st June the besiegers received further reinforcements from Ludlow.

On the 2nd June Whalley sent ten colours of foot down to Roger's Hill, to the new works there.   A great iron culverin was planted on St. Martin's Gate, to dislodge the besiegers from Roger's Hill.   It burst on discharge, wounding the chief engineer.   A sortie was made against Hallow, but nothing came of it.   It was said that a mistake was made in making an attack in front instead of sending the men round by the Broadheath to take the besiegers in the rear.

On June 3rd the besiegers extended their works from Windmill Hill to Barbourne, and thus on to the river.   Some letters passed between the governor and the besiegers.   The letter from the Parliamentarians is signed by Whalley, Thomas Rous, William Dingley, William Lygon, Edward Smith, Joseph Edgiock, and Henry Hunt; the list of signatures shewing who the County Parliamentarians then were.

On June 4th the besiegers went on with their works at Barbourne, some skirmishing took place on Pitchcroft.   This resulted in the besiegers bringing down next day 500 foot and 200 horse as a guard to protect their works.   In the city a council of war was held.   They ordered all shovels, spades, and mattocks to be seized and brought to certain named places.   All the coal, wood, and lime in St. John's was brought into the city.   All unnecessary people were sent out.   A clearance round the walls, so as to make a road for cavalry to pass all round the town, was made.   No one was allowed to enter or to leave without a pass.   The next three days were quiet.

On June 9th the besiegers pushed on into Henwick, and some as far as St. John's; one of their officers was killed. The next day a flag of truce was sent to ask for the body; it was given up, and escorted to the besiegers' lines by a number of gentlemen and a troop of horse. They were met by a number of the besiegers and drank wine together. Baxter, who was present with the besiegers, as chaplain to one of the regiments, utilised the occasion by discussing points of divinity with one of the Royalist chaplains (Dr. Warmestry). The first was "whether there is any difference between a church and any common place." After several hours' controversy the two divines are said to have parted good friends.

June 11th, the besiegers began the bombardment with their great guns, some of the shots from which weighed 17, 19, 24, and 31 lbs. One ball fell in the pantry of the Bishop's Palace. In the afternoon the guns the besiegers had placed at St. Martin's and the Blockhouse opened on the town, but did no damage. In their turn the besieged made a sortie against Henwick, but no result followed. The next day (the 12th) the besiegers occupied St. John's, lined the village with musketeers, and about 3 p.m. placed a number of foot behind the church tower, hoping by this to complete the investment of the city to the west. But, to prevent this, at 11 p.m., a sortie in force of 500 foot and 200 horse was made to dislodge the besiegers from St. John's, and to destroy Cripplegate and the houses that gave shelter up to the bridge. The entrances to all the houses and streets were barricaded, but the Royalists, some by the highways, some by the backs of the houses, some by the courts and passages, drove the Parliamentarians out. Some of them fled into St. John's church, 100 of the besiegers were killed, 10 prisoners were taken, with three colours and a drum. The colours were hung up on the bridge and on the leaden steeple of the Cathedral. The besiegers, on the 12th, opened fire on the town from St. John's and from the guns on Rainbow Hill. Some of the shots fell into the town, one on a bed in which persons were sleeping.

On the 13th all was quiet except a few shots which fell into the town, one of them killing a man and his wife as they lay in bed in a house in the Trinity. A good deal of chaff passed between the two sides. The besiegers called the garrison "Papists," "Russell's apes," and asked "Where is your tottering King?" The besieged retorted with "Traitors," "Go and preach in a crab tree," "Where are the Scots you hired to fight against the King?"

The 14th June was a quiet day except for occasional shots, one of which damaged Sir Rowland Berkeley's house in the Corn Market. The besiegers finished a bridge of boats they were making near the top corner of Pitchcroft, and threw up a breastwork on each side of the river to protect it.

Early in the morning of the 16th, Captain Hodgkins, or "Wicked Will," being very drunk, sallied out over the bridge to St. John's, attacked the guard of the besiegers, killed one, and came back in safety. He was so drunk he fell off his horse twice, and had to be taken back across the river in a boat. The guns the garrison placed on the quay kept up a fire on St John's and killed four men at the back of the Swan Inn. All the south side of the town, beyond the Sidbury Gate, was still open to the garrison. They went out beyond the walls to make hay, which they brought in by the river, and turned out their cattle to graze.

On the 16th the besiegers paraded in full force, fired three volleys, and lit a bonfire in St. John's to induce the garrison to believe Oxford had surrendered; the actual surrender did not take place until the 20th June, when the Princes Rupert and Maurice, who were in it, accepted passes to go abroad, which they did on the 5th July.

On the 17th thirteen guns were fired at St. Martin's Church and the Cross Inn. Whalley sent in a buck as a present to the governor. The citizens' wives and some of the citizen members of the Council, urged the governor to treat. This Washington refused. He caused a foray to be made by the garrison towards Kempsey and Pirton, to bring in all the cattle they could catch. As the Irish soldiers in the garrison began to give trouble the governor's task was becoming more and more difficult. To better secure the defence he had the parapets of the bridge over the river raised and loopholed for musketry.

On June 19th the governor's footman was taken prisoner. The besiegers began throwing up new works in St. John's. All useless persons were made to leave the city. These numbered some 1500, who it was said had only one meal a day. Another strong party was sent out to make a further foray, seize all the provisions they could collect, and compel persons to bring in whatever eatables they had. Report came to the place as to the hopelessness of resistance, and a female messenger was sent off to the King to learn his pleasure about the garrison resisting. Complaints were made of the scarcity of bread, a scarcity arising not merely from the lack of flour but from the refusal of the bakers to bake, no less than sixteen flatly declining to do so. A cannon ball hit the mayor's house.

On June 22nd the governor tried to strengthen the defences on the north side the city wall, near Pitchcroft. In the part next the butts, between Foregate Street and St. Clement's Church, poles, rafters, cross-pieces and hurdles were fixed and the spaces filled up with earth and horse dung. To still further carry out the investment the besiegers occupied Kempsey and Barnshall.

On the 23rd the force at Barnshall was much strengthened, the investment carried down to the river on the south side, and so completed. On that night, the city was once more summoned to surrender, and told of their hopeless condition as Oxford had fallen. This last news Washington refused to believe and asked leave to send a messenger to Oxford. On hearing of the summons the people pressed the governor to capitulate, but this he refused to do. On his refusal the besiegers began constructing new works at Battenhall, so as to make the investment quite secure. An iron saker, at the Blockhouse burst, doing much damage. A piece of it, weighing 160lbs., fell on the "Rose and Crown," near St. Helen's Church, and other pieces in Broad Street, wounding various persons. The garrison showed strong signs of insubordination, a good deal of plundering went on, much discontent prevailed, and the officers were not able, even if they were inclined, to check it. The governor had a list made of all the provisions in the town, so that some idea might be gained as to how long they could hold out. The besiegers hit upon an ingenious but cruel device to capture the city cows which were turned out to graze under the walls. They tied a cow to a stake, made a fire round it, so that the cow began to bellow. This, it was thought, would bring the other cows to see what was the matter, and that then the besiegers could get between them and the city and so cut them off. The attempt, however, failed. A further letter came in from the besiegers, and on its being read a doubt was raised if Oxford had really surrendered. But at night Prince Maurice's secretary, Anthony Kempson, who had been taken prisoner at Oxford, but had a pass given him, arrived, and told them that the fall of Oxford was true and it was utterly hopeless to look for relief.

So on the next day, the 26th June, Washington called a council of war, to meet at the Bishop's Palace, to consider their position and hear Kempson's statement. He told them they were in a hopeless state, as Fairfax, with 10,000 foot and 5000 horse was marching on Worcester, so that they had better at once accept the best terms they could get. The council, on this, sent Kempson to see Whalley. He did so, and Whalley wrote offering to treat.

On the 27th June another council was held to consider Whalley's letter, the result of their deliberations was the Governor sending the following letter:—

"Sir,

"Upon overture of a treaty from you, intelligence of the delivery of Oxford, "and the sight of His Majesty's letters there printed for the surrender of this "garrison, amongst others, upon honourable terms, I have named the gentle-"men underwritten to meet with those that are or shall be named by you for

" that purpose, and instead of hostages I am contented to take your engagement
" of honour, under your hand, for the safe conduct of those gentlemen and their
" necessary attendants. To-morrow being Sunday, unfit for business. I leave
" the time and place to your appointment.

" Your servant,

" June 27th.   Hen. Washington.

" For Major-Gen. Whalley."

Considerable discussion arose as to who should be the
" treaters." The military men named Sir Robert Leigh, Sir
Jordan Crosland, Sir William Bridges, and Major Thomas
Savage.

The gentlemen named " Lord " William Brereton, Sir Ralph
Clare, Sir Rowland Berkeley, and Mr. Ralph Goodwin.

The citizens named Sir Daniel Tyas (who, as Mayor, had
been knighted by Charles in 1644), Mr. Francis Street, the
Town Clerk, Alderman Hacket, and Alderman Heming. To
the last-named objection was taken, so Lieut.-Colonel Soley
was appointed in his place.

The clergy named Dr. Downe (Dean of Chichester), and Dr.
Warmestry (son of the registrar of the diocese), a member of
an old Worcester family, whose name survives in the street
known as " Warmestry's Slip." He was afterwards Dean of
Worcester.

Mr. Fitzwilliam Conyngsby, the head of the recusants and
reformadoes, a man of good property in Herefordshire, objected
to any idea of surrender until they heard from the King.
Conyngsby had been the Royalist Governor of Hereford, and
he now considered it to be his duty to insist on " no surrender."
Great heat ensued. The governor, who was a very passionate
man, asked

" if they would live and die with him upon the walls, and fight it out to the last
" man ? "

Conyngsby said they would, and asked that all those who were
not of the same mind should be thrown over the walls. The
governor said it should be put to the vote whether they
surrendered or not. This the bishop and the moderate men
opposed, saying that the governor should hold a council of
war and get the military reasons for what should be done. The
governor said he would do as he pleased, and proposed to
break off all negotiations, and fire a gun from the walls himself to shew that this was done. Swearing a great oath, he
went off to do it, but the bishop and some others ran
after, stopped him, and at last persuaded him to appoint six
gentlemen, six soldiers, six citizens, together with the bishop
and Dr. Warmestry, to decide if they should or should not
treat. After some debate, the committee were unanimous to
treat, and the governor's letter was sent. Whalley replied :—

" Sir,

" Since our proposed treaty is condescended to by you, and the time and

"place left to me, I desire your commissioners would give the gentlemen under-
"written a meeting at Hindlip House, belonging to Mr. Abingdon, on Monday
"morning, 10 o'clock. I do hereby engage myself for the safe coming and
"returning of them. I except against Lieut.-Colonel Soley as a citizen, being
"also a soldier.

"   "I rest, your servant,
"June 27th, 1646.   Edward Whalley."

For soldiers and citizens : Colonel Bridges, Colonel Dingley,
Colonel Starr, Colonel Lygon, Colonel Betsworth, Lieut.-
Colonel Torkington, Major Fiennes, Major Hungerford.

For the gentry: Sir Thomas Rous, Mr. Lechmere, Mr. Hunt
and Mr. Moore.

For the ministry: Mr. Moore and Mr. Baxter.

An armistice was agreed upon. The governor sent to
Colonel Dingley, with whom he had served in the Low
Countries, to meet him outside the city in the Foregate.

"They met with many other friends, and drank plentifully till 10 at
"night."

This act of the governor's was much censured, as it encouraged others to go out of the garrison and allowed the
besiegers to come within pistol shot of the works.

June 28th. The enemy on Windmill Hill, on the south of
the town, came down and examined the works, and at the
Foregate many on both sides met and conversed. In the
afternoon the articles of the treaty were sent in and read.
This caused violent scenes between the governor and the
officers.

On the 29th Whalley, who was at Hallow, sent a safe
conduct for the treaters to come then to Mrs. Fleet's house.
A dispute arose as to whether there should be a cessation
of hostilities during the negotiations for surrender. At last
Whalley wrote the governor the following letter :—

"The kingdom is at great layings out after you and the city, and much
"increased by the addition of forces. I intend to be a good husband for you,
"and not to lose time, which may be improved by the reducing Worcester,
"therefore give you notice the cessation is at an end.
"   "Your servant,
"   "Edward Whalley."

At this the governor was "nettled." He at once set a
cannon and fired it himself, and the city's guns began a
regular cannonade, which did some execution. The Foregate
guns killed some at Newchurch (?), the fire from the bridge
killed some of those on Pitchcroft, the guns from the Castle
Hill shot the steeple at St. John's. One of the culverins in
the Severn hit the great gun mounted by the hedge at Roger's
Hill.

The governor sent a trumpeter for the treaters to meet.
This was agreed, and Whalley sent attendants to meet the
treaters in St. John's. When the Parliament treaters read the

proposed terms of surrender, Colonel Bridges said they were terms for men if the King had his towns, castles, and armies, not for such as were the only city left, and were actually better terms than had been given to Oxford or any other place, and could Worcester, the last garrison, expect better terms for her obstinacy? Sir Ralph Clare said sooner than surrender on dishonourable terms they would see the city and the garrison in ashes. Colonel Betsworth said it was better in ashes than received on such terms. Colonel Bridges said the Parliament forces would lay all their bones under the walls rather than agree to such terms.

On July 2nd an attempt was made to capture Colonel Betsworth, who was quartered at Kempsey, but the party were delayed as it was a dark, wet night. Betsworth got word and escaped, and all the result of the sortie was to capture five horses and men.

Things were going badly with the city. There was great difficulty in maintaining discipline, or keeping the troops at their posts. On July 4th some four troopers came up from Mrs. Andrews, at Barnshall, under the Diglis works, drove away seven head of cattle, as no sentinel was on guard. In the afternoon 30 horse came within carbine shot of the sconce, but there was no guard. One man who was there picked up a musket and shot a gentleman of note, whose body the Parliament compounded for.

On July 5th the enemy again came up against the sconce, and a sharp skirmish took place, which ended in the besiegers drawing off.

On the 6th July Captain "Wicked Will" made a sally, behaved most gallantly, and brought in seven prisoners.

On the 8th the governor gave public notice he must open the magazine, which was done.

Whalley's connection with the siege was now ended, Colonel Rainsborough was appointed to take over the command. On the 9th July he held a general review of the besieging force on Rainbow Hill or Wheeler's Hill. Thirty-one carriages, ten of which were ordnance, were drawn up at Barbourne House.

On the 10th the besiegers joined up their works from Perry Wood to Red Hill Cross. One of the shots hit Edgar Tower, a long mile from the works. The besiegers made an effort to raise a new fort on Wall's furlong, but this was opposed, and after some fighting successfully opposed, by the besieged. Civil messages passed between Rainsborough and the governor.

On the 10th Rainsborough opened a fresh treaty. The besieged strengthened their works on the Castle Hill, placed two brass field pieces on the top of the tower commanding Windmill Hill to answer the new works there, and at the Knowle, nearer Mrs. Andrews', where the besiegers had been erecting

Day - Today

Touchpark Service Station
Castlebar, Co. Roscommon
Phone 09066366642
Till No 0390iE

	€

Diesel
24.616 ltr × €3.250/1 ltr = 80.00
80.00
80.00

1

NETT	VAT AMOUNT
65.04	14.96
65.04	14.96

January 03, 2017 12:25:52
Terminal 01

Trading As Main Street
Company Vat Number 6579991E

further batteries. Tents were set up at Barbourne House, which was Rainsborough's head-quarters.

Provisions were becoming scarce. Fresh meat—beef, mutton, and veal—sold at 8d. per lb., about 3s. 4d. at present prices. Sir John Knotsford gave 30s. (£7 10s. od.) for a piece of roasting beef. On the 11th July, the fire from Roger's Hill caused great annoyance. One ball hit the Town Hall and rolled to the Earl's post, a distance of 40 yards. Another hit Mr. Street's (the Town Clerk's) house.

On the 13th the works on Castle Hill were strengthened.

On the 15th a small brass gun was placed on the top of the Cathedral, which, it is added, "will gall the besiegers." Rainsborough sent in a letter offering to treat. The governor consented to treat on honourable terms, and a cessation of hostilities was agreed upon. On the 16th the negotiations went on. A private letter intimated they might have honourable terms, but the gentry and soldiers said they should hold out to the last, so that, as Worcester had been the first city to declare for the King, it should be the last to give up his cause. The negotiations went on, the besieged insisting that Whalley should not be appointed governor if there was a surrender.

On the 18th Rainsborough sent in his terms, saying they were final. On this it was proposed to fight it out, but the governor told them if it came to a storm he had only powder to last an hour's fight, but he was quite willing to hazard his own person.

The following letter was then agreed upon:—

" Sir,
"Your propositions are so obscure to me that I shall desire you to grant a "pass to Mr. Goodwin to receive a clear sense of them, and upon his return "you shall receive further answer from your humble servant,
" Henry Washington."

Within two hours Rainsborough sent this reply:—

" Sir,
"Although I am not sensible of the least obscurity in the articles, yet, that I "may not be wanting in anything which is civility, I have sent a pass for Mr. "Goodwin according to your desire, and remain.
" Your humble servant.
" T. Rainsborough."

The mayor called a common council of the citizens to discuss the terms, and they agreed to accept terms if they were the best to be got.

The terms were:

"Articles of agreement for the surrender of the garrison of Worcester, con-"cluded July 19th, between Colonel Thomas Rainsborough, general in that "behalf of Sir Thomas Fairfax, general of the forces raised by Parliament. "and Colonel Henry Washington, governor of Worcester.

" That the City of Worcester, with all forts, ordnance, arms, ammunition, "stores and provisions of war thereunto belonging, shall be delivered up, "without wilful spoil or embezzlement, unto His Excellency Sir Thomas Fairfax, "or whom he shall appoint to receive the same, upon the 22nd July, at 10 a.m.,

"in such manner and with such exceptions as are contained in the ensuing
"articles.

"That on the 23rd July the governor and all officers and soldiers of the
"garrison, with all other persons that will, shall march out of Worcester with
"their horses, arms, and baggage, that properly belong to them, to any place
"within one mile of Worcester, which the governor shall choose, where all their
"horses and arms, except such as are in the ensuing articles, shall be delivered
"up to such as His Excellency Sir Thomas Fairfax shall appoint. All the
"soldiers shall be disbanded, and all such, both officers and soldiers, and others
"as shall engage themselves by promise never to bear arms against the Par-
"liament of England, nor to do anything wilfully to the prejudice of their
"affairs, shall have the benefit of these ensuing articles.

"That all such as desire to go to their own houses or private friends shall
"have the general's passes and protection for their peaceable repair to and
"abode at the several places they shall so desire to go unto. The governor to
"pass with all horses, arms, and baggage properly belonging unto him. Each
"colonel to pass with three horses, each lieut.-colonel and sergeant-major with
"two horses, each captain, lieutenant, and cornet with one horse, and every
"person not under the degree of an esquire with three horses, and all of them,
"with their arms and goods properly belonging to them, to be carried upon
"their horses, and all soldiers, with their swords and such baggage as properly
"belongs to them, which they carry about them.

"That all persons who are to have the benefit of these articles shall, if they
"desire it, have passes to go beyond sea, provided they depart this kingdom
"within two months after the surrender of the town.

"That the City of Worcester and all the inhabitants thereof shall be pre-
"served from all plunder or violence of the soldiers.

"That Sir William Russell, now resident within the City of Worcester, be
"exempted from any benefit of these articles.

"That the garrisons of Worcester, Evesham, Strensham, Hartlebury and
"Madresfield be disgarrisoned, and the Bishop of Worcester, Sir William
"Russell, and Colonel Lygon be restored to their houses and estates."*

Goodwin urged that by the articles of Oxford all other
garrisons were entitled to as good terms, but these were in
some of the details worse, and expressly objected to the exception of Sir William Russell as something quite unheard of.

Rainsborough replied that Worcester had lost the benefit of
the Oxford articles by continuing to fight and not surrendering.
He refused to alter the articles, or to give more than two days
for the surrender.

On the governor finding that the citizens would not fight, he
informed the gentlemen and officers that he had only three
barrels of great powder for ordnance, five barrels of musket
powder, and one of pistol powder left, scarcely enough for one
day's hot service and storming for 3000 men; that during the
cessation of hostilities many of the men had deserted; that the
provisions would not last above a fortnight; that no help could
be looked for from the King. On this it was decided to accept
the terms. Accordingly, Washington wrote consenting to the
terms, and agreeing to surrender on the 22nd, but begging to
be allowed to send a messenger to Fairfax to try and get better
conditions.

---

* Rushworth, VI., 286.

A number of the officers and gentlemen protested against
Sir William Russell being excepted, saying it was consenting to
his murder, and it was almost unheard of to except anyone. It
had only been done in the Bridgnorth case, which differed
from this. Washington asked if the whole city and all the
people in it were to be destroyed for one man's benefit?
Russell cut the matter short, saying he should walk out and
surrender himself.

" He neither feared nor cared what the enemy could do unto him ; he had but
" a life to lose, and it could not be better spent."

The gentlemen, however, determined to send a letter to
Fairfax, asking that Russell should not be exempted from
the terms of the surrender. This the citizens opposed.
While they were disputing Rainborough wrote to the
governor :—

" Sir,
    " I shall no ways remit any civility to you, but can by no means admit the
" gentlemen to go the general with your message desired ; yet, if you please to
" send them, or any other persons, to see the general sign the articles accepted
" by you they shall receive such safe conduct. In the meantime I shall, in the
" presence of whom you shall appoint, sign the articles myself with engagement
" for the general's confirmation thereof ; and I do (together with such hostages
" as you please to send me) expect the like from you, and for that you desire a
" pass for Colonel Bridges and Colonel O'Kay.
                        " I remain, your humble servant,
                                " Thos. Rainsborough."*

On the 20th, Sir Edward Littleton and Sir William Bridges
went to Rainsborough's quarters to see him sign the agreement.

On the 22nd, the troops in St. John's burnt their huts and
marched off. The Parliamentary Committee took up their
quarters in the gentlemen's houses round who were their
friends. Heath arrived from Sir Thomas Fairfax with an
assurance they should have large passes and protection sent
them next day; that Sir William Russell should be used as a
gentleman, and should be Rainsborough's prisoner.

The 23rd was the last day of the siege. The Cathedral
organ had already been taken down, but at 6 a.m. a service was
held in the Cathedral, the last Anglican service held there
for 14 years. It was largely attended by gentlemen and
officers, and was for many of them the last time they were
ever to hear service said according to the use of the Church
of England This over, Washington, at the head of his
own regiment, Sir William Russell's regiment, and the remainder of Colonel Sandys' regiment, under Major Moore,
marched out to the Round Mount, on Rainbow Hill, the place
Rainsborough had fixed for the formal ceremony. With them
came the civilians: the Earl of Shrewsbury and his son, Lord

---

* Nash, II., civ.

Talbot, from Grafton; Sir Edward Littleton, Sir Edward Barrett, of Droitwich; Henry Townshend, of Elmley Lovett; Edward Penel, of Woodson; Anthony Langston, of Sedgeberrow; Edward Sheldon, of Beoley; Sir Martyn Sandys, of Worcester; Joseph Walsh, of Abberley; Russell, of Little Malvern; William Habingdon, of Hindlip; the Bishop (Prideaux); the Sheriff (Henry Ingram, of Earls Court); Sir William Russell, of Strensham; Sir Rowland Berkeley, of Cotheridge; Sir John Winford, of Astley; Henry Bromley, of Holt; Thomas Acton, of Burton; Thomas Hornyold, of Blackmore; Robert Wylde, of the Commandery; John Cockes, of Crowle; Major Thomas Wylde, Major John Ingram, Colonel Herbert Prior, of Pedmore; George Acton, William Walsh, of Abberley; George Welch, Thomas Berkeley, of Spetchley; William Langston, of Henley (? Hanley); French, of Pershore, and John Lane, alderman of the city.*

Some hitch occurred; they arrived at Rainbow Hill at 10 a.m., but there were no passes. So they had to wait till the passes arrived; the time elapsed but no passes came. At last, at 1 p.m., they were received. Then they were handed to Hugh Peters, the fanatical minister, whom the Royalists hated with the bitterest hatred, to distribute. The choice of such a person could not have made for order or peace. Each man was asked if he promised not to bear arms against the Parliament, and if he gave the promise then, but not till then, was his pass handed over to him. This is never remembered when the rising under Charles II. is spoken of. Had any of these men then fought for Charles they would have deliberately broken their parole, for rightly or wrongly the promise given was general, not confined to that war. On receipt of the passes they marched off.

About 5 p.m. Rainsborough entered the city. He had already sent in some of his troops, and he thus finished the first Civil War, so far as Worcestershire went.

No time was lost in getting rid of the besieging army. It was determined to retain in Worcestershire only one regiment of foot, 100 horse, and some dragoons, as a guard for the Sheriff. The rest were marched off into other Counties.

But, although the fighting was over, Worcester was made to feel the heavy hand of the conqueror.

On July 24th Rainsborough ordered all arms to be brought in on pain of death; all Royalist soldiers to depart the city within ten days; and that, while in the town, no Royalist should wear a sword.

Having disarmed the citizens the committee got to work the next day, the 25th, by beginning to make an inventory of all estates, demanding a contribution of 25 per cent. Any man

---

* Nash, II., cv.

they pleased to call so became a delinquent, and was "then so squeezed that he could not recover in an age."

The committee consisted of Sir Thomas Rous, Nicholas Lechmere, of Hanley; Daniel Dobyns, of Kidderminster; Colonel William Lygon, of Madresfield; John Egiock, of Feckenham; Major Richard Salwey, second son of Humphrey Salwey, of Stanford; Captain Thomas Milward, of Alvechurch; Thomas Cookes, of Bentley; William Moore, of Alvechurch; Major Edward Smith, William Collins, of King's Norton; William Younge, of Evesham; John Younge, servant to Lord Brooke; John Fownes, of Dodford; John Giles, of Astley; Colonel William Dingley, governor of Evesham.*

The prisoners the Parliament took and obliged to compound included among others: Sherington Talbot, of Salwarp; Edward Vernon, of Hanbury; Philip Brace, of Dovedale; John Washborne, of Wichenford; Francis Finch, of Rushock; Sir Thomas Littleton, late governor of Bewdley; Edward Sheldon, of Beoley, a condition of whose composition was that he should stay at home; Mrs. Pakington, of Harvington, who had leave to stay at home. Sir John Pakington, of Hampton Lovett, who was the then member for Aylesbury; and Sir Henry Herbert, of Ribbesford, who was then member for Bewdley, voluntarily went and compounded.†

The committee got rapidly to work. They first dealt with the Mayor of Worcester (Mr. Evitts).

"By the committee of the county and city of Worcester it is ordered that M. "Evet, the malignant mayor of Worcester, be confined to his house, and the "sword, mace, and seal of the corporation, in possession of the mayor, be "seized on and delivered to this committee, and that M. Writer and M. John "Tilt signify this order to the mayor and demand the sword and other the "above mentioned implements of magistracy."

It was as conquerors that the task was carried out. The Worcestershire Royalists were made to feel that they were the conquered. There was no more fighting. The time was spent in fining, compounding, sequestrating. So far as war was concerned there was a lull. There was to be no more fighting within the borders of the County for the next five years.

---

* Nash, II., cvi.   † Ib.

CHAPTER VI.

1647—1650.

At the end of 1646 the Worcestershire Royalists were for the time crushed, it could not well be otherwise. Such of those who openly favoured Charles and were in Worcester at the surrender had given their parole not to make war against the Parliament, so could not in honour, even if they would, have been willing to run the risk of fines, forfeitures, and sequestrations, break their word. The list given in the last chapter of those in Worcester at the surrender, and the fact that a number of others had compounded but had not yet paid the whole of their composition, and were seeking to get it reduced, would tend to keep them quiet. Added to this, for the present further resistance was hopeless, so obviously so that only men who had nothing to lose by war and rebellion would dream of it. Although gloomy as was the outlook there was not wanting persons who plotted and planned against the Government, with a view of being in readiness to strike a blow when occasion arose.

The history of the next four years is very obscure and must, obviously, be so, as it is the history of plots which would, as far as it was possible, be kept secret, and further, after the Restoration, every person who was in any way connected with these plots and designs, did not fail to put forward a claim for compensation. When once it was realised that those who had helped the cause of monarchy would be rewarded, and substantially rewarded, the number of claimants grew even in a quicker ratio than their alleged services. Nor did the claimants allow the value of their services to remain obscured. They were not slow to magnify their importance. It is, therefore, hardly possible to give an accurate account of the details of what really took place during this time.

The broad outlines are, however, fairly clear, and are as follows :

With the surrender of Worcester the resistance of the County came to an end. No sooner did Parliament hear of it than they at once, on the 24th July, 1646, made an order:

"That all garrisons in Worcestershire, except Worcester City, were to be "slighted, and all the horse there, were to be disbanded, except 80 to "attend on the High Sheriff."*

---

* Whitelock, p. 222.

This was carried out to a certain extent, but Hartlebury was only very partially " slighted," and was easily restored.

In order to understand the subsequent events, some reference to matters outside the County must be made.

It was not until the 30th March, 1647, when Harlech Castle surrendered,* that the task of reducing the Royalist garrisons was completed.

In September, 1646, Essex died. His death was a very serious loss to the Presbyterian party in depriving them of their chief leader, who, had he lived, might possibly have modified, or at least delayed, the coming storm.

The Scots, on receiving the arrears of their pay, handed Charles over to the Presbyterians, and he had been taken to Holmeby House, in Northamptonshire, from whence, on the 3rd June, 1647, he was carried off by Cornet Joyce, on behalf of the army, and ultimately taken to Hampton Court. Charles considered that the divisions among his opponents gave him his opportunity. He tried to use it, with the result that he only succeeded in convincing all parties of one thing, that it was quite impossible to trust him.

The state of the Royalists in the County is very well shewn by the petition of Dame Frances Russell, the wife of Sir William Russell, of Strensham, and Thomas Russell, son of the said Sir William. It states that

" Sir William is under sequestration for delinquency, and is at present " indicted for murder at Worcester for an act done in relation to the war, so " that he cannot as yet compound. Meantime his timber is being cut down " and his estate wasted. The petitioners pray that they may be allowed to " compound for the estate, so that it may be preserved from ruin."

Russell's assessment was fixed at £3000, but it was ordered, on his deposing that £80 represented his twentieth, that his assessment should be discharged for £500.

He was arrested and imprisoned in the King's Bench for debt under several executions, and in 1649 his wife again petitioned that she might be at liberty to compound. In February, 1649, Russell's fine was fixed at one-third (£2071) of his estate, to be reduced to £1800 if he would convey the Rectory of Birlingham, which belonged to him, to the parish.

The Worcester Committee reported in September, 1647,

" that several persons sequestered by them from the Chamber of Worcester as " delinquent persist in holding their estates, and by the prevalence of the " malignant party have procured the election of George Heminge, the " principal amongst them, a noted delinquent, as mayor for the ensuing year, " to the great grief and discouragement of the well-affected."

All these complaints would not tend to make the Royalists more satisfied with the existing Government.

Early in November the King left Hampton Court and went

---

* Whitelock, p. 245.

to the Isle of Wight.　While there he concluded a treaty with the Scots.　The fact of this treaty became known, but not its contents.　It was said, but unjustly, that the treaty was a breach of faith.　So strongly did the Republicans feel this that they proposed " to lay the King by and settle the Government without him."　A vote in Parliament for no more addresses to be sent to the King was carried on the 3rd January, 1648, by 141 to 92.　This anti-monarchical step brought together and united not only all Royalists, but also all those who objected to such a fundamental change in the Constitution as getting rid of the Kingly office, and all who desired to see England a Monarchy.　In fact it produced a new division of parties, into Monarchists and Republicans.　Numerically the Republicans were far the weakest, actually they were far the strongest, as they could rely upon the army to support them.

This new division caused disturbances of all kinds, riots and tumults occurring all over the country, often from such small matters as sports and games, which, although quite harmless, the fanatical zeal of the Puritans desired should be put down.

As a result of Charles' treaty it was known that the Scots would invade the country to restore the King, on the terms they had dictated.　It was felt that to regain power the King would consent, at least in name, to any terms that might be proposed.　In Wales, Kent, Essex, Herefordshire, Nottinghamshire, and Cornwall risings actually took place.　In other Counties active preparations were made for risings.

Worcestershire was among the latter class.　No regular narrative of the Worcestershire plottings seems ever to have been written.　Information as to them has to be picked up from isolated accounts of different occurrences.　It is, therefore, quite possible that the following statement is not accurate, either in all its details or in the order in which they occurred. But as far as at present can be said, the plan of operations in this County was somewhat as follows.

As has been stated, in 1646, after the surrender of Worcester, Parliament settled that all the County garrisons but Worcester should be disgarrisoned.　In March, 1647, they made an order as to Gloucestershire, by which it was fixed :—

" That Gloucester City be continued a garrison and 600 men kept in it, and "no other garrison in that County."*

" That Colonel Morgan should continue governor of Gloucester."†

A little later his pay was fixed at 12s. a day as governor, and 8s. a day as captain.‡

So far all went well, and possibly if the Government had been able to have paid their troops regularly all would have gone well, and there would have been little if any trouble.

---

* *Perfect Diurnal*, March 1—8, 1646-7.　† Ib., March 13.　‡ Ib., April 12—19, 1647.

But money was scarce with the Parliament. They could not pay their troops, and so the men became mutinous. The lesson, the evil lesson, that they had been taught by the example of various places that if they only mutinied for their pay they would get, if not all, at least some of it, had sunk into the minds of the Gloucester garrison. Acting on it, they thought the best way to get their pay was at once to mutiny. The Royalists took advantage of this discontent. In January, 1648, the Presbyterian officers of the Gloucester and other garrisons, who had, like Massey, become Monarchists as opposed to Republicans, took action.

From its position there were few places in Worcestershire that had seen more of the war, and were better suited for the rendezvous of troops than Broadway. Under the Cotswold Hills, on the direct road from Wales to Oxford, not far from the spot where the road from Warwick to Gloucester crossed, it was a locality of no small importance. Being on the borders of three Counties it made a most convenient centre. It is, therefore, not surprising that at Broadway those who were discontented with the existing state of things met to consider if it was possible that anything could be done. The following is the mention of this meeting by Rushworth :—*

" 'A letter was read to the House of Commons concerning the complotting of " some officers in a dangerous design about Gloucestershire and the shires " adjacent.' Sent by an eminent person, the copy whereof followeth."

" A council was held at Broadway the greatest part of last week by about " 80 officers of Colonel Kempson's, Colonel Ayre's, Colonel Herbert's, and " another regiment of foot, and of Colonel Cooke's regiment of horse. Their " debate was upon their discontents, the surprisal of Gloucester, it being " alleged that there were 300 barrels of powder there, and they knew where to " come at it, and that the works being bad they could easily surprise the town " by night. Hartlebury Castle, they conceived, would be delivered to them " by Colonel Turton. If not, they held that easily to be surprised, too. " They had some discourse at [as to] Ludlow, Shrewsbury, and Hereford, " and an assurance that Langbourne would join with them, and that they would " have 2000 capmen from Bewdley, and also that the discontented citizens of " London would furnish them with present monies. To this debate there " were about 20 dissenters, so that Saturday last they broke up their council, " but it is thought that the rest who were for it will meet again, or have met " sometime the beginning of this week. I am assured by the gentleman that " the general is acquainted herewith by some of the dissenters. The governor " and the officers are acquainted herewith, and I find nothing but all fair and " well with them, they being now willing to admit of the general's forces in " upon the payment of common soldiers their two months, which we shall " provide, although we have scarce £300 (now) in of the assessments. " Captain Bayly's horse was forgotten in the establishment. The commis- " sioners sent for £2000, so that to the end we may have orders for money " enough. We will desire you for another order for the issuing out of £1000 " more out of the assessments. Captain Bayly's horse hath done good " service here, and therefore I shall desire that they may have their two " months pay (according to the establishment), but in this we look for " directions from you. I hope that they shall find your favour. I have sent

* Rushworth VII., p. 974. *Perfect Occurrences*, January 21—28, 1647.

"a messenger away to my brother with the former intelligence, to the intent
"that they may look to Hereford, Shrewsbury, and Ludlow.   The messenger
"stays for this, so I must end, resting.

                                        "Signed by a person of note.
    "Gloucester,
        "Jan. 19, 1647."

    "The House, on debate hereof, ordered to refer the business to the Com-
"mittee of the Kingdom at Derby House, and the letters to be communi-
"cated."*

The Parliament were alarmed at this communication. They
at once took steps to check the conspiracy. They resolved
that the Gloucester garrison should be forthwith changed.

    "Sir William Constable's regiment marched into Gloucester on Thursday
"last, the 28th January; Colonel Morgan (the governor) and his officers
"marched out.   There was shewed loving respect on both sides, and Colonel
"Morgan's force are now quartered about Stow-on-the-Wold."†

Placing Morgan and his men on the London Road, to intercept any force that the conspirators might send towards
London, shows how alarmed Parliament was at the plots, and
their belief that in Worcestershire there was a strong Mon-
archical movement, and that it was due to accident more than
to anything else that this County did not take part in the
second Civil War.

The reference to Bewdley connects the Broadway plot with
the subsequent movement. The cap trade was then a great
Bewdley industry. The Sessions Records shew that the cap-
pers were not the most peaceable people, and were ready,
doubtless, to rise when occasion required them to do so.

What was the next step in the Broadway Plot does not
appear, but on Monday, February 28th, there is a statement
in the proceedings in the House of Commons, that

    "There was also something published, in one of the weekly sheets not long
"since, of a design amongst some officers holding a council at Broadway, in
"Worcestershire, against Gloucester, wherein amongst others some officers of
"Colonel Herbert's regiment were said to be concerned, but very unjustly
"accused, as may appear by the certificates following which we publish for
"better satisfaction.

    "Forasmuch as it hath been set forth in several printed papers, that the
"officers of the regiment of foot, under the command of Colonel Herbert,
"amongst others, held a debate at Broadway, in Worcestershire, about the
"22nd January last, for the surprisal of Gloucester and Hartlebury Castle,
"etc.   These are therefore, at their desire, to certify whom it may concern,
"that Captain Short, together with the Lieut.-Colonel, the Major, Captain,
"and other commission officers and soldiers of the said regiment entered
"into this County of Somerset upon the 13th January last to quarter, and have
"ever since continued here, attending from time to time upon us and the rest
"of the commissioners of Parliament for the receipt of such monies as have
"been allotted them upon their disbanding.   Whereby it manifestly appears
"that the imputation laid upon them is altogether untrue.
    Witness our hands at Somerton, the 11th February, 1647.

        "W. Strode, Geo. Hornek, John Buckland, Thomas Hippesley."‡

It is obvious, from this disclaimer, that there must have

---

* Rushworth, VII., 975.   † Rushworth, VII., 979.   ‡ Rushworth, VII., 1012.

been a good deal in the Broadway Plot, otherwise an absent regiment would not have taken such pains to prove their absence. Whatever there was, it was checked for the time. Nothing more is now mentioned of it.

It does not appear how far the discontent had gone, nor if its real cause was anything more than delay in receiving pay. Nor whether it had any bearing on the next incident, the disbandment of Major Richard Hopton's Regiment. This was carried out at Whittington, near Hereford, on the 19th March.* The regiment was about 500 strong. Acting under the orders of Parliament, directing regiments to be disbanded, preparations were made to do this, but when ordered to disband these men mutinied, and it was only by strategy, combined with a hogshead of wine provided by their commander, that the disbandment was carried out. The account of it proceeds:

" After they had refrained their tears they refreshed their spirits with the " wine, and departed every man to his house with abundance of love and " civility."

The discovery and failure of these plots made some of the Royalists despondent. On the 16th March, 1647, it was reported† that Sir Andrew Knighton and Sir Humble Ward took the benefit of the Dudley articles and their sequestrations were then taken off.

Whatever the weaker vessels might do there were still some sturdy Royalists ready, in spite of everything, to rise for the King, and of such men Parliament stood in wholesome dread, and acted accordingly. In May it was ordered that the County Committees in Gloucester and Hereford should arrest the disaffected. On the 19th May Parliament ordered that steps be taken to secure Ludlow. On the 23rd May an ordinance was passed for settling the Hereford Militia. On the 30th June the Worcestershire Committee

" was authorised to raise such horse and foot as they should think fit for " suppressing all tumults and insurrections in the County and preserving the " peace thereof."‡

Early in July the governor of Hartlebury Castle, Colonel Turton, suspected something was wrong in the district. On the 11th July letters ‖

" were read to the House of a design of a rising by malignants in Worcester-" shire, Shropshire, Staffordshire, and Herefordshire, and to possess several " strong places to make them garrisons for the King, but the design was " discovered and through the vigilancy of the governor of Hartlebury Castle, " prevented, Major Harcot (a chief actor for the King), and some others " taken prisoners, who confessed the whole design."

This statement is only part of the truth. The design of the Royalists was stated as §

---

* Rushworth, VII., 1042.   † Ib., 1030.   ‡ Rushworth, VII., 1171.   ‖ Ib., 1185.
§ See a tract: "A Letter from the Committee of Worcester," &c.

" an association of divers knights, colonels, gentlemen, and others for the
" king."

It consisted of divers

" cavaliers of Worcestershire, Salop, Stafford, and Hereford for surprising
" Hereford. Colonel Dudley, Sir Francis Oakley, Colonel Lane, Major
" Elliott, Major Harcot, Broughton (the parson of Wolverley), and divers
" others were in the plot to surprise Dawley Castle and the house of Sir
" Bazill Brooke near adjacent."

A Captain Jenet went, or was sent, to Wolverley, to the
house of the Parson, Broughton, and, on making a search,
found in a corn field behind the house half-a-hundred-weight
of powder. On this, Major Harcot was arrested and brought
to Hartlebury Castle. Here, on his refusing to confess and say
who his associates were, and what were their plans, he was
tortured by having lighted musket fuses placed to the soles of
his feet. This drove him to make a confession, which was
reported to the House and thoroughly alarmed them. They
at once made an order approving of

" the regarrisoning of Worcester by Colonel Dingley, and the well affected
" gentlemen of that County, ordered the regarrisoning of Hartlebury, and
" referred it to the committee to decide how monies might be raised for the
" maintenance of the forces of those garrisons."*

Parliament had reason to be alarmed; a wide-spread conspiracy was on foot. A movement, possibly a continuance of
the Broadway plot, was going on round Bewdley to raise men
and find arms. The men were to be raised by the well-known
Colonel Dud Dudley, who has given his own account of his
part in this and other affairs.

Dud Dudley was the fourth son of Edward, Lord Dudley,
who died 1643, by his mistress, Elizabeth, daughter of William
Tomlinson, of Dudley. Although illegitimate, his pedigree is
recorded in the Staffordshire Visitation of 1663-4. He is
mostly known as the inventor of the method of smelting iron
with coal instead of wood, a process he describes in his
" Metallum Martis." But he should also be known for the
active part he took on the King's side as " colonel of a
regiment in the army of King Charles I., and general of the
ordinance to Prince Maurice for his said Majesty's service."
After the surrender of Worcester, in 1646, nothing is heard
of him until July, 1648, about which time he began to raise
men for the King in Worcestershire and Staffordshire, it is
only right to add, at his own cost. The Staffordshire men were
being drilled in the Boscobel Woods, near Madeley, and from
information wrung from Harcot by torture the place and time
of the drilling were disclosed. This led to them being surrounded, attacked, and captured whilst drilling. They were
some 200 in number, and all were either dispersed or taken

---

* Rushworth, VII., 1185.

prisoners. Among those taken was Dud himself, Major Elliott, Captain Long, and Cornet Hodgetts. They were carried off to Hartlebury Castle and confined there. Dud says that he and the others were stripped naked, or nearly so, and subjected to all sorts of insults and contumely. After a time they were sent on to the prison at Worcester. On the journey they were made to ride almost naked through the streets, and subjected to every possible indignity. On arriving at Worcester they were kept close prisoners. The fact of their being confined there caused considerable alarm in the city, so much so that the guards, both at the castle and at the city gates, were doubled. Nothing daunted by these precautions, Dud and Elliott determined to escape. In this they were successful. They got out from the gaol on to the roof of an adjoining house ; from there they made their way along the roofs of the nearest houses, so as to pass the castle guard and gate and also the south gate of the town (the Sidbury Gate), and so got clear away into the country. They were closely pursued, and were obliged to hide in trees in the daytime and travel only at night. Continuing in this way for some days, they at last reached London in safety. Their luck now changed. After a few days Elliott was discovered and arrested, and very soon Dud shared the same fate. They were brought before the Lord Mayor (Sir John Warner), who at once remanded them to appear before the committee that was then sitting to deal with all matters relating to the war— "that cursed committee" as Dud calls them. The committee dealt with the prisoners in a very summary manner ; both were at once sentenced to be shot. Pending their execution they were sent to the Gatehouse, Westminster. The following Monday, 26th August, 1648, was the day fixed for their death. On the Sunday morning, during the time of divine service and sermon, about 10 a.m., a number of Royalists, including Dud, overpowered the few guards who were not attending the sermon and broke out of prison. Dud at once separated from the rest, and made for the open country. He had a wound in his leg, probably received in his escape, so was only able to walk with great difficulty, and on crutches. With remarkable pluck and determination he pushed on. He had numerous escapes, some of them very narrow indeed. Among others, "he fed three weeks in private in an enemy's hay mow," but he escaped detection and reached Worcester in safety. On his arrival there he found his wife and children gone, his house sold, his ironworks destroyed. He heard his wife and family were at Bristol, so he set off to go there, and with delays and difficulties reached it in safety. There he dwelt for some time, living a most retired life, until the Restoration. He died in 1684 and is buried in St. Helen's Church,

Worcester, where there is a monument to him on the wall of the south aisle, with a long inscription which has been allowed to scale off, but which, when legible, set out his career as

" *regiæ majestatis fidissimus subditus et servus in asserendo regem in* " *vindicando ecclesiam in propugnando legen ac libertatem Anglicanam sæpe* " *captus, anno 1648, semel condemnatus et tamen non decollatus.*"*

How far this is an accurate account of Dud it is difficult to say, as almost the only version we have of Dud's adventures is his own, not drawn up until years after, when the King was restored, and it was Dud's interest to magnify all that he had done and suffered for Royalty. Rewards were then going for those who had helped the King. So it would not be right to expect absolute accuracy in every detail of Dud's account of himself and his actions. But of this there can be no doubt that in 1648 he was arrested while drilling men who were being raised to enable them to strike a blow in Worcestershire for the King, and which, if he had not been arrested, would probably have been struck. Whitelock describes it†

" A design of malignants in Worcestershire prevented, and Mr. Harcourt and " others apprehended for it. Orders for garrisoning Worcester by Colonel " Dineley, and Hartlebury."

Men were useless without arms. The next incident tells how the arms were being provided. It is contained in a document among the Sessions Records. The declaration of Edward Reynolds, of Kidderminster, taken before Gervase Birch and John Latham, two Justices of the Peace for the County, as to Edward Broad, of Duncklin [Dunclent], Esq.‡

" About seven days before Sir Henry Lingen did rise against the Parlia- " ment "

(this was in August, 1648, when Lingen collected a body of horse, attacked Harley's County troop near Leominster, and took 80 prisoners. But two or three days later Harley and Horton surprised Lingen between Radnor and Montgomery, routed his force, retook the prisoners),§

" and surprised and took the County troops of Hereford. The said Edward " Broad spoke to this informant being his tenant, and his warriner to go to " John Brancill's dwelling at Kidderminster, being a joiner and well skilled in " stocking of guns, to come with all speed to stock guns for him, and willing, " this informant also himself to be in readiness. And this informant asking " him what use there would be for so many guns, the said Edward Broad " answered there would be use for them very speedily. and further said that " Mr. Hugh Viconidge, of Comberton, and Mr. Thomas Wannerton, and " other Roundheaded rogues should be hanged to begin withall. And the " said Brancill came to Duncklyn accordingly, but how many guns he stocked " their informant knoweth not. And afterwards, when the news was first that " Sir Henry Lingen had surprised Hereford County troops, the said Edward " Broad asked this informant whither Sir Henry Lingen was gone, whereunto " this informant answering that he did not know, the said Edward Broad

---

* Nash, II., cxlix.　　† Memorials, p. 315.　　‡ Worcestershire Sessions Records, 1651.
§ Whitelock, p. 325.

"replied and said Sir Henry Lingen was not so good as his word, and about a
" week after Sir Henry Lingen was surprised; the said Edward Broad hid
" divers guns, which he had provided as aforesaid, under a rick of hay, and
" afterwards removed them thence and hid them in a corn mow in one of the
" barns at Dunclin, where they were seen within a year-and-a-half by one
" Thomas Lude, a coachman belonging to that house, as he told this
" informer."

This declaration was not made until 1651, three years later.
It is prefaced with an account of what Broad had done in
opposition to Fox and the garrison at Stourton Castle. It is
so obviously made to gain the favours of the powers that then
were, that its entire accuracy, especially as to details, must be
regarded with a degree of suspicion, but it may be accepted as
an indication of what would have taken place if the chance of
regaining their position had ever been given to the Worcestershire Royalists. Nothing more appears of this affair of
Broad's than the tract, the statement by Dud Dudley, and
the information of Reynolds. Parliament, however, considered the state of things in the County so serious as to
render it necessary to raise a force for the defence of
Worcestershire. A petition of Colonel Dineley, who was the
Parliamentary governor of Evesham while it was garrisoned,
and afterwards of Worcester, shews this. Dineley states, in
1649,

" that he is in great arrears of pay for service in the County, that he had done
" good service during the late war, and *got into debt by raising forces last*
" *summer, when this County and other parts were in danger.*"

This obviously refers to the Hartlebury Plot. The Council
of State communicated with the Sequestration Committee in
Worcestershire as to Dineley's petition, and added

" that the sequestrations of that County are in your disposal by ordinance of
" Parliament, for payment of the forces of your County. We commend
" Colonel Dineley and others to you for retribution, that he and others may
" more cheerfully serve the Commonwealth."

To help Dineley he was made an additional member of the
Committee of Sequestrations for the County.

Parliament also made an order in September, 1648,

" for raising 100 horse and 300 foot in the County of Worcester, and pro-
" viding a sum of money not exceeding £100 a week for their maintenance."

This might be expected from the past history of the
County. The plot would tend to make Parliament see the
necessity of keeping a very tight hold on it. The effect very
possibly was that when in August, 1651, trouble did actually
come, and the King of the Scots called upon Worcestershire Royalists to rise, they were not able, even if they had
been willing to do so, being kept down by force and
deprived of all weapons and means of offence. To " encourage
the others" one example was made to shew what they
might expect if they broke their parole and rebelled. Major

William Pitcher had formed one of the Worcester garrison when the surrender took place in July, 1646. He served again against the Parliament in Wales, thus breaking his parole. Being arrested in London he was promptly tried by a Council of War, found guilty and shot.*

Colonel Morgan petitioned the House of Lords to carry out his arrangement with Colonel Samuel Sandys, of Ombersley, under which Sandys surrendered Hartlebury Castle to him in 1646, to take off the sequestration on Sandys estate, without fine or composition. Morgan begs the House to be tender of his honour and to grant a performance of his promise.

Parliament felt that something should be done to make good the damage the city and the County had sustained by the war. An ordinance was made for the sale of the leaden steeple on the north-east of the Cathedral Church.

"18th February, 1647. The Lords and Commons being informed that in "the Cathedral Church Yard of the said city there is a steeple called the "leaden steeple, [not] fixed to the said church, nor employed in any other "use than a woodhouse, the lead and other materials of which steeple are "estimated at above 1200*l*, therefore ordered and ordained that certain "persons be empowered to sell the steeple and employ the money for re- "edifying of the said alms houses . . . . and for the repairs of the "churches of St. John in Bedwardine . . . . Dodderhill, and Castle- "morton." †

In consequence the steeple was sold; it brought £617 4s. 2d. The money was not by any means all devoted to repair of churches and almshouses. A surplus remained in hand. £10 in 1651, after the battle, was ordered to be paid to Mr. James Warwick, minister of Hanley Castle, and £20 to Mr. Symon Moore, minister of the College at Worcester,

"being a very faithful preacher of God's word, and of singular good affection "to the Government of this Commonwealth, who had suffered great losses by "the Scotch army at Worcester."‡

One of the Committee of Sequestration for the County was Sergeant Wylde, or Chief Baron Wylde, as he had now become. From the Bewdley accounts it would appear that he was not wholly averse to " having a drink" at the expense of those who came before him, as there are the following entries§ in those accounts:—

"Pd. our charge, riding to Judge Wilde, at Worcester   oo o1 o5
"Pd. for wine bestowed on Judge Wilde   oo o2 o8
"Money laid out at Worcester to 21st December, 1648, to attend
    the Commission whom the County sent to oppose the order
    charging them   oo o9 o1

In the beginning of 1648 a valuable gold cup was carried away from Belvoir to Oxford, and then to Worcester, by Paul, the Governor of Belvoir Castle. Although there was a good

---

* Rushworth VII., 1377.   Whitelock, 360.   † H.M.R., XIV. Rep., VIII. App., p. 188.
        ‡ XIV. Rep., p. 188.   § Burton's Bewdley.

deal of fuss made about the cup, it never seems to have been found, or really known who the thief was.*

So far as Worcestershire was concerned the plot of the Royalists to ensure a rising was quite frustrated by the failure of the plotters to carry out their plans. For a time this must have had a very marked effect upon the gentry of Worcestershire. But, whatever they may have felt, they were not prepared to take the plunge into Republicanism, and were most likely more loyal to the King in January, 1649, than they had ever been. One thing may have made them so. Among the numerous men who are said to have been

"those two persons who, being disguised by frocks and vizards, did appear "upon the scaffold erected before Whitehall, upon the 30th of January, "1649, and who were out of the Act of Oblivion wholly excepted and "foreprised." †

one is said to have been a Worcestershire man, Thomas Fox, the tinker, but there is absolutely no evidence come down to us that could in any way account for such a suspicion. There is, in fact, no evidence to connect the "Tinker" with the King's death beyond the fact that he was a most zealous Parliamentarian.

Whoever the persons were their act, or rather the act of one of them, led to a strong Royalist reaction. Parliament now found that they had gone so far that they were obliged to go further. The House of Commons took on itself the power of Parliament. It declared the House of Lords "useless and dangerous," the office of King " unnecessary, burdensome, and dangerous," so it abolished both. A Council of State was appointed, with full executive power in all home and foreign affairs. Among its members was one Worcestershire man, the Chief Baron Wilde. Another High Court of Justice was formed to try the prisoners taken in the second Civil War, at Colchester: Hamilton, Holland, Norwich, Capel, and Owen. Bradshaw again acted as president, and the servants found it was sufficient to be as their master. Two, Owen and Norwich, were reprieved, and the remainder, in addition to Lucas and Lisle, executed. Probably the stern way in which these men were dealt with was the truest mercy, as it shewed plainly what was the certain fate of rebels. It had its effect. For the time Monarchy was dead in England.

It was otherwise both in Ireland and Scotland. In Ireland strong hopes of a Royalist rising prevailed. In Scotland, on his father's death, Charles was at once provisionally proclaimed King. The question that pressed hardest on the Royalists was, where should the struggle begin, Ireland or Scotland? Each had its strong supporters, and each had

---

* Hist. MSS. Com., XII. Rep., / pp. V.
† 12 Car. II., c. 11, sec. 34.

strong arguments to adduce in its favour.   Charles and his
advisers decided on Ireland.   As soon· as this appeared,
Parliament determined to put down Monarchy in Ireland once
and for ever.   Cromwell was sent over, and ordered to remove
the unclean thing with the sword.   This work took him until
the 26th May, 1650, when he returned from Ireland to England.   How he did his task is best shewn by the fact that even
now, two centuries and a half after the work has been finished,
the bitterest Irish imprecation is : " The curse of Cromwell be
upon you."
     In England the Royalists were in a sad state.   The pro-
ceedings in the matter of Sir Martyn Sandys will give an
instance :—

     " The Council of State ordered its Secretary to write to the Lord Chief
" Justice that Sir Martyn Sandys, against whom a warrant had been issued,
" he being outlawed for the murder of Mr. Stayner, of Worcester, was then in
" safe custody, in the Gate house, to be proceeded against as a dangerous
" person."

     Sandys had been arrested in rather a peculiar way.   One
Hastings was a person the Council were desirous of arresting.
They heard he was somewhere in Essex, disguised.   Hearing of
the whereabouts of a disguised Royalist, they sent to arrest him,
and to their great surprise found when they brought their
prisoner to head-quarters that they had arrested, not Hastings,
but Sandys.   To justify his detention a charge of murder, for
something he had done during the war, was made against him.
Two of the Council, Sir Henry Mildmay and Sir William
Masham, were appointed to further examine into it.   Mildmay,
the Registrar, and Committee at Goldsmith's Hall were ordered
to certify the sum at which Sir Martyn had compounded, and
if he had prosecuted his composition into effect.
     In November, 1649, John Compton applied for and obtained
leave to bring an action against Sandys,

" provided he be not thereupon removed to any other prison without warrant
" from the Council or Lord Chief Justice, or hindered answering to justice in
" what he stood committed for."

     A further complaint was made by the Council of State to
the Worcestershire Committee in consequence of

" a complaint formerly made of waste of timber in Bewdley Park, we gave
" order for preventing thereof.   Since then some persons have proposed
" buying the timber, and a claim has also been made on it by Sir Ralph Clare,
" to whom (as he pretends his evidences are in the country) we have given
" him two months to prove his title to that wood and timber.   Take
" care that none of it be felled or disposed of until the title be evidenced and
" further orders taken in it.

     On December 8th, 1649, the Council of State wrote to the
trustees for the sale of the Dean and Chapter lands, ordering
them to give notice to the Council before they offered for
sale Aymore Wood, Worcestershire, near the Severn, the

Council being informed that they lie conveniently for building of ships.

Having crushed Ireland it now became necessary to do something in Scotland. The Scotch had begun negotiations with Charles. Montrose had raised a party for the King. The English Royalists shewed signs of uniting if not of rising. There was, however, one great obstacle to union, the Solemn League and Covenant. Without it, Scotland would not move; with it, England would not stir. Charles was prepared to take the Covenant or anything else to gain the crown. He stated he was a Presbyterian, he subscribed the Covenant, he came to Scotland. A few days before his arrival his most faithful follower, Montrose, who had invaded Scotland on his behalf, was defeated at Carlisdale, taken prisoner and executed (21st May, 1650). On the 23rd June, 1650, Charles landed at Speymouth. Solemnly and publicly he took the covenant. On the 6th July, he reached the Royal Palace of Falkland. All Charles now wanted was an English rising, for this he waited. The English Parliament became thoroughly alarmed. All Papist soldiers of fortune and delinquents were ordered to leave London, and not to come within 20 miles of it. The number of those who left greatly astonished Parliament, and greatly increased the alarm. A new High Court of Justice was set up, new regiments were raised, Cromwell was thanked by Parliament for his services in Ireland, and he with Fairfax appointed to put down the rebellion in Scotland. After accepting the position Fairfax resigned, so Cromwell went alone (26th June, 1650), taking as his lieut.-general Fleetwood, and as his major-general Lambert. As before, the Scotch army was nominally commanded by the Earl of Leven, but the real commander was David Leslie.

On July 22nd, 1650, Cromwell advanced from Berwick into Scotland. A series of manœuvres ensued, terminating on the 3rd September, 1650, by the rout of the Scots at Dunbar. This for a time discouraged the Royalists.

The Scots began to quarrel among themselves. The command was taken from Leslie and given to Middleton, but after a while given back to Leslie. Cromwell took Edinburgh, and gradually forced the Scotch northwards.

All the summer and autumn there had been Royalist plottings in England, some of which the Government detected. If there was any plotting in Worcestershire—which it is most probable there was—no record of it appears to have survived. A Captain Levinz was arrested for bringing commissions from Charles Stuart into the country, tried by a court-martial, and hanged. Eusebius Andrews, a barrister, and one Benson, were, for an alleged plot, tried before the High Court of Justice, convicted and executed. In December a Royalist outbreak took place in Norfolk, the result of which was a series of executions. All these plots thoroughly alarmed the Parliament, as they clearly shewed if Charles did invade England, unless special steps were taken, there would be a very serious rising, which would try their resources to the utmost.

Parliament urged their spies to special activity, so the Government received information of the alleged details of Royalist plots, details which were stated as the result of the late rising in Norfolk. Whether the information was true or false, the Government acted upon it and arrested very freely. Among other persons was one Birkenhead, whom, it was said, was engaged in preparing a rising in Lancashire. Steps, decisive steps, were promptly taken to secure that County, steps so severe but so effectual that when the Scots did come the support they received in Lancashire was reduced to the lowest dimensions, and which probably made the subsequent attempt of the Earl of Derby to raise the County hopeless. Arrest followed arrest. Some of the persons arrested were Presbyterians, some were ministers, two of them (Love and Gibbons) were tried for treason, sentenced to death, and executed.

It is quite possible if this so-called plot had not been discovered, and these stern steps not taken, when Charles did come his expedition would not have failed; Lancashire would have risen. The feeling that this was so caused the Parliament to try to strangle the Royalist movement by placing their leaders inside prison walls, instead of allowing them to remain outside and able to help.

The cause of monarchy did not look hopeful. The Scots were far from enthusiastic. At that date Highlanders and Lowlanders were as far apart as Englishmen and Scotchmen now are. The Highlander did not care for Charles or his cause. The Lowlander had his doubts as to whether Charles was in deed and in truth " a covenanted King." In one thing and in one thing only were the two agreed, in feeling no confidence whatever in their King. In a less degree, but only in a less degree, neither party had confidence in their general. That Leslie was an able soldier no one who reads the history of that time can have any doubt. That had Leslie had a free hand he would have proved more than a match for Cromwell seems most probable. But to the Highlander Leslie was incompetent, as his defensive tactics were regarded as treachery. To the Lowlander he was treacherous, as he had permitted the saints of the Lord to die on the Dunbar Hills. If it is desired to know how it was that the defeat at Worcester was so crushing and so complete it is essential to keep these things in mind.

Although there was no actual rising in Worcestershire in 1650 yet there was a great deal of discontent, and discontent which led to bloodshed, mainly owing to the exactions and oppressions of the Commissioners of Excise. Early in the year, in February, the Council of State wrote to the Committee of Excise :—

"that the persons formerly employed in Worcestershire as Sub-Commisioner's "for Excise may not be employed again, there having been some bloodshed "in the County through the default of these men."

About a fortnight later the Council of State wrote to the Commissioners of Excise :

"Some disturbance has lately happened in the County and City of Wor-"cester by the violent proceedings of Captain Prescott and some other Sub-"Commissioners of the Excise, wherein several men were slain and others "wounded, to the breach of the peace and breeding of great disaffection. "The Parliament, upon the desire of some of that County, ordered that some "others should be Commissioners of the Excise there and the others laid "aside, which is not yet done, and the said persons still go on in their "employment, with which the County is much discontented. Fearing it may "produce some ill-effects if speedy care be not taken, we desire you forthwith "to discharge the said Commissioners, and appoint in their places Edward "Elmers (Alderman of Worcester), William Collins and William Stephens "(Sub-Commissioners), and Gervase Buck (Comptroller), men well-affected to "the Commonwealth."

This looks as if the Royalists had been using the Commissioners to stir up strife with a view to eventualities. Gervase Buck was a most active magistrate and a very strong Parliamentarian. Parliament was still uneasy about the state of the County. In June the Council of State wrote to Major-General Harrison, who, from this, must then have been at Worcester or in the County,

"to consider whether 'Matchfield' [Madresfield] House, in Worcestershire, "is fit to be demolished."

On the 11th June the Council of State directed

"Sir William Constable (the Governor of Gloucester), and Colonels Harrison, "Saunders, and Dingley, to view the strength of Matchfield House, four "miles from Worcester, and if anything be necessary to make it untenable, to "signify the charge and what loss it will be to the proprietor."

For some reason Madresfield was the centre of disturbance. Parliament was in dread of a rising and of the house being seized and held as a fort. Details of the reasons why attention was so closely directed to this quarter are wanting, but from 1650 to April 1651, Parliament was most anxious that Madresfield should be made untenable.

At the end of the year there is a petition from an old Cavalier, John Washbourne, of Wichenford, which well illustrates the conditions under which the "Malignants" had to live. Washbourne asked to be allowed to come to London, but this was only to be granted

" if upon enquiry the Lord Chief Baron Wylde conceive him fit to be suffered'
" to come hither, and likewise certifying what security Washbourne should put
" in."

That is, the malignants could not leave their County without
it was thought fit, and not then without special bail, and such
bail for safe appearance as their neighbours, who were their
opponents, considered sufficient.

No. 2.

THE WORCESTER CAMPAIGN.
22nd August to 3rd September 1651.

To Droitwich

To Kidderminster

R. Severn

Bransford Bridge

River Teme

Powick Bridge

Powick

WORCESTER
Charles, 22 August

SPETCHLEY
Cromwell, 30 Aug.

White Ladies Aston.
Cromwell, 29 August.

River Severn

Madresfield

Blackmore Park

Pershore

Cromwell, 28 August
MOOR

River Avon.

Evesham
Cromwell, 27 August

R. Severn

Lambert, Aug. 29

Severn end

Massey
Upton on Severn.

River Avon

CHAPTER VII.

1651.

On the 1st January, 1651, Charles was crowned at Scone King of Scotland. He had now become formidable, having, to use the words of a recent historian, " succeeded in lying his way into a commanding position."*

For some reason, why—unless it was on the road to Wales—it is difficult to discover, as Worcestershire was not on the direct route between Scotland and London, the Parliament were very anxious about the County, and took all the steps in their power to ensure a tight hand being kept on it. On the 13th January, 1651, the Council of State ordered :

"That special care be taken for the security of Worcester, Gloucester and "Hereford, that all dangerous and suspicious persons be removed, and an "account taken of all arms and ammunition."

In March, 1651, the Council of State

"directed Lord Grey to move Parliament to give orders for making the city "of Worcester untenable, for preventing the dangers that may come to the "Commonwealth thereby."

This shews the continued anxiety of Parliament with regard to Worcester and their fear of disturbance, but, curiously enough, no account of the movement against which Parliament and the Council of State were now trying to guard has, apparently, come down to us.

On 19th March, Parliament made a further order :

"That the Council of State take care the City of Worcester be forthwith "made untenable."

On the same day (19th March) the Council of State wrote to the Militia Commissioners for the County of Worcester :

"Parliament, for special reasons, has ordered the City of Worcester to 'be made untenable, and has referred it to the Council to give order for it, "and also to the special care of Lord Chief Baron Wylde and Mr. Lechmere, "to see it done. As there are some designs on foot by the enemy against "that place it should be speedily and effectually done. We desire you to "give all assistance therein."

The alarm did not subside, for on 19th April, 1651, the Council of State wrote to the Governor of Gloucester (Sir William Constable):

"The business touching Worcester is under consideration, and we all know "ye will have a watchful eye upon it and all parts about you, for prevention

---

* Gardiner, Commonwealth, I., 353.

"of any portended disturbance.　Matchfield House belongs to Colonel
"Lyggin (*sic*), formerly a garrison for the King, and whether it has been
"made untenable, and give a speedy account thereof"

On the 31st March, the Council of State wrote to Colonel
John James, issuing a commission to him to raise and command the forces in Worcestershire under the Militia Acts.
James set about his task with a will.　The Council also wrote
to the Militia Commissioners for the County :—

"Hearing how much it would conduce to the advantage of the service if
"the horse and dragoons in your County, raised on the Act for the militia,
"were under the command of John James, we have issued a commission for
"that purpose and sent it to him, and desire you to use all diligence in
"raising the forces.

In May, the Militia Commissioners for the County wrote to
the Council of State as to impressing men for Ireland.　This
was referred to the Irish Committee, and this Committee was
instructed to prepare letters to the Commissioners for Worcestershire, the City of Worcester to send their proportion.
Worcestershire had always been a recruiting ground for
Ireland, and the fact that it was now so used would seem to
point to the inference that the immediate danger, whatever it
was, that had so alarmed the Government about the County
had passed away.　None of their precautions were, however,
relaxed.　On the 19th May there is an order relating to the
well-known Royalist, Colonel Samuel Sandys :—

"Whereas Colonel Samuel Sandys was, by order of the Council, not to de-
"part out of the limits of Oxfordshire without special licence, and was not to
"go into Worcestershire.　The Council thereby intends that he shall not go
"out of Oxfordshire without special occasion to be made known and approved
"of by four Justices of the Peace of that County, and that then he may not
"go into Worcestershire."

Major Savage, of Worcestershire, probably the Savage of
Elmley Castle, who had gone to live at Malvern and who had
been so hardly used, and for whom Massey had interceded,
was discharged on entering into a recognizance for £500, with
two sureties of £250 each, on the usual terms.

Colonel Dineley, one of the Commissioners, was able to
work that body for his own affairs.　In June the Militia Commissioners were instructed by the Council of State

"That there being money due to Colonel Dingley, as he alleged, for services
"in that County, they were to examine into that business and certify the
"state thereof to the Council, and also what money was remaining in that
"County that was raised under the late Militia Act, whereupon further direc-
"tions could be given."

Taken by themselves these incidents are of slight importance, but taken together they give some idea of the condition
of the County.

The plots of the Worcestershire Royalists had caused the
County to be thoroughly distrusted, as was shown by
raising soldiers to keep it quiet.　It will be remembered that

the soldiers had to be paid, and the money to pay them was raised in the County, often out of the estates of the Royalists. It is also clear that the Government, most likely wisely, were determined to keep the County free from Royalist leaders, so that there should be no rising, as, however much the Royalists might desire to aid the King, without leaders they were powerless. This is shown in the refusal to allow Sandys to enter the County. While hard on the leaders the Government did not, if they kept quiet, press hardly on the ordinary gentleman, the rank and file of the Royalist party, such as Savage, of Elmley Castle, as is shown by allowing him out on bail. While those who, like Colonel Dineley, loyally supported the Government, had their reward, even what they alleged they had expended was repaid them to the last farthing, possibly out of delinquents' estates. It was therefore an object lesson for the County how much better it was for all alike to support the Government, and the lesson was learnt..

There is one point of some importance that is not at all clear. Had the Government any reason to believe that in the coming invasion of England, which they knew must take place sooner or later, there was a probability of the County being the scene of any of the fighting, and so special precautions were taken? Or were the precautions that doubtless were taken to keep the County quiet merely the result of the labours of the Government spies? That there were "many malignants" in the County, and it was desired to keep it from rising, if possible is clear. From the evidence that exists the latter seems the true opinion, otherwise it is difficult to see why nothing was done to repair the walls of Worcester, and why some troops were not posted there. This is confirmed by the letters of the exiled Royalists, who do not in their correspondence even hint that it was part of the original plan of the Scots that on the invasion of England they should march into the County. The question is one of much interest, and has not as yet received the notice it deserves.* But in estimating the action of the Worcestershire Royalists and their conduct towards the Scots, all these facts should be borne in mind if a just judgment is to be formed on the question

In the spring and summer of 1651 Cromwell, by a series of manœuvres and skirmishes, was gradually pressing the Scotch army northwards. Leslie had, however, taken up a very strong position round Stirling, and from this Cromwell was unable to dislodge him. Finding that a frontal attack was hopeless Cromwell is said to have formed the plan that by taking his army across the Forth and getting between Leslie

---

* See Ludlow, p. 139.

and the Highlands he would compel him to evacuate his position at Stirling, and retreat either westward or northward, or otherwise be cut off from his base and unable to obtain supplies. This is the usually accepted idea, and it is mentioned as a great instance of Cromwell's strategy.

There is, however, another and a more probable explanation. The English Government were then fully persuaded that sooner or later they would have to meet an invasion by Charles and the Scots, they were now ready to do so. They would never again be in a better position. The majority of the leading English Royalists were either exiles or prisoners. However inclined the English might be to rise, a rising was then if not impossible yet reduced to its smallest possible dimensions. If the Scots were given the chance to invade England, would they not take it? Then the question could be decided once and for all. As long as Cromwell remained south of Stirling invasion of England was impossible. If he crossed the Forth Leslie would have an opportunity of marching to his doom.

This view is borne out by the fact that Cromwell sent for Harrison, who was commanding in Northumberland, and on the 23rd July they had a conference at Linlithgow. The result was that Harrison was ordered to bring up Colonel Rich's horse from Nottinghamshire to unite with his own in Northumberland and Cumberland,

" so that Harrison would be in a capacity to engage, or impede the march of " the Scots if they attempt that way."[*]

Cromwell's plan was, therefore, to leave the way to England open for the Scots if they chose to take it, and if so by marching after them with his own force, place them between Harrison and himself, and so surround or destroy them when they had got far enough into England.

On the 24th July Cromwell crossed the Forth, marched on through Fife, and took Perth. A week later, on August 1st, he heard that Leslie had fallen into the trap set for him and marched south. Leaving Monk with a small force to hold Perth, Cromwell started southwards in pursuit of Leslie. He sent Lambert in advance with 3000 men to hang on the Scots' rear, instructing him to impede and harass the enemy as much as possible. He ordered Harrison to concentrate his force, march down the east coast until he could strike across to the west, and get between the Scots and London. Harrison rose to the occasion. Writing to the Yorkshire Committee, he said :—

"The enemy's hope is that Englishmen will be so mad as to join them."

---

* *Army Intelligencer*, cited by Gardiner, II., 291.

If there had ever been any grounds for such hope it had been frustrated by the action of the Government, in the spring and early summer, in imprisoning all those who were likely to be the leaders in a Royalist rising.

On the 31st July, that part of the Scotch army that had agreed to follow Charles marched from Stirling to the south. It was by no means the whole strength of the Scots, as some were unwilling to undertake the English march. Argyle and Loudoun declined to come, Leven and Lord Crawford were left behind to enlist recruits, and, if it were possible, to rouse the north. With these defections, the Scots' army could not have exceeded 12,000 men. They had with them 16 leather guns. Lauderdale and Hamilton marched south, but Hamilton was most doubtful as to the result. Writing in an almost prophetic tone, he said :—

"I cannot tell whether our hopes or fears are greatest, but we have one "stout argument, despair."

On the 9th August the first English town (Carlisle) was reached and occupied, and then Penrith. Acting on his orders, Lambert followed up closely and cut off many straggling Scots on the march through Cumberland and Lancashire. Very few recruits were received, such as came in were badly armed, Charles had neither arms or money wherewith to buy them to give the recruits. The Royalist leaders who might have raised some substantial number of recruits were in prison. In the absence of leaders there was nothing to remove the natural aversion felt against the Scots. Harrison carried out his orders. Having got far enough south he struck across the country to the west, and was now able to attack the Scots in front while Lambert attacked their rear. Hearing that Cromwell was pushing on, Lambert marched by the Scots' flank, joined his forces with Harrison's, and the two now considered themselves strong enough to make a stand to check the advance.

Parliament, meanwhile, was making every preparation in its power to receive the Scots. Coventry was fixed on as the place where the forces were to rendezvous and assemble, and it was hoped to collect a considerable number there.

On the 15th August the Council of State wrote to Militia Commissioners for Worcestershire :—

"We have been informed by Mr. Lechmere, one of your number, of the "good posture of that County in this conjuncture, and of your great diligence "to provide for the common safety and your own. Many other places have "also shewn good forwardness. Had all done so it would have been a great "discouragement to further attempts when the enemy saw all men so unani-"mously resolved against them. We approve of what you have done in "pursuance of our former instructions, and doubt not you have received our "directions since sent. We shall not need anything further to excite you to "put them into execution. We hope that the business will have a speedy

" end, and that God will settle peace on this Commonwealth, but desire you,
" nevertheless, to use your utmost care and diligence meantime in the execu-
" tion of your trust."

The united forces of Harrison and Lambert, reinforced by
some 3000 militia from Staffordshire and Cheshire, amounting
in the whole to some 3000 foot and 9000 horse, on the 13th of
August took up a position at the bridge at Warrington, over
the Mersey, where it divides the Counties of Lancashire and
Cheshire, and prepared to resist its passage by the Scots. On
reaching the bridge the Scots at once attacked, and a sharp
fight ensued between their advance guard and Harrison's
army. When Lambert found the Scots were in considerable
force he fell back; his retreat being quickened by pressure
from the Scots' attack. Lambert, thus rapidly retiring,
enabled the Scots to say with truth that they had forced the
bridge, notwithstanding the resistance of the combined forces
of Harrison and Lambert. This fight at Warrington was the
first and only success the Scots achieved. Having carried the
bridge the Scots were unable to settle what course to take.
The boldest, a dash on London, would probably have been the
best. In the East of England the Scots had never been
quartered. Nothing was known against them, the country
had not been their feeding ground like Worcestershire and
Herefordshire. Whitelock*says that

" after passing Warrington the Scots began to plunder extremely, and many
" of them were weak."

It was hopeless to expect that in the Counties where the
Scots had been quartered, and where their plundering habits
were well known, any great enthusiasm would be felt for them.
Charles was in dire need of supplies and recruits. A more
effectual way of not getting them could hardly have been
devised than to march to the very Counties which the
Scotch army, a few years before, had pillaged so effectually.
This was, however, the course decided upon. It was not done
without some difference of opinion; Hamilton urged Charles
to march at once on London. But his views were overborne
by those who expected reinforcements would come in,
especially from Wales, and who urged that they should make
for some place where they could be joined by those reinforcements. This idea, a somewhat similar one to that which had
proved so successful to Charles I. in 1643, led the Scots to
make Worcester the point on which to march, especially as
they were told that there they would receive very substantial
reinforcements. So Worcester was fixed upon.

On the 17th August the Scots were joined by the Earl of
Derby with a small reinforcement of some 250 foot and 60

horse—a very disappointing number to those who had expected the full force of Lancashire to rise for the King. Charles was most eager to collect more, and it is quite possible that if he could have stayed for a short time in the County more men would have come in ; but it was no part of Cromwell's plan to give the Scots time to collect recruits. He had sent Colonel Lilburne to Lancashire to prevent any recruiting by the Scots, so nothing remained but to press forward.

From Warrington the Scots marched to Nantwich, from Nantwich to Whitchurch. On the march from Whitchurch to Newport they passed within a short distance of Shrewsbury. A party was sent to summon it to surrender. Macworth (the governor) refused. From Newport the Scots marched to Lichfield, thence to Wolverhampton. From there, through Kidderminster, Hartlebury, Ombersley, to Worcester, where they arrived on August 22nd.

On the 21st August the Council of State wrote to the Militia Commissions of Dorset, Devon, and Cornwall, inform-ing them that the Scotch army, by making great marches, had come as far as Worcester, and requiring them to bring forth their forces to the rendezvous.

On the 22nd the Council wrote to Cromwell that the Scotch army were bending its course to Worcester, and urging alacrity; and on the same day they wrote to the Lord Chief Baron Wylde and the Militia Commissioners for Worcester-shire :—

" We have received yours of the 20th, and think that you should detain " your own forces, notwithstanding the former appointment made when the " enemy was conceived to be bending his course this way. We have recom-" mended Major-General Lambert, who has a good body of horse and foot " near Coventry, to have a special eye to the enemy's motions and to the " safety of your city, and hope that by such as shall be appointed to retard " the enemy's march, and the army which is designed to pursue and fight " them there will be a seasonable prevention of any intention against you or " other places. We approve your endeavours in your own defence, but not " being upon the place must leave it to you to discern what is fittest to be " done in order to your safety, and to make such preparations as you shall " judge requisite."

Charles' friends abroad were greatly pleased with the course of events in England. John Lord Byron, writing to Ormonde from Paris, 9th September, 1651, says :—

" I doubt not but your excellency knows of the King's happy progress in " England by several hands and ways, and to give us the better ground to " believe it there are letters come to the Duke of York out of Holland, which " were brought hither by an express from Scotland, which assured us that the " King marched into England, not only with a flying body of horse, as we " first heard, but with his whole army, consisting of 15,000 foot, 6000 horse, " with a good train of artillery, of which a particular list was sent his High-" ness. His Majesty's army is much increased since his coming into England, " and at Warrington Bridge he forced his passage with so great a slaughter of

" the army that opposed him, under the command of Harrison and Lambert,
" that, by their own confession, they were forced to run as far as Uttoxeter, in
" Staffordshire, leaving the King a fair and uninterrupted march to London,
"from whence, in all probability, he cannot now be far distant."*

Another letter, dated Paris, of the 12th September, from
Henry Bennett to the Duke of Ormonde, says :—

" Though there be in all likelihood grave pains taken to keep us from the
" knowledge of good news in England, yet from these very pains we find the
" King's affairs are in a good condition, however, having beaten out the
" rebels garrison to receive his; if His Majesty prospers proportionately to
" what he has done this last six weeks, this crown will certainly need a con-
" junction with him, much more than he does now with them."†

On the 4th September Ormonde wrote from Caen to Sir E.
Nicholas :

" We have nothing out of England but from the rebels or from very pas-
" sionate friends.   The first, I think, begin to find it necessary to resume the
" foundation of their state, lying, and the latter I doubt not give us good wishes
" for good events.   I could not hold pace with them in the belief that brought
" the King near London, but am content to compound between them and the
" rebels, placing him in Worcester and upon the Marches of Wales, en-
" deavouring to seat himself so as to receive assistance, and to be out of
" danger of fighting at the will of his enemy, which if he compass we may
" hope for such natural advances as God usually gives to so great a work as
" that I trust he is doing for our King and us.   If the print say true of the
" rebels' advance towards the King, you will hear of action before this comes
" to your hands.   Sir, though battles are I think to be avoided, round en-
" counters cannot without quitting the cause.   God prosper him."‡

These letters shew how little the Royalist party knew
the real state of things.   How the King wanted more arms,
ammunition, in fact everything that troops require, and that
the badly equipped force, inferior in numbers and in everything else, was about to be pitted against the finest infantry of
that day, men who boasted their backs had never been seen by
their foes.

On Friday, August 22nd, the Scots arrived at Worcester on
the north side the city.   Lambert had garrisoned the place
with a small body of 500 horse, but they, feeling they were
outnumbered and that it was useless to resist, retired to
Gloucester without a fight.   Whitelock,§ however, says:—

" the country forces made a gallant resistance and beat back the enemy several
" times.   But the townsmen, having laid down their arms, and some shooting at
" the Parliament soldiers out of the windows, they removed their ammuni-
" tion while 30 men only resisted the enemy, and then, having actually beaten
" them back, withdrew, leaving the town to the enemy and came to Gloucester."

The garrison being withdrawn, on Saturday, the 23rd
August, Charles entered Worcester.   He was met by the
Mayor, Thomas Lysons, and the Sheriff, James Brydges.   The
Mayor rode before the King to the Guild Hall, carrying the
city sword.   Charles was there proclaimed as King of Great

---

* Hist. MSS. Com., Marquis of Ormonde's Papers, N.S. I., 200.
† Ib., p. 204.   ‡ Ib., p. 206.   § p. 477.

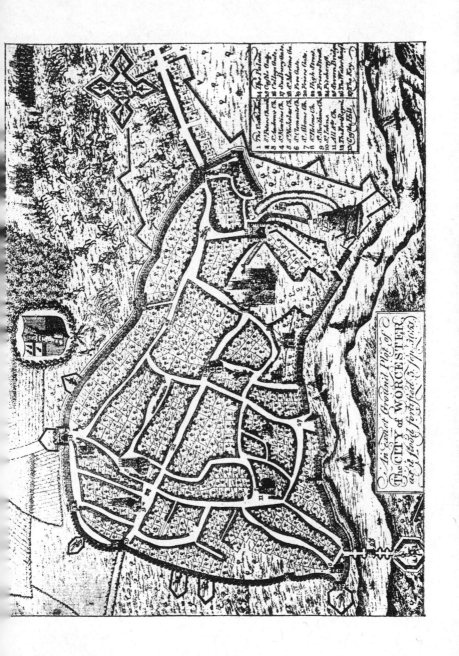

An Exact Ground Plot of
The CITY of WORCESTER
as it stood fortified 3. Sep. 1651

Britain, France, and Ireland, by Anthony Jackson, with loud acclamations. The Mayor, on his knees, tendered to the King the keys of the city and the city mace, which were returned to him, the Mayor adding a proper welcome to the King on his arrival in his " ancient and loyal city." On this the King knighted the Mayor. So far as the city officials could do anything they did all in their power for the King. But the Scots were greatly depressed by the fact that there was great lack of support, both in supplies and recruits. Their state was pitiable. They had marched 300 miles in three weeks and were worn out. Shoes and stockings were provided for them. Tired with their march, they demanded a halt, and Charles was in no condition to refuse. Yet to halt was a serious step, as it was doubtful if the advance was not made at once if it could ever be made at all. On Sunday, the 24th, the King attended the service at the Cathedral, the preacher, Mr. Crosby, a strong Cavalier, used the bidding prayer, that the King was,

" in this his realm, and in all other places his Dominions and Countries, over
" all persons, and in all causes, ecclesiastical as well as civil, supreme,"

and held forth in glowing terms on the Royal supremacy— quite inconsistent with the ideas of " a Covenanted King." The Scots were offended, and the preacher had to be admonished.

On the same day the Council of State wrote to Sir William Constable, the Governor of Gloucester. After acknowledging the receipt of his letter giving them notice of the King having entered Worcester, the letter continues :

" The few well-affected there are likely to suffer by it. As for those who
" were so ready to invite and receive such guests, they will find enough of
" them by the time they have done with them and that the State has reckoned
" with them for it."

The Council of State also wrote the same day to Colonel Pyne and the Somerset Commissioners, complaining that

" through the treachery of the townsmen the Scots are possessed of Worcester,
" and bend their course westward, and urging the committee to unite their
" forces to pursue the enemy."

The words as to the direction of the Scots' march were obviously inserted to incite the Somerset people to activity, lest the Scots should visit them.

Having taken the city it was necessary to hold it, and for that purpose to repair the fortifications and throw up new ones. On the 24th August (Sunday) orders were issued to the constables of the different parishes round Worcester to send in men on the Monday morning to begin this work. The order as to Salwarpe, one of the parishes, ran thus :

" Charles R.
" You are hereby required to send out of your parish 30 able men to work
" at the fortifications of this city, and in regard of the necessity to begin

"to-morrow morning (Monday), at five o'clock, whereof you and they are not
"to fail, as you tender our displeasure.
    "Given at our Court at Worcester, the 24th August, 1651.
    "To the Constables and tything men of Salwarpe.
"And you are to bring with you spades, shovels, and pick axes."*

The Court at Worcester was probably held in the house in the old Corn Market, still standing, where the King lodged. The Duke of Hamilton and some of the Scotch lords were quartered on the Wyldes, at the Commandery,† this branch of the family being Royalists, as opposed to those of Kempsey and Droitwich, to which the Lord Chief Baron belonged, but little is known where the other officers were quartered.

The determination to fortify Worcester shews that the Scotch had resolved to fight the inevitable fight here. Steps were accordingly taken for that purpose. It is not quite clear when this intention was arrived at, but it could not have been later than the 24th August.

Charles issued another order, calling out the *posse comitatus* of the County, requiring all men between 16 and 60 to attend him on Pitchcroft on Tuesday, 26th August, to aid in the defence of the throne and the liberties of the country.

On the Monday parties were sent out to seize and break down the bridges over the Severn at Bewdley and Upton, and over the Teme at Powick and Bransford. At least, this is so stated in Nicholas Lechmere's diary. He says:

"The King, with a numerous army, most Scots, some English, by long
"uninterrupted marches from Stirling, in Scotland, to Worcester, suddenly
"possessed himself of the City of Worcester, and in a few days fortified it
"beyond imagination. At the same time the Scots possessed themselves and
"break down Upton, Bewdley, Powick, and Bransford bridges."

Two things must have caused the King much anxiety. His generals were quarrelling with each other, especially Leslie and Middleton. The Royal force was already far too small for what it had to do, and the generals practically declining to co-operate made matters worse. This quarrel had serious results. If Leslie had loyally supported Middleton on the 3rd September, at Wick, the result of the battle might have been different; had Leslie supported the Duke of Hamilton in his attack on the Parliament centre, Worcester would have been a Royalist victory; as it was Leslie's horse took no part in the fight. The other was quite as disappointing. The King had been expecting the Earl of Derby to bring him strong reinforcements. Derby had remained behind to collect them. He had actually raised 1500 men, and expected to be joined at Wigan by another 500. Instead of this he was met

---

* Noake, Worcester in Olden Times, p. 157.
† The Commandery, now Mr. Littlebury's, is the best remaining relic of the battle. It has been much altered, but the broad outline of this house, the only remaining one that stood outside the city walls, but inside the Scotch lines, and which was the receptacle for the troops and the wounded, are very clear.

there by Lilburne with a strong force, completely defeated, his men routed, scattered, 400 of them made prisoners, and he himself, wounded and deserted, escaped with difficulty to join the King at Worcester and carry the news of his utter discomfiture. This source of supply, therefore, failed the King. It did more, it discouraged all the Royalist gentry from coming in. They saw that the end was certain, and it was useless to ruin themselves by joining a predestined failure.

Charles went on with his preparations. On the 25th August Massey was sent to take possession of the bridge at Upton. Lechmere, who lived near, at Hanley, thus states the fact :

> "Massie, Major-General to the King, with about 130 Scottish horse, "quartered in my house at Hanley. He treated my people civilly, but "threatened extirpation to me and my posterity for having joined the "Parliament."

On Tuesday, 26th, the King attended on Pitchcroft to meet his loyal subjects of Worcestershire, but very few obeyed the Royal summons. It is said that Lord Talbot, Sir John Pakington, Sir Walter Blount, Sir Ralph Clare, Sir Rowland Berkeley, and Sir John Winford were among those who attended, but this is most doubtful. It can be proved almost conclusively, that if Sir Rowland Berkeley spoke the truth he was not there, and the accuracy of the list is therefore very questionable. It is even less likely that men like Lord Talbot, who had given their parole after the surrender of Worcester not to serve against the Parliament, would deliberately break it, especially having regard to the fact that with so hopeless, obviously hopeless, a prospect before them a breach of parole would be the height of absurdity. The list has all the appearance of being manufactured after the Restoration, when everyone was desirous of saying what they had done for the King. Even if the list is correct, it must have been most disappointing to the Scots, for the total force that came in was not more than 2000 at the outside, ill-armed, and without any enthusiasm.

A Royal manifesto was issued after the fiasco of August 26th, urging that men should come in and support the King. It produced little if any result. A further proclamation was issued, offering to settle religion according to the Covenant, to satisfy the arrears of pay of all the soldiers who would come over to the King from Cromwell's army, to assent to an Act of Oblivion to all who would join the King, and solemnly promising that as soon as he had defeated the rebels, the Scots should return to their own country—obviously to allay the fears of Worcestershire and Herefordshire as to a renewal or Scottish plundering.

This manifesto produced practically no result. It became

obvious to Charles that, as against all the forces that the Parliament could bring against him, he would have to rely on the Scots, and on the Scots alone ; that the English would have nothing to do with them.

The Scots and the few reinforcements the King had received did not, all told, number over 16,000 ; a force wholly inadequate to defend the fortifications of Worcester, still less to engage an army in the field.   If the expedition had seemed doomed at first, that doom was now made certain.

Charles realised the utter hopelessness of his position. All ideas of assuming the offensive, of continuing his march, of leaving Worcester, had to be abandoned.   All that remained to be done was to wait to be attacked, and then to make the most stubborn defence that could possibly be made.   To do this orders were given to make some entrenchments on the Royalist right at Wick, in the fields and near the bridge at Powick.

Although to those who knew the facts the most gloomy view must have been taken, the exiles seemed to think that the King's prospects looked bright.   Byron, writing from Paris to Ormonde, on the 6th September, says :

" So that my hopes of any good to be done that way being so faint (*i.e.*, "foreign help), I comfort myself with the belief that God will do the great "work without any foreign assistance, having already made a progress in it "far beyond anything we could have hoped for, and by what the printed "papers tells us this week we may conclude that the King will either be past "help, or will need none, before any can come to him.   They speak of some "disaster befallen my Lord of Derby in Lancashire, which I am extreme "sorry for, but some private letters wish us not to believe the *Diurnals* this "week, and assure us that the King hath totally defeated Fleetwood at Upton "Bridge, near Worcester, who had a tertia of Cromwell's army with him, con- "sisting of 12,000 men."*

Meanwhile, further Parliament forces were collecting at Warwick.   Fleetwood and Desborough were there; men were coming in daily.   Fleetwood had written to Parliament :

" The Scotch had left a party in Worcester, and had transported their army "over Severn, intending to secure the passes, and invite their friends to them "and refresh all their wearied army.   That their army is 12,000 horse and "foot effective, and the foot so much harassed by often and frequent marches, "that they did importune the King to take pity on them, who answered that "they should suddenly have refreshment, gave them good words, and told "them what help he expected from his friends."

On the 24th August the Council of State ordered

" the Parliamentary forces in Essex, Norfolk, Suffolk, and Cambridge to "march to Oxford, and there attend orders from the Lord General, who was "supposed to be near Worcester."

On the 27th the Council of State wrote to all the militia authorities as to the false rumours circulated by the enemy,

" for the prevention of which, although we doubt not that a few days will put

---

* Hist. MSS. Rep., Ormonde Papers, N.S. I., 207.

" an end to that business, the enemy being yet in Worcester and not able to
" prosecute any design, and our army being now come to a conjunction, and
" able to divide and attack the enemy on both sides of the Severn, we recom-
" mend you to use special diligence against vendors of false news."

Cromwell had followed the east coast route on his march
from Scotland. Starting from Edinburgh, he marched by
Kelso, Newburn, Durham, Ferrybridge, Rotherham, Chester-
field, Burton, Tamworth to Coventry, thence to Warwick,
which he reached on the 24th August. He was met there
by Lambert, Harrison, Fleetwood, Desborough, and Lord
Grey, of Groby.

On the 26th August Cromwell marched to Stratford-on-
Avon and Fleetwood to Shipston-on-Stour. Reinforcements,
mainly militia, were constantly arriving, so that when, on the
27th Angust, Cromwell and Fleetwood united their forces at
Evesham, Cromwell found himself at the head of some 28,000
men. He was now in a position to carry out the pre-arranged
plan :—

(1) To place his army between the Scots and London.

(2) To cut off the King from Wales and the Welsh
Marches.

(3) To fall on the Scotch army with a greatly superior force,
surround it, and destroy it.

On reaching Evesham he had attained the first object. He
had now to carry out his second—cut the Scots off from
Wales, so as to prevent any help coming to them from there
or from the west. It is uncertain if Charles and his officers
had any idea of Cromwell's plan. Breaking down the Teme
bridges, at first sight, looks as if they had anticipated it, but
the fact that so small a force was sent to Upton makes this
very doubtful, for, if the Royalists had realised the idea,
Upton would certainly have been more strongly held than
by a force of only 300 men.

Charles was badly served in the matter of scouts. Possibly
the general despondency that was settling down on him and
on his army took away all reasonable care and caution. With
Massey, who knew every inch of the ground, as an adviser, it
is almost incredible that Charles should not have taken the
most ordinary precautions. The situation of nine years before
was repeated in almost exact detail. Again a Royalist force
held Worcester; a Parliament force was advancing against
it along the London road. Was Charles about to allow,
as Byron had been forced to allow, an enemy to appear
in force on the west bank of the Severn and turn his right
flank? Massey proposed to give a negative answer to the
question. He marched down the river with his men nearly to
Gloucester, hoping that on his coming his old friends would
join him. This, however, was not the case. He found that

his name no longer worked wonders. He crossed the river between Tewkesbury and Gloucester, met a party of women, who said there had been some fighting at Upton, and Massey had been wounded in the hand and legs and his horse killed under him.

The repairs and additions to the Worcester fortifications proceeded rapidly. Earthworks were thrown up outside the walls; some of the more important points, especially the city gates, were strengthened. The north, or Foregate, was blocked up, leaving St. Martin's Gate the only entrance from or exit to the north. An elaborate series of earthworks were constructed across the London road, covering the south side of the town, the one which Cromwell was about to attack. Inside the works, on a hill overlooking the town, a large, star-shaped fort was thrown up, called the Fort Royal. This was connected by an earthen rampart with the city walls, one end of which joined the wall at a spot near where the old City Gaol now stands at the Blockhouse, and the other, crossing the Bath Road and part of the site of the present porcelain works, ended at the river below the Castle mound. The fort and this rampart were the main defences, covering the Sidbury Gate and south side of the town. The works do not seem to have been fully finished ; certainly they were not fully armed. It is most doubtful, even if there had been time to complete them, whether the King could have found guns for them, and if he had, probably there was not sufficient ammunition to effectively work the guns. The new works were also subject to this defect : they were commanded by any battery that might be placed in Perry Wood or on Red Hill. But for this, they dominated the south-east of the city.

The Scots' army was divided into two parts. The largest was kept in the city to man the walls and defend the new fortifications. The other was sent across the Severn and placed on the tongue of land formed by the rivers Severn and Teme to secure the right flank of the Scots. Whether from want of supplies, or for some other reason, these men were badly cared for, and obliged to camp out, having only such shelter as they could throw up.

To further strengthen the defences, the bridge at Powick was broken down, two arches, the two next to the St. John's bank, being demolished. The bridge at Bransford, three miles higher up the river, was also broken down; here the arches destroyed were those on the side furthest from Worcester. To this day the arches have never been rebuilt.

Cromwell's force at Evesham was increasing daily. As he now out-numbered the Scots by nearly two to one, he was able to carry out the second part of his plan, to cut off the Scots from Wales and the west. As has been said, Cromwell reached Evesham on the 27th August. His first act was to occupy the west bank of the Severn. To do this, on the 28th August a strong division, both horse and foot, under the command of Lambert, was ordered to march from Evesham to Upton, drive Massey from there, take possession of the bridge and occupy the town.

Leaving Evesham, they marched the 13 miles, arriving at Upton in the evening they found the bridge broken down, but a plank had been left across the ruined arches by which it was possible that one or two bold and daring men might, with some danger and difficulty, effect a passage and surprise the Scots. Lambert resolved to try. Massey was quartered at Hanley, at Severn End, a house of the Lechmere s, about a mile away, on the Worcester Road; his men were billeted in the town. Some slight earthworks had been thrown up between the town and the brook on the Worcester Road, which formed a strong position to resist any advance made along the road.

Lambert saw that if the place was defended it would be impossible to carry it in its then state. There was just one chance : the Scots might keep a bad look-out, as no sentries were posted, possibly they had no idea any enemy was near. To cross the river was a service of difficulty and danger, but unless the river was crossed the plan laid down could not proceed. Lambert, therefore, determined to take the risk.

During the night he kept his men out of sight at Ryall, so as to raise no suspicion or alarm. At daybreak, selecting 18 picked men out of his force, he ordered them to cross the bridge, and, as soon as they had done so, to seek some shelter in Upton, so as to be able to hold the bridge head until they were reinforced.

On the 29th August, in the grey morning light, as dawn was breaking, the 18 started on their mission. Never were troops given a harder task than Lambert's men were now called upon to perform. In dim daylight to walk in single file over a long, narrow plank, high above a deep, rapid river, with the prospect each moment of being fired upon, was a task before which the bravest might quail. It is no disgrace to Lambert's men to say they did not like it; yet they did not shrink; they knew that at all hazards the river must be crossed, and that they had to cross it. When they got on to the plank, and began to march in single file, they could not stand the running water below them; their heads swam, and they were in danger of falling. So they sat down on the plank, straddling across it, scrambling along.

"They mounted it as though it was their wooden Pegasus, and so scrambled "across to the opposite side."

After some delay all reached the Upton bank in safety.

There some hot work awaited them. As they formed up the
Scots perceived and at once fiercely attacked them. Carrying
out their orders Lambert's men retreated, first into the
churchyard, then, finding that their numbers were too few to
enable them to defend it with success, into the church itself,
fastened the door, and fired through the windows on the
Scots. The attack was fierce. The Scots pushed on up
to the church, but, unable to effect an entrance, set fire
to the church, and shot at the survivors of the 18 through
the windows, trying to thrust them with their pikes, or
cut them down with their swords. The 18 held out
bravely, returned their assailants' fire, causing them some loss.
Massey, woke by the sound of the firing, at once set off to his
men and directed the attack on the church. The 18 were, to
all appearances, doomed. Over the bridge, with the Scots now
on the alert, no passage was possible. Under the fire that
would be poured on it no one would live to walk the plank.
Lambert was loth to leave his men without an effort to save
them. The river was low, the tide was out. It was said to be
fordable, but that the ford was difficult and dangerous, but
possible. Lambert decided it should be risked. At the spot
below the bridge, known now as Fisher's Row, where the ford
was said to be, Lambert ordered his dragoons to enter the river,
get through at all risks, and relieve the men in the church.
The dragoons entered the river; floundering about, partly
fording, partly swimming, in some way they got through.
Forming up on the Upton bank, they charged on the rear of
the Scots, who were attacking the church. Surprised at this
unexpected and sudden charge, the Scots at first gave way, but,
recovering from their surprise, rallied, and in their turn charged
the dragoons, drove them back, killing several men, and many
horses. But Lambert, having found that it was possible to
ford the river, did not leave his men unsupported; he sent
more horse across, so the Scots rapidly became out-numbered.
Fighting fiercely, they were only driven away from the church
by Lambert's superior numbers; but they were driven back,
and such of the 18 as remained were rescued.

Not satisfied with the rescue, Lambert resolved to complete
his work. The Scots retired into their entrenchments; they
were to be driven out. Lambert ordered the entrenchments to be stormed. Again the fight was sharp. The Scots,
now on the defensive, fought well, and had the fight been on
anything like equal terms Lambert would have failed to carry
the works; but to the Scots no reinforcements could come,
while the assailants were constantly increasing in number.
Planks had been placed over the arches, the troops could
now pass easily over the bridge into Upton. Massey already
had had a horse shot under him, now fell sorely wounded.

Discouraged by the loss of their leader, the increasing number of the enemy, their continuous and sustained attacks, the 300 Scots at last gave way. Lambert's men carried the earthworks, the Scots, abandoning camp, baggage, and wounded, made off as fast as possible along the Worcester Road.

It is said that the rout was so complete that each horseman took up a footman behind him so that they might make off with greater rapidity. But this can hardly be true. Not only were very few prisoners taken by Lambert's horse, but Massey got back safely to Worcester. He was so badly wounded in his head and thigh that he could not sit on his horse without support, and could not suffer his horse go out of a walk.

Lechmere, in his diary, thus records the affair. August 28th :—

" The Parliament army, under the command of the Lord General, advanced " before Worcester, and at the same time Major-General Lambert gained " Upton Bridge from the Scots, in which enterprise Massey was wounded and " some few of the enemy slain."

The Upton fight had been sharp while it lasted. Lambert deserved his success by the bold way he executed his orders and the tenacious grip by which he held on to Upton when once he got a foothold there. In all the Worcestershire fighting in the Civil War no braver act is recorded than that of the 18 who crossed the bridge, held the burning church against 300 Scots, and enabled Lambert to win his victory.

But neither its severity, nor its duration, nor the bravery of Lambert's troops, mark the real importance of the Upton fight. It enabled the turning movement, cutting off the Scots from Wales and the west, to be carried out. It was also the first step towards driving in and crushing the right wing of the Scots, enabling the encircling movement to be begun, and the elaborate defences which the Scots had taken such pains to construct to be turned.

How important Cromwell regarded it is shewn by the fact that later in the day he came himself to Upton to thank Lambert's men for their courageous behaviour, and to see the best use was made of their triumph. As he passed, says Whitelock,*

"from one guard or regiment to another, he was received with abundance of "joy and extraordinary shouting."

Cromwell ordered the bridge at once to be repaired and made passable for troops. Cromwell, the same day, sent his second in command (General Fleetwood) to take the command at Upton, ordering him at once to march there with a large force of troops, the whole of Lambert's and Dean's brigades.

---

* p. 481.

In pursuance of these orders in the course of the next day a Parliamentary force some 12,000 strong was encamped on the west bank of the Severn. Its outposts were pushed forward to the Old Hills and nearly to Powick. Its vedettes were sent up the Teme valley to cut off all attempts the Scots might make to communicate with Wales or the west.

The defeat at Upton and the disablement of Massey was a great discouragement to the Scots. They perceived that the net was closing round them, and that hope was practically gone. Massey is reputed to have said, after Upton, that "he wished Charles was safe in a foreign land."

The main body of the Scots were now drawn in to the right bank of the Teme; a detached picket holding Powick. News was continually being received of the arrival of more troops to reinforce Cromwell, who, consequent on this, was constantly occupying fresh points, to the prejudice of the King. Cromwell was joined by the militia from Essex and Suffolk, some 3000 strong; even Worcestershire men, who had refused to rise for the Scots, were now rising for the Parliament.

Cromwell had thus carried out the second part of the plan : the Scots were cut off from Wales, their right flank could be turned. He had now to begin the third and most difficult part, to enclose the Scotch army, efface it, or destroy it. To do this certain preparations were necessary. These Cromwell now proceeded to make.

It is a matter of interest, if it could be ascertained, to know who was the real author of the plan of the Worcester operations. It is always assumed to have been Cromwell, but this is doubtful, for it must have been prepared in London and the instructions to carry it out sent down to Cromwell, as it is clear that the broad lines of the plan had been all arranged before Cromwell arrived at Evesham. On August 27th, the day Cromwell reached that place, the Council of State wrote to all the militia authorities a letter as to dealing with purveyors of false news, in which this passage occurs :—

"Our army being now come to a conjunction, and able to divide and attack "the enemy on both sides of the Severn."

This was before Lambert had attacked Upton, and must have been written before Cromwell had arrived in the County, so the idea of sending a force across the river was apparently settled before Cromwell's appearance.

The Council of State wrote to General Blake:—

"The Scots' army is in or about Worcester, most of them in the town every "night. The Lord General is before the town east of the Severn, and "Fleetwood west. There is a bridge of boats preparing above the confluence "of the Teme and Severn. When ready this will be a line of communication "between the two armies, and we shall speedily force them to fight, or starve, "or run if they can break through ; the latter will be most likely. There are

"forces in all the passes if they slip away before we have fully invested the
"town. The Counties have risen readily against them, and few come to them,
"and those generally the scum of the people. They are in great want,
"especially of ammunition. We expect a speedy end, but you shall know all
"that happens."

This shews that the plan of the Parliament was to drive the
Scots from the west of the Severn into Worcester. Unite the
two wings of the Parliament force, as had been done in the
former siege by a bridge of boats, Cromwell extending his right
from Elbury Hill to Barbourne and Pitchcroft, Fleetwood
occupying Henwick and joining Cromwell's force on Pitchcroft,
while the bridge of boats over the Severn, near Teme's mouth,
would unite Lambert and Cromwell, and so complete the
investment. If this could have been carried out the city
would have been completely surrounded, and, as the letter
says, the Scots must have starved or broken through. This
seems to have been the original plan, but the battle, as it
developed, made material alterations in it; in fact, its result
was not part of the plan laid down, but the consequence
of Cromwell taking advantage of his opportunities. This is
further borne out by another letter from the Council of
State to Monk, dated 2nd September, the day before the
battle :—

" The Scottish King's army with their King is now in Worcester, the Lord
" General with his army on this side of the river, and Lieut.-General Fleetwood
" with another army on the other side of the river, ready to march from Upton
" (which bridge we have) towards the enemy. The Counties in general have
" come in with very great cheerfulness and alacrity, and in great numbers, so
" that the affairs of the Commonwealth here are in good condition, both as to
" the number of men and as to their readiness and affection to the work in
" hand, and we hope to have a very good issue of it speedily."

The same day the Council of State wrote to the Militia
Commissioners in Yorkshire :—

" The main work we have now in hand is to destroy their army about
" Worcester, which our army waits to do. A few days will put them to a
" necessity either to fight or fly, and the latter is most likely. The army will
" use all possible care to prevent it, and therefore have ordered forces with the
" greatest advantage they can ; yet because none know which way the Scots
" will take when they have entered upon that course, there will be need of
" many forces in several places."

From these letters and instructions it seems fairly clear that
the " general idea" was to surround Worcester, shut in the
Scots and starve them out, while such stragglers as escaped
would be intercepted and dealt with.

On the 29th August the Council of State wrote to the Lord
General, desiring him

" to send a commission of martial law into Scotland for the trial of such as
" had assisted Charles Stewart, some of whom were then in restraint, and in
" case the City of Worcester, or any of its inhabitants who had been instru-
" mental in betraying of it to Charles Stewart, fall into your hands, you
" should proceed with their trial according to law."

On the same day one James Waynwright wrote to his friend in Hamburgh :—

"The King has got to Worcester with his army, some say very strong. He "hath fortified Worcester, and entrenched at Upton, within eight miles. "There, some say, he will choose whether he will fight. The Lord General "is about Worcester, I think about 30,000 horse and foot. Some say the "King has 20,000, or above. It may prove a winter war. As they do lie, we "shall be put soon at it. The next week will scarce tell us anything, being "all our old soldiers are weary except our fresh men, which is not to be con- "fided in."

Mr. Waynwright had not the gift of prophecy. While he was writing Lambert was taking Upton, and so far from the Scots having the chance of selecting the battlefield, it was already settled for them. So far from a winter war, in a week it was all over.

Having established himself in force on the west bank of the Severn, Fleetwood was ordered to send vedettes up the Teme valley to cut off any reinforcements or supplies that might possibly be coming to Worcester from Wales. It is said that

"a party of Scots had moved up into Herefordshire, pulled down two bridges "of the Teme, but being flanked by a party of Lieut.-General Fleetwood's, "supposing they intended to march away, they retreated."*

Lambert was ordered to search the river as far down as Gloucester for boats, and bring up to Teme's mouth all he could find.

Having made these preparations, Cromwell left Evesham on the 28th August. It is not quite certain where he passed that night. Some of his troops were quartered at Pershore, but Cromwell kept the upper road, through Pinvin, and did not cross the Avon. While for the sake of the subsequent rewards and honour of having sheltered the King, innumerable persons claimed that Charles slept in their houses before the battle of Worcester, none cared to say they had sheltered the arch traitor. Thus the names of the houses that had the honour of sheltering Cromwell are not recorded. There is a local legend that he slept the night of August 28th in the Old Manor House at Moor, a village on the way from Evesham to Worcester. It has this in its favour, it is on Cromwell's direct line of march, and he must have stayed somewhere in the neighbourhood. On the next night he slept at Mr. Symonds', at White Ladies Aston, a house between Moor and Worcester. Symonds was, and had always been, a strong Parliamentarian, and his house was on the line of march.

On the 30th Cromwell came to Spetchley, the house of Mr. Justice Berkeley, three miles from Worcester, where he is said to have established himself during the subsequent operations.

* Whitelock, 482.

Other accounts say that Mr. Berkeley burnt the house down sooner than it should be defiled by sheltering a regicide.

Wherever he slept, Cromwell at once set to work to complete his preparations. He did nothing on the right of his position, obviously waiting till he had driven in the Royalists. His furthest outpost on this side was Elbury Hill, and from thence his line extended to the Severn at Bund's Hill, near the Ketch, opposite the confluence of the Teme and the Severn. This was his extreme left on the east of the river, a distance from Elbury Hill of about $2\frac{1}{2}$ miles. When Cromwell arrived the Parliament troops were chiefly placed at Red Hill and Perry Wood, but his first step was to extend his line to the left by Battenhall to Bund's Hill. Here he was only separated by the Severn from Fleetwood's advanced posts near Powick. Cromwell's great object was to establish some means of communication with Fleetwood. For this purpose he waited anxiously for the boats Lambert had been sent to collect. As soon as they arrived Cromwell began to make a bridge over the Severn at a point just above Teme's mouth, and to connect up with Fleetwood he made a second bridge across the Teme, about 50 yards up that river.

Nothing could shew the depression of the Scots better than the fact that, so far as appears, they allowed these bridges to be constructed, which they must have known to be so important, without making an effort to oppose or obstruct their construction, unless the sortie on the night of 31st August was in part directed against the Bund's Hill works. To distract the attention of the Scots while he was constructing his bridges Cromwell ordered his guns on Red Hill and in Perry Wood to keep up a desultory fire on the town and works. The new Fort Royal replied so briskly that the Parliament gunners observed that " the Scots acted as if they feared never to want powder or bullets."

The Scots were a good deal harassed by this fire, so at a council of war it was decided, if possible, to put an end to it by a sortie on the guns. This night attack was to consist of two columns. One, the chief and strongest body, was to attack the position on Red Hill, the other was to attack a post held by about 200 of the Parliamentary musketeers. The locality of this post is not stated, but it seems to have been somewhere between Red Hill and the Ketch, as the slain were found on the Kempsey road, and was, possibly, the post placed on Bund's Hill, above the Severn bridge of boats, to protect its construction, so if carried would have enabled the Scots to have destroyed this bridge without difficulty; but as to this there is no definite information as to where the fort was situated.

The night was dark, and the Scots hoped to effect a

surprise. That they might know their own men in the darkness they agreed that they should wear their shirts over their
breast and back pieces. The whole business seems to have
been skilfully arranged, and it deserved to succeed, but there
was in the loyal city one Guise, who combined the vocations of
tailor and spy. He, hearing of the intended sortie, took a full
report to the Parliamentarians, with the result that they were
on the alert. So, on the sortie being made, instead of the
Scots surprising the Parliamentarians they were themselves
surprised by the vigour of the resistance. The Scots who
reached the outpost were unable to do anything but retreat.
They were repulsed with some loss, 11 dead bodies being
found in the Kempsey Road next day. Nor did the sortie
that was made on Red Hill fare any better. Led by one Major
Knox, they came up fearlessly to the attack. They were met
by Fairfax's regiment, and were rather staggered by finding
these men ready to receive them. Knox, however, urged
them on very boldly. In bringing them up to the charge
he had to get over a hedge. He leapt across it and landed
on a stand of pikes, " and so lost his life in a vapour." Seeing
their leader fallen the Scots gave way, and, though making a
gallant struggle, were driven back into their lines with considerable loss. The failure of the sortie was due to Guise's
treachery. He was at once arrested and hung.

This failure discouraged the Scots. No further sortie was
attempted.

Meanwhile, reinforcements kept coming in to swell
Cromwell's force. Some were very enthusiastic; some plainly
desired to be on the winning side. Of this last were the
Surrey Militia, commanded by Sir Richard Onslow, whose
grandson gives this account of Sir Richard's proceedings:—*

"It is true Sir Richard Onslow was again Colonel of the Surrey Regiment
"in the year 1651, and was ordered to join Cromwell at Worcester, but he
"had no good-will towards the service, and did not come up to the army till
"after the fight, which Cromwell imputed to his not being hearty in the cause,
"and said, in a passion, ' that he should be one time or another even with
"that fox of Surrey;' though Whitelock, in his ' Memorial,' says he marched
"hard to come up to the engagement. Yet, by a paper in his own hand-
"writing, among the Clarendon Papers, it appears he was put upon the
"service to try him and ruin him, and that he hovered about with his
"regiment until the battle was over, and that Cromwell said after, in the
"House of Commons, if he had come up before the fight it would have been
"uncertain which side he would have taken."

The passage in Whitelock† is :—

"The Regiment of Surrey, under Sir Richard Onslow, and the troops
"under Captain Walter St. John, marched hard to come up to the engage-
"ment."

Whatever the views of the reinforcements may have been

---

the continuous arrival, day by day, of more and more troops for the Parliament, served to rouse their confidence, while the Scots settled down to a dogged despondency.

After four days' hard work Cromwell's bridges were finished, ready for the passage of troops, so he was now in a position to begin the third part of his work: to drive across the Severn the right wing of the Scots into Worcester. Cromwell did not delay. On September 2nd the bridges were finished; he gave orders the same day that the attack should be made on the next, and made on the right of the Scots' position. No orders were given for any movement elsewhere.

To carry out these orders, Fleetwood ordered Lambert and Deane, whose divisions were on the west bank of the Severn, to occupy Powick, drive the Scots across the Teme. Deane was to carry the bridge at Powick, Lambert to cross by the bridge of boats at Teme's mouth, and then, pressing on the attack against the Scots, force them out of Wick, through St. John's, across the Severn into Worcester. To keep the Scots engaged while this movement was carried out, the guns on Red Hill and Perry Wood were to fire on the city, the lines, and the Fort Royal.

The Scots' right, which had to meet the attack of Fleetwood, was commanded by Montgomery. It consisted of Keith's brigade, who held Powick Bridge; Piscotty's Highlanders, who were stationed near Teme's mouth, opposite the bridge of boats over the Teme; with Dalziel's brigade in reserve placed in Wickfield, on the high ground overlooking the places where Keith and Piscotty were stationed, and on the spot where, in 1642, Rupert had defeated Fiennes.

On the east of the Severn the Duke of Hamilton was in command at the Fort Royal, where the main body of the Scots was placed. On the Castle Mound Lord Rothes had a strong detachment, while the whole of the Scotch horse, under Leslie, were drawn up on Pitchcroft, well out of the way of any fighting, but in a position where they could be sent to support either the right or the centre, as might be required.

Lambert and Dean began their march from Upton early in the morning of the 3rd to Powick. They were supported by Goff and Gibbons, but there were various delays; it was about noon when they reached Powick and came in touch with the Scotch outposts, who fell back from hedge to hedge. The first stand was made in the churchyard. Here a sharp fight took place, the Scotch endeavouring to hold it while the rest of their detachment made their way to the bridge. The church tower still shews the marks of the bullets fired by Dean's soldiers. Dean's superior force caused the Scotch to gradually retire from the churchyard towards the bridge upon Keith's brigade.

Having carried Powick, Dean proceeded to try to carry the bridge. Here the real struggle began. Keith had been ordered to hold the bridge to extremity, and he did so, successfully repulsing in turn the repeated attacks that Dean's men made against him; Dean was therefore not able to make any way.

Lambert was posted near Teme's mouth. Crossing the bridge of boats over the Teme, he attacked the Highlanders, who were drawn up in readiness to receive him. As Lambert's men came across the river the Highlanders drove them back. Lambert was no more successful than Dean; at neither point could the Parliament forces make any way.

On the firing beginning Charles and his staff had ascended the Cathedral tower to watch the movements of the troops. His officers soon saw what was the object of Cromwell's move against their right, and that it was of vital importance to prevent the right being crushed. Charles, therefore, rode off at speed to Powick to encourage the Scots in their defence. On arriving at Powick Bridge he urged Keith to hold it to the last, and received the assurance that he would do so.

For some unexplained reason Charles did not go down to Piscotty's Highlanders, on whom the stress of the fight had fallen and was to fall. They were the only part of the force he did not visit. Before returning to Worcester he went to Dalziel's men on the high ground in Wickfield and begged them to stand firm and fight to the end.

Lambert renewed his attacks on the Highlanders in greater and greater force, trying to drive them back on to Worcester, which, if he could do, Keith would be forced to retire, as he must either retreat or be cut off; and if Dean forced the bridge at Powick the same result would be brought about as to Piscotty. But although both attacks were made in force, and with desperate daring, they did not succeed; both Keith and Piscotty were able to hold their ground.

Things were becoming serious for Fleetwood. It had now all the appearance that the attack would fail, and that the right wing of the Scots could not be driven into Worcester, so all the plans to shut up the Scots would be useless. Cromwell perceived that the crisis of the fight had come. Without some help Fleetwood would have to retreat, and even with help the result was doubtful; for if Cromwell too seriously weakened his centre and right the Royalists might sally out and drive his men from Red Hill. But Cromwell's superiority in numbers was so great, and the crisis so serious, that he determined to risk everything and detached a large force to Fleetwood's help. To ensure the movement being properly carried out he led the men himself to attack Piscotty's flank, ordering Lambert to bring up more men and renew the attack on the Highlanders in front. Cromwell marched three brigades over the bridge of

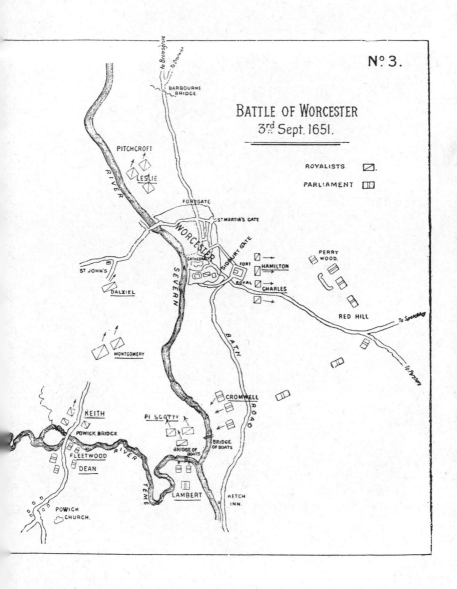

BATTLE OF WORCESTER
3rd Sept. 1651.

ROYALISTS
PARLIAMENT

boats across the Severn, formed them up on the west bank, ordered them to bring their right shoulder forward, and led them on to charge the left flank of the Highlanders, Lambert attacking in front. The Highlanders fought well, assaulted by an overpowering force in front, assailed by a fresh force on their flank, they stood firm until at last out-numbered and out-manœuvred, they began to give ground. Fleetwood and Cromwell pressed them harder and harder, still the Scots stood and fought, obeying their orders to fight to extremity. No reinforcements either from Dalziel or Leslie came to them, but fresh troops were continually advancing to help Lambert and Cromwell. The weight of numbers told at last. Fighting every inch, the Scots were gradually driven back; Montgomery fell, desperately wounded, there was no one to take his place. The retreat began to get disorderly as Lambert pressed the Scots harder and harder. It was soon to become a rout, as Cromwell had foreseen, Piscotty, being driven back towards Worcester, had isolated Keith's brigade. Dean's repeated attacks on it now had their reward. Keith was taken prisoner, his men, seeing or believing they were cut off and likely to be surrounded, gave way. Dean then carried Powick Bridge, drove the Scots back on to the remains of Piscotty's Highlanders and Dalziel's reserves. This increased the confusion. The joint pressure of Lambert and Dean converted the retreat from being disorderly into a rout, which Dalziel was unable to check. The Scots fled into St. John's in great disorder. Here Dalziel tried to rally them, but failed. With Lambert's and Dean's troops at their heels they made the best of their way helter skelter into Worcester.

So at last, after a hard struggle, the third part of the work had been done, the right flank of the Scots was turned and apparently Cromwell had finished his day's work. To prevent any reinforcements coming from Wales, or any escape of the Scots there, he at once ordered Major Mercer, with a troop of horse, to advance up the west bank of the river, seize Bewdley, and guard the bridge. Cromwell afterwards wrote to Parliament :—

"I believe the force that lay, through Providence, at Bewdley, were in a "condition to intercept the flying enemy."

But Cromwell's work for the day was not nearly over. It seems fairly clear he did not mean to do any more than he had done so effectually. He had only now to join his force at Henwick with that at Elbury Hill by another bridge of boats and the Scots were in a trap. He, however, was not anxious to close it; he was not to have the opportunity of doing so.

When the stress of the fight was apparent to Charles' officers at Worcester, they felt that something should be done to relieve Montgomery, and relax the pressure that was overwhelming him. The obvious course was that Leslie's horse, the whole Scotch cavalry, or some part of them, should go to his relief. They were drawn up close to the bridge at Worcester and could have advanced without difficulty, but although ordered to do so they refused to move. Why, it is difficult to say. It may have been the result of the quarrel between the Scotch Generals. It may have been that Leslie was right. When speaking of his horse he said that, " well as they look they will not fight." Whatever it was they remained stationary on Pitchcroft, and allowed Montgomery to be overwhelmed within a mile of them, without an effort to save him. Had that effort been made the result of the battle would probably have been different.

As Leslie would not move, Charles' staff considered what else could be done. They resolved, and rightly, that an attack on the Parliament centre, which Cromwell had so seriously weakened by going to Lambert's help, would prevent any more men being sent to support Cromwell, and might relax the pressure on Montgomery, while, if it succeeded, the Parliament army would be in great danger. It was resolved to make the attack.

Collecting all his available force, Charles marched out of the city, through the Sidbury Gate, up the London Road, over the new lines of the Fort Royal against the Parliament centre on Red Hill, while the Duke of Hamilton led a column of his own regiment to the left, up a lane to Perry Wood. The lane was lined with musketeers and a body of horse were in the field at the end, but Hamilton and his men rushed the lane, drove off the horse, charged home to the Parliament guns in Perry Wood and captured them. The other column attacking Red Hill was likewise successful, and drove back the Parliament troops, forcing them to retire to the top of the hill. There was now a general retreat of the Parliament line, and if the attack could have been pushed home the Parliament troops would have been routed. Once more, if instead of standing on Pitchcroft doing nothing, Leslie's horse had charged, the day was won. But there was no support, the Parliament troops, not being pressed, began to rally, and the Parliament men, finding they were in greatly superior force, stayed their retreat. A pause came over the fighting owing to the Scots not pressing home their success. Word was brought to Cromwell of what was taking place. He saw the danger and the necessity of at once averting it. Leaving Fleetwood to deal with the right wing, he ordered the brigades he had brought over the Severn at once as rapidly as possible to re-cross. Galloping back to his broken centre, he re-formed his men, ordering them to stand up to the Scots. His arrival stopped any idea of retreat, inspiring his men with confidence, so they not only withstood but also repulsed the Scots. Meanwhile Hamilton found himself in a difficulty. No reinforcements, or hope of reinforcements, appeared, his ammunition had given out, and his advance being checked his men began to retreat. The Parliament troops were re-crossing the river, so Cromwell now considered himself strong enough to assume the offensive against the wavering Scots. Every minute was improving his position. He gave the order to advance. Ashamed of having given way before the Scots, fighting in the presence and under the influence of their favourite leader, the Saints of the Lord charged furiously. Hamilton fell, mortally wounded, and his column, disheartened and dispirited, gave way. This caused a retreat of the Scots all along their line. Cromwell's opportunity had now come and he did not neglect it. Pressing on, he drove the Scots back to their entrenchments, which he at once gave the order to storm. His men responded bravely to his call, rushing in over the Scot's lines they engaged in a hand to hand conflict. The Essex Militia, in a frenzy of enthusiasm, in spite of a stubborn resistance, bore down the defenders, pushed on, and entered the Fort Royal. Sir Alexander Forbes, the commander, was struck down while rallying his men. The King's standard,

> "   .   .   .   proud Scotland's royal shield,
> "The ruddy Lion ramped in gold,"

was torn down and the blue Parliament flag hoisted on the fort. Overwhelmed by numbers, slowly and stubbornly, the Scots gave way, but while trying to hold back the swelling tide of troops they heard cries on their right flank and in their rear. Cromwell's men, from the St. John's side of the river, had recrossed the Severn, marched up past Diglis, broken into the lines between the Fort Royal and the Sidbury Gate, thus taking the Scots in flank and rear. Fearful of being cut off, with their leader disabled, with no hope of rescue, giving way before the ever-increasing mass of the Parliament troops, they rushed down the hill for the Sidbury Gate, only to increase the already hopeless confusion that there existed. Cromwell, ordering the guns of the Fort Royal to be turned on the town, advanced with his victorious host against the disordered mass of fugitives, striving and struggling to enter the Sidbury Gate, so falling an easy prey to the swords of the Saints. Here the great slaughter took place. Cromwell's troops thronged the inside of the works. The Scots could not get outside except through the pikes of the Ironsides. They could not get inside as the gate was so narrow that only a few could pass at a time. So they stood, as it were in a shambles, were cut down and died.

In spite of all, Charles declined to believe that the battle was lost. He refused to seek safety inside Worcester, desiring

to rally his men for a final charge, but that mob neither would
rally or could be rallied. It was even a more hopeless task
than that undertaken by his father at Naseby, or his great
nephew at Culloden. Riding down on the fugitives were
Cromwell's horsemen, pressing in, stern, relentless, smiting
hip and thigh, shewing no mercy to the children of Amalek.
The danger had been so great that now the chance had come
they were determined to do the Lord's work thoroughly and
to the end.

Pressing on, they nearly altered the whole course of English
history. Charles still trying, vainly trying, to rally the Scots
to induce them to show a front to the enemy, was at the
entrance to the Commandery, before the Sidbury Gate. One of
Cromwell's troopers recognised the man of Belial, rode at him,
and would have cut him down, had not William Bagnall, a Worcester citizen, so runs the legend, seized the bridle of the
leaders of a team of oxen attached to an ammunition waggon,
which had stopped there through one of the wheelers of
the team being killed, and drawing them across the road enabled Charles to slip through the narrow space between the
entrance to the Commandery, the city walls, and the team,
a space too narrow for the trooper to follow, and so to escape.
Bagnall always afterwards boasted that he had saved the King.
Possibly it was the worst thing he could have done, for if
the King had died at the Sidbury Gate, " happy in the occasion of his death," Charles II. would have been the favourite
hero of English history.

If this was not enough to satisfy Charles that all was
lost, when he got inside the gate almost the first sight
that he saw was the remains of his cavalry fleeing down
Lich Street. The Earl of Cleveland, Sir James Hamilton,
Colonel Wogan, Colonel Careless, Peter Blount, and others
had rallied these troopers in the High Street for another
charge, but were taken in the rear by Fleetwood's men,
who, having carried the bridge, poured into Worcester up
Broad Street, following up the beaten fugitives from Wick
and St. John's. To their eternal disgrace, this was done under
the eyes of Leslie's horse, whilst they refused to move, but
at length, seeing that all was lost, they wheeled about and
made off for Scotland. It was almost poetic justice that this
force, which twice on that day might have changed the
fortunes of the battle, but either from cowardice or calculation
of chances refused to fight, were never destined to see Scotland.
In one way or another they were killed or taken almost to a
man.

Charles made for his quarters in the Corn Market. As he
did so Fleetwood's troopers, coming up the Broad Street and
down Mealcheapen Street, got into the Scots' rear and so cut

off any chance of escape.   The Foregate (the north gate) had been built up, Sidbury (the south gate) was in the hands of Cromwell's troopers, the Bridge Gate (the west gate) in those of Fleetwood's, Friar's Gate (on the east) led into the lines where the victorious Parliament troops were celebrating their triumph.   The only possible exit was St. Martin's Gate. Fortunately for Charles it adjoined his quarters.   Wilmot led a horse to the back door next St. Martin's Gate;   Colonel Corbett with his troopers came into the house at the front door of Charles' quarters, and he was able, but only just able, to slip out at the back door, mount his horse, pass through St. Martin's Gate, along a lane to Barbourne Bridge, where he gained the north road at the point where it divides into the roads to Kidderminster and Droitwich.

All was now over.   The only point where there remained any resistance was the Castle Mound, near the Sidbury Gate. Here Lord Rothes, Sir William Hammond, and Colonel Drummond defended themselves against repeated attacks. This they did so long and so bravely that Cromwell offered them terms to surrender, which they accepted.

So ended the Battle of Worcester, and the third part of the task Cromwell had been set to do, although possibly not finished as he had intended it should be.   By seizing the right moment to attack the Scots' centre, he turned what promised to have been a defeat into a victory, greater than even the most sanguine could have expected.   It was more than a victory, it was an annihilation.   The Scots' army no longer existed.   Out of the 15,000 men of which on that morning it had been composed, 3000 were lying dead either at Wick or the Sidbury Gate, 10,000 were prisoners, and the remaining 2000 were scattered fugitives, helpless wanderers. As the Council of State wrote to the Militia Commissioners of the different Counties:—

"It is probable that such as can scatter homewards will endeavour to do so
"Use your best endeavours to gather them up."

The number of wounded was enormous;   of the officers nearly every one of note.   Among the officers who were prisoners were Generals Massey, Middleton, Montgomery, Piscotty, and Keith, Sir Alexander Forbes, Lords Kelly, Carnwarth, St. Clare, Grandison, the King's Secretary (Fanshaw), six colonels of horse, thirteen of foot;   nine lieut.-colonels of horse, eight of foot;   six majors of horse, thirteen of foot;   eighty-seven captains of horse, and seventy-two of foot. The others of minor rank were too numerous to mention. Among the trophies were the banner "which Scotland's Royal Scutcheon bore," the King's S.S. collar, his coach and horses, all his artillery, 158 colours, and the arms, ammunition, and stores of the army.

Glorying in their shame, to this day the City of Worcester exhibit in their Guildhall a cannon, certain head, front, and back pieces, which they say King Charles left them after the battle.

The wounded soldiers were beyond count. Possibly the number will be best appreciated from the fact that for years after the Restoration, whenever application was made by a pauper for relief to the Court of Quarter Sessions he invariably stated, almost as a common form, that he had been wounded at Worcester. If the parish registers of the County are carefully searched entries of the burial will be found of many a wounded soldier who, after the fight, had wandered there to die. One instance may be given. In 1902, at Himbleton, a skeleton was found in a very shallow grave in the churchyard, and with it a decayed leather purse full of "bawbees," a number of Scotch and a few French farthings, obviously the remains of a Scot soldier who had strayed there after Worcester and died.

The victors were merciless, and did not spare to use that sword

"that was forged at Long Marston, tempered at Naseby, welded at Drogheda, "ground at Dunbar, and was now polished at Worcester," *

Victory always brought out the worst side of the Puritan character. They did not want to be guilty of the sin of Saul in sparing the Amalakites, and they were not. The victors consisted largely of local militia men, who were full of zeal for the Lord. Three thousand militia had come from Essex and Suffolk. These were the men who when the battle hung in the balance, had, in spite of every difficulty, done the Lord's work and carried the Fort Royal. They shewed their gratitude by a free use of their swords. There were other militia regiments—Cheshire, Staffordshire, Leicestershire, Warwickshire—who had come to assist and had assisted, and who, when they thereafter boasted they had been at Worcester, were unwilling to render themselves open to the reproach that they had used the sword in vain and had been slack in the work. For some time the Scots had been held over England as a terror, which she might expect for her sin. The terror had come and should never come again. It was a duty to make Scotch invasions impossible for the future. This was considered to be true mercy, and the tender mercies of the Puritans were cruel.

There are various accounts of the battle which are of interest, given by those who either took part in it or were on the spot. First are two despatches on the part of the Parliament. The one written by Stapleton is dated September 3rd, 1651, the day of the battle. †

---

* Woodstock   † Whitelock, 482

" Sir,

" This has been a glorious day. This day twelve months was glorious at
" Dunbar. This day hath been glorious before Worcester. The word was
" then the Lord of Hosts, and so it was now, and indeed the Lord of Hosts
" was wonderfully with us. The same signal we had then as now, which was
" to have no white about us and indeed the Lord hath clothed us with white
" garments, though to the enemy they have been bloody. In the morning,
" 3rd September, Lieut.-General Fleetwood had orders to advance with his
" brigade on the other side Severn, and all things being prepared for the making
" of a bridge, and having cleared our passage with a forlorn we laid a bridge
" over Severn and another over Teme. Our foot disputed the hedges with
" much courage and resolution. The fight began on the other side Severn,
" and our foot from this side began it, they clearing the way for the rest to
" come over after them. The right wing of Lieut.-General Fleetwood's force
" came over the,bridge of Teme, while the left wing disputed the bridge at
" Powick, which dispute lasted a long time and was very hot. But the Lord
" gave our men to gain ground of the enemy till we had beaten them out of
" the ground. While this was doing the enemy rallying made a very bold
" sally out on this side of the town, and came with great bodies of horse and
" foot. Supposing most of our army had been drawn out on the other side
" they gave our men a very hot salute and put them to a little retreat and
" disorder. But in a short while the Lord gave us victory on this side also,
" our foot did very noble and gallant service, and they disputed with them,
" not only the hedges but followed them boldly to the very mouth of the
" cannon, which was planted on the mountain works. At length we gained
" their works and planted their guns against them in the town, and we hear
" that some of our horse and foot are in the north and east end of the town.
" The night came on so fast that we could not pursue further. Most of the
" horse escaped, but my Lord General despatched Major-General Harrison's
" Brigade after them. We cannot yet give an account who are taken or slain,
" but we conceive the number of the slain far exceeds the number of the
" prisoners, but I guess the number of the killed and taken to be about 8 or
" 10,000. To-morrow we shall be able to give you fuller relation. Our
" Quartermaster-General and Captain Jones is slain, and Mr. Howard,
" captain of the Life Guard, is wounded, and Major-General Lambert's horse
" was shot under him.

                                        " Yours to serve you,
        " September 3rd, 1651.   " Robert Stapleton."

The other despatch is Cromwell's. He sent a short letter to
the Speaker, directly after the battle, announcing his victory,
which was received in London on September 5th, but the day
after the fight he sent the following detailed account :—

" I am not yet able to give you an exact account of the great things the
" Lord hath done for this Commonwealth and for His people, and yet I am
" unwilling to be silent, but according to my duty shall represent it to you as
" it comes to hand. This battle was fought with various success for some
" hours, but still hopeful on your part, and in the end became an absolute
" victory, and so full an one as proved a total defeat and ruin of the enemies'
" army and possession of the town, our men entering at the enemies' heels and
" fighting with them in the streets with very great courage, took all their
" baggage and artillery. What the slain are I can give you no account,
" because we have not taken an exact view, but they are very many, and
" must needs be so, because the dispute was long and very near at hand, and
" often at push of pike, and from one defence to another. There are about 6
" or 7000 prisoners taken here, and many officers and noblemen of quality,
" Duke Hamilton, the Earl of Rothes, and divers other noblemen ; I hear the
" Earl of Lauderdale, many officers of great quality, and some that will be fit
" subjects of your justice. We have sent very considerable parties after the

" flying enemy. I hear they have taken considerable number of prisoners,
" and are very close in the pursuit. Indeed, I hear the country riseth upon
" them everywhere, and I believe the forces that lay, through Providence, at
" Bewdley, and in Shropshire and Staffordshire, and those with Colonel
" Lillburn, were in a condition, as if this had been foreseen, to intercept what
" should return.

" A more particular account than this will be prepared for you as we are
" able. I heard they had not many more than 1000 horse in their body that
" fled, and I believe we have near 4000 forces following and interposing
" between them and home. Their army was about 16000 strong, and fought
" ours on Worcester side of Severn almost with their whole, whilst we had en-
" gaged half our army on the other side but with parties of theirs. Indeed, it
" was a stiff business, yet I do not think we have lost 200 men. Your new-
" raised forces did perform singular good service, for which they deserve a
" very high estimation and acknowledgment, as also for their willingness
" thereunto. For as much as the same has added so much to the reputation
" of your affairs, they are all despatched home again, which I hope will be
" much to the ease and satisfaction of the Country, which is a great fruit of the
" successes. The dimensions of this mercy are above my thoughts; it is, for
" ought I know, a crowning mercy. Surely, if it be not, such a one we shall
" have if this provoke those that are concerned in it to thankfulness, and the
" Parliament to do the will of Him who hath done His will for it and for the
" nation, and whose good pleasure is to establish the nation and the change of
" the Government by making the people so willing to the defence thereof, and
" so signally to bless the endeavours of your servants in this late great work.
" I am bold humbly to beg that all thoughts may tend to the promoting of
" His honour, Who hath wrought so great salvation, and that the fatness of
" these continued mercies may not occasion pride and wantonness as formerly
" the like hath done to a chosen people ; but that the fear of the Lord, even
" for His mercies, may keep an authority and a people so prospered and
" blessed, and witnessed to, humble and faithful, that justice and righteous-
" ness, mercy and truth, may flow from you as a thankful return to our
" glorious God. This shall be the prayer of

                                    " Sir,
              " Your most humble and obedient servant,
" Worcester, September 4th, 1651.   O. Cromwell."*

On the receipt of this despatch the Parliament ordered a
thanksgiving day, and that the letter of the General should be
read by the ministers in the churches. A proclamation was
issued for apprehending the King, and a reward of £1000
promised to anyone that did it.† Charles is described as

" A tall man, about two yards high, his hair a deep brown, near to black, and
" has been cut off since the destruction of his army at Worcester, so that it is
" not very long."

Nicholas Lechmere, in his diary, says:

" It has pleased God to give a total overthrow to this Scottish army. The
" battle began on the west of the city in those very fields where my brother-in-
" law, Colonel Sandys, in 1642, fought with Prince Rupert and received
" wounds whereof he died, but was ended and was sharpest on the east side.
" The morning the battle was fought the General made a bridge over the
" river of Severn, a little above Teme's mouth, whereby he passed over his
" army from side to side as he saw occasion. The battle began about one of
" the clock and lasted till night. I was present at it in pursuit of the victory.
" The city of Worcester was taken by storm and all the wealth in it became
" booty to the soldiers."

---

* Whitelock, 483.   † Whitelock, 484.

The Council of State sent out the following official account to the Militia Commissioners of the different Counties:

" It has pleased God to give us a great victory against the Scotch army at " Worcester yesterday. The fight was on both sides of the town. It began " about 2 p.m. and continued until they could see no longer to prosecute it. " The slain are estimated at 4000, but there are not 100 of ours. The enemy " were wholly routed on both sides of the town, and some of their horse are ' fled which our horse are pursuing, Their great fort is taken, such as are " left of them are yet in the town, into a part of which some of our force " entered yesterday night. It is probable that such as can scatter homewards " will endeavour to do so. Use your best endeavours to gather them up."

Another account gives a picture of Worcester after the battle, it is dated 6th September.

" Things at Worcester are in great confusion. Lords, knights, and gentle- " men were there plucked out of holes by the soldiers. The common " prisoners they were driving into the Cathedral, and what with the dead " bodies of the men and dead horses of the enemy filling the streets there was " such nastiness that a man could hardly abide in the town. Yet the Lord " General had his head-quarters in Worcester, the walls whereof he hath " ordered to be pulled down to the ground, and the dykes filled up."

With regard to this last item the Council of State ordered, on September 13th, that Major Salway should

" Report to the House the Council's opinion that orders should be forthwith " given for the speedy taking down the walls of Worcester and the demolition " of the great fort there."

On September 16th the Council of State wrote to the Lord Chief Baron Wylde:

"We see by yours the great diligence of yourselves and the rest of the " Militia Commissioners in that County and the state of affairs there, and " that you are about demolishing the walls of Worcester and the rest of the " works there, which we desire may be speedily and effectually done, and laid " so flat that they may not be in a position to be again made defensible. We " doubt not that the country will be willing to come to the work and that " you and the rest of the Commissioners will speedily and effectually finish it."

No time was lost. On the 25th September the Council of State wrote to the Lord Chief Baron and the other Militia Commissioners thanking them

" For the care they had taken in the affairs of the County, and particularly " for demolishing the walls of Worcester. Proceed," it adds, " in effectually " completing this."

The thoroughness of the victory embarrassed the Parliament. The number of prisoners was so large they did not know what to do with them. Orders had been given directly after the battle for the Middlesex troops to be placed

" On the roads about London to apprehend such of the enemy who had been " routed and scattered at Worcester, and who might endeavour to enter " London."

The first difficulty was where to put the prisoners. Those in Worcester were temporarily put in the Cathedral, but this was obviously only a makeshift. Orders were issued within a few days of the battle to bring some of them up to London. Colonel

Berkstead, who was commanding in London, was ordered on September 9th

"to view the artillery ground in Tothill Fields and see what part of the "prisoners of Worcester might be kept there, and what charge would be "necessary for fitting it."

The Council of State wrote to the Commander-in-chief of the convoy bringing up prisoners from Worcester desiring him to correspond with Colonel Berkstead with a view to the orderly bringing of the prisoners to London.

But on the way up the guard escorting the prisoners was "very slender," by reason thereof many had escaped, particularly Anthony Jackson, who proclaimed Charles Stuart King of England. He was, however, afterwards arrested again. There seems to be some doubt if he was the real man who did this, as the Militia Committee for Hereford wrote to the Council of State saying they had secured the man who had proclaimed the King. The Council replied:

"We understand by yours that amongst the prisoners taken in your County "since the defeat at Worcester you have secured one who proclaimed Charles "Stuart King of England, concerning whom you desire our direction. The "matter should be thus examined, and if you find he did it, otherwise than "through fear or by constraint, he is to be proceeded against according to "law."

As soon as the prisoners were got rid of the town was disinfected. The City records have this entry:—

"Paid for pitch and rosen to perfume the hall after the Scots."

From some of the prisoners bonds and engagements were taken, others were detained locally and tried locally by military courts. The Mayor of Worcester (Lysons) and the Sheriff (Bridges) were, it was said, fit to be made an example of justice, and Cromwell was directed to issue commissions to some officers at Warwick or Coventry for their trial. However, subsequent orders directed that General Massey, the Mayor and Sheriff of Worcester, and other prisoners then in Warwick Castle, should be conveyed by Major Knight's troop to London, which was done.

The general's letter concerning such of the County, as well of the quality as of the meaner sort, who, having been engaged in the former war, did now appear in arms against Parliament was ordered to be referred to the Council of State. A Committee was appointed

"to consider how the English prisoners, then at 'Gower House,' taken at the "late engagement at Worcester, might be disposed of, as there was no con- "venience for keeping them there."

The Committee was also instructed to dispose of the prisoners who were captains or under:

"At Chester, Shrewsbury, Stafford, Ludlow, Worcester, or in any Counties "near the Severn, upon the proposition made to send 1000 to Bristol, in order "to sending them to New England."

The Council of State then ordered the Governor of Bristol:

" That the prisoners from Worcester and other towns were to be taken to
" Bristol in order to their transportation as opportunity should present, and
" upon their arrival at Bristol provision should be made for them at the rate
" of 2½d. a day per man."

Sir Henry Vane, Mr. Salway, and others were authorised

" to dispose to plantations all the prisoners under the degree of a field officer
" taken at Worcester, and report to the Council of State how they were dis-
" posed of."

What number were actually transported it is impossible to
say, but probably it was considerable. The price of men to
export to the plantations fell after the battle. It is stated, as a
grievance, that after the battle at Worcester a prisoner for ex-
portation could be bought as cheap as £1. At Bristol,
however, he would fetch £5, but the number of men to be
exported was so considerable that prices fell so low for slaves—
or rather, exiles—that there was no profit on the transaction.

One of those who were sent, one of the Lancashire recruits,
survived to return to England after 14 years in Barbadoes.
When, in 1665, Thomas Jackson, of Bury, Lancashire, was
travelling from Whitehaven homewards he was arrested, and
gave an account of himself. He was taken prisoner at
Worcester, and from there sent to Barbadoes, where he stayed
near 14 years, from whence he came into Ireland, and from
there unto Whitehaven, and so hither (Rydal).*

Whatever may have been the other virtues of Cromwell's
soldiers, they did not hesitate to utilise their opportunities.
According to the ideas of those days, as the city had been
taken by storm, the booty belonged to the soldiers, who proceeded to gather in their property. It is stated, possibly it is
an exaggeration, that every house in Worcester, whether
belonging to friend or foe, was plundered. It is certain there
was something like a general " loot," and no doubt mistakes
and " regrettable incidents " occurred.

There was also some difficulty in dealing with the dead.
A letter from Worcester, written on September 6th—three
days after the battle—says that from the dead bodies of the
men and horses, filling the streets, there was such nastiness a
man could hardly abide in the town. How the dead were all got
rid of is not clear; some were buried in the Cathedral churchyard, which was then in St. Michael's parish, for it appears
that a sum of £2 9s. 4d. was paid to St. Michael's in Bedwardine, in which the Cathedral is situated, by the County, it
being then a County parish,

" for burial of the Scots that were slain and died in our Parish, the Palace,
" the College, College Green, Castle Hill, and the precincts of the said
" several places, and of divers others that were brought out of the City of
" Worcester and laid in the churchyard."

* Hist. MSS. Com., XII. Rep., App. 7, p. 35.

It is not clear where the others who fell were buried. On the Ham, at Powick, are two hollows in the ground, which, tradition says, are two pits into which the dead who fell at the battle were placed.

One burial is recorded, that of the Duke of Hamilton. He fell wounded, shot in the leg, near Perry Wood, while trying to rally his men when the Parliament troops began to press them back. After the battle he was carried down to the Commandery. His blood was until recent years shewn on a board in a room on the ground floor. The King's surgeon, who attended him, said the leg must be amputated. Cromwell sent his own surgeon, who said amputation was not necessary. Another Royalist doctor said it was. While they differed as to the method of treatment to be followed the Duke died. His servant applied to the Council of State for leave to take the body to Hamilton Palace, and place it there with those of the other dukes, but the Council ordered the corpse should be buried at Worcester, and nowhere else; so it was buried in the Cathedral, within the altar rails on the north side. During the restoration in 1862, when so much was altered and not replaced, the altar pavement was taken up and the Duke's body, wrapt in lead, was found. Even in death he was not to rest, for a workman's pick-axe struck through the lead.*

Parliament were elated, rightly elated, at their victory. The servant of the Lord Chief Baron Wylde is said to have brought the first news of the victory. For this he received £30. Constantine Heath, a messenger, conditionally received £30, and Lieutenant Audley £10 for bringing the good news of the taking of the town of Worcester, "in case it be confirmed tomorrow." A bonfire was ordered to be made at Whitehall Gate for the good news of the routing of the enemy near Worcester. Colonel Berkstead was ordered to take charge of the bonfire, and to shoot off the guns of his regiment.

Orders were made by Parliament:

"That £100 be given to Captain Edward Orpin, as a gratuity from Parlia-" ment, for taking at the fight at Worcester the colours which he brought with " him to the bar."

"That the Council of State give reasonable gratuities to such persons as " gave intelligence to our forces of the transactions in Worcester, especially to " the little maid mentioned by Major Salway in his narrative to the House."

There does not appear to be any record of what it precisely was this little maid did, but it must have been something of considerable importance, as the Council of State ordered:

"That £140 be paid to such persons as gave intelligence at Worcester, " whereof £100 to the little maid, and the other £40 to such persons as Mr. " Salway and Mr. Scott appoint."

---

* I saw the body, and have a piece of the lead.

The rejoicings were not confined to London. They seem to have been very wide-spread.

At Bewdley the Mayor gave

" to the ringers at the 3 churches at the news of the good success at Worcester
" £1 10 0."

At Beverley the churchwardens of St. Mary's

" Pd. the ringers on the day of thanksgiving for the great victory over the
" Scots at Worcester, 20s."

At Leicester they went further than bell-ringing:

" Paid William Newton for 14 gentlemen's dinners, and for wine, strong beer,
" and tobacco at a dinner there. upon the day of thanksgiving for the great
" victory at Worcester, £4 14 4."

They also paid for a quart of sack to drink with Colonel Haskew when he came from Worcester fight.

There are similar entries at Reading and other places, which make it clear that there was general rejoicing, not at the defeat of the Royalists, but at the defeat of the Scots.

One reward given by the Parliament must have greatly exasperated the Royalists. It will be remembered that the Scots' sortie failed from the treachery of Guise, a tailor, who informed the Parliament troops of the intention to make the sortie. The next morning Guise was hanged. After the battle it was thought right to make some provision for Mrs. Guise, so on Thursday, September 9th, it was ordered that

" Mrs. Guise, whose husband was executed by the King of Scots at Worcester
" for giving our forces intelligence of the enemies' signal, should have £200
" in money and £200 a year. The £200 a year payable out of the estate
" of Thomas Hornihold, a delinquent."

Unfortunately for Mrs. Guise, Hornihold had only a life estate in the property, so she was in danger of losing her annuity. She therefore, in 1654, petitioned Cromwell to be allowed a sum out of the sale of Hornihold's woods in Hanley and Great Malvern. On this petition an order was made allowing Mrs. Guise £500 a year from money arising from the sale of land to be discovered by Captain N. Happerley, after his quota was paid, to be paid in lieu of a grant made to her in September, 1651, of £100 a year, on lands in Ireland, to her and her children, for her husband's faithfulness to the State, and in lieu of a grant by Parliament of £100 a year from the estates of persons who had adhered to the enemy in the business at Worcester.

Mrs. Guise seems to have had further security. Sir John Pakington, a delinquent, was fined. After a time the sum of £1000 was accepted as a full discharge for his fine. Mrs. Guise was successful in getting an order that the £1000 paid by Sir John Pakington should be applied to satisfy her demands.

At Barbourne bridge Charles had to decide what he would

do.   He says he was anxious to go to London, but he was
dissuaded by his friends from doing this   There were a large
number of fugitives, including most of the Scotch horse, who
had refused to fight when wanted, and when not wanted would
not leave the King.   Charles had a difficulty in shaking them
off.   They all went on together through Ombersley to Hartlebury.   There, where the Stourbridge road turns off to the
right from the Kidderminster road, Charles, with Wilmot, the
Duke of Buckingham, and a few others, left the mass of
fugitives to go on to Kidderminster, and turned down through
Chaddesley Corbett parish, past Hagley and Pedmore, to
Stourbridge, or as Charles says himself :

"We slipt away out of the high road that goes to Lancashire, and kept on
"the right hand, letting all the beaten men go along the front road . . .
"So we rode through a town short of Wolverhampton, betwixt that and
"Worcester."

At Stourbridge there was a troop of Parliament horse, but
they were not keeping any look out and Charles was able to
get by without causing an alarm.   From Stourbridge he went
on to Kinver and there got into Staffordshire.

It was fortunate that he changed his route from the main road
to the right.   Those who went on to Kidderminster were not
so lucky.   Riding at a rapid rate they woke up the townsmen
as they passed through.   According to Baxter's account :

"Kidderminster being but 11 miles from Worcester the flying army passed,
"some of them through the town and some by it.   I was newly gone to bed
"when the noise of the flying horse acquainted me with the overthrow, and a
"few of one of Cromwell's troops that guarded Bewdley Bridge, having
"tidings of it, came into our street and stood in the open market place, before
"my door, to susprise them that passed by.   And so when many hundreds of
"the flying army came together, when the 30 troopers cried 'stand' and fired
"at them, they either hasted away or cried quarter, not knowing in the dark
"the number it was that charged.   And so as many were taken there as so
"few men could lay hold on, and till midnight the bullets flying towards my
"door and windows, and the sorrowful fugitives hastening by for their lives,
"did tell me of the calamitousness of war."

The usually accepted version, which agrees with Charles'
own account, is that he passed through Stourbridge, but a place
is shown at Wolverley, in the dell below the bank on which
Lea Castle stands, as the precise spot over which Charles
crossed on his way to Kinver and Boscobel.*

Wherever the spot was where Charles left the County it is
doubtful if he ever returned to it.   But Mr. Fea says,† or
rather conjectures, that an incident on the journey with Jane
Lane from Bentley to Bristol, recorded in Charles' narrative of
his escape, took place at Bromsgrove.   Charles says :—‡ From
Bentley

"we took our journey towards Bristol, resolving to lie at a place called Long

---

* Noake, Notes and Queries for Worcestershire, 325.
† The Flight of the King.   ‡ Boscobel Tracts, 145.

" Marson, in the Vale of Evesham.   We had not gone two hours on our way
" before the mare I rode cast a shoe, so we were forced to ride to get another shoe
" at a scattering village, whose name began with something like ' Long——,'
" and as I was holding my horse's foot I asked the smith the news.   He told
" there was no news that he knew of, since the good news of the beating of the
" rogues, the Scots.   I asked him whether there were none of the English
" taken that joined with the Scots.   He answered that he did not hear that
" rogue, Charles Stuart, was taken, but some of the others, he said, were
" taken, but not Charles Stuart.   I told him if that rogue were taken he
" deserved to be hanged more than all the rest for bringing in the Scots, upon
" which he said I spoke like an honest man, and so we parted."

Mr. Fea suggests that this incident occurred at Bromsgrove, which is a long, straggling village, not far out of the line between Bentley and Stratford-on-Avon   All that can be said is that it is possible it may be so.   If it did it brings the romantic story of Charles' escape into Worcestershire history.

In concluding the story of the Battle of Worcester there are two remarks that should be made.   The first is that the idea of so-called loyalty, which after the Restoration made everyone in Worcestershire so loyal, has worked great injustice on the men who, in the days of trial, fought for what they believed were the liberties of England.   No one can read the claims that were put forward for rewards for services to Charles after the Battle of Worcester without something approaching disgust.   Take, for instance, the claims of Captain George Lascelles :

" After Worcester his near relative, Henry Lascelles, was instrumental in
" saving the King from violence."*

Or the case of Elizabeth Smith, who,

" when your Majesty lay at Moseley, in your happy escape from Worcester,
" made your Majesty's fire and bed, and who, when your Majesty was asleep
" and Cromwell's soldiers were about, rubbed softly your Majesty upon the
" feet and legs to wake your Majesty and warn you thereof."

Then loyalty paid, so everyone was loyal, and everyone was connected with the Battle of Worcester.   But it is hardly fair on the Worcestershire gentry to make out, as is usually done, that they were supporters of Charles II. when he came to Worcester with the Scots.   The Worcestershire gentry fought and bled for Charles I.   Some of the present Worcestershire families, like the Lytteltons, can rightly boast of what they did, of what they suffered, and of what they endured for that King.   The Worcestershire gentry hated the Solemn League and Covenant, and next to it they hated its supporters, the men

"   .   .   .   who sold
" Their King for gold,
" As Judas sold his God."

For them they could not fight; by their side they would not fight.   A covenanted King was to them a contradiction

---

* Hist. MSS., XI. Rep., App. 7, p. 92.

in terms. The Royal Martyr had died for the Church of England and Divine right. They would not forfeit their honour or break their parole for a cause he had refused to accept in his direst need. Yet this is what their descendants at the present day are only too proud to say their alleged ancestors did.

One instance will suffice to show how family legends of this kind have grown up. Sir Rowland Berkeley, of Cotheridge, was a strong Cavalier, who certainly helped to hold Worcester for Charles I., and is *said* to have attended the muster on Pitchcroft on August 26th, and have fought hard on the 3rd September for Charles II. No account of the battle is ever considered complete that does not relate the story of his two piebald horses and the trick he is alleged to have played on Cromwell's soldiers.

The story was started, possibly invented, by Nash,* and, as told by him, is as follows :—

"I shall mention a trifling anecdote of the escape of my grandmother's "father, who, after the battle was lost, met the King and a council of some of "the leaders, held on Barbourne bridge, when they agreed every one should "shift for himself. Sir Rowland Berkeley with speed galloped home to "Cotteridge, but, thinking he should be marked by the peculiarity of a pied "horse, he immediately sent the horse he rode in battle to a farm he had "at some distance, and put another horse of the same colour, fresh, and "in body clothes, pretending himself to be very ill and unable to go abroad. "It was not long before a detachment came to seize him. On his pleading "his infirmity, and that it was impossible for him to be at Worcester, they "replied he was particularly marked by a piebald horse he rode. Sir Rowland "said he had indeed such a horse, but if they would go into his stable and "examine the horse they would be convinced that the horse had not been out "that day, which they did and, being satisfied, went back to Worcester with- "out their prey, leaving Sir Rowland in his night-cap and slippers, though he "was afterwards forced to compound for his estate, paying £2030."

The story is a pretty one, but, unfortunately for its credit, the Historical Manuscripts Commissioners have published two letters of Sir Rowland Berkeley's which shew how it arose, and how utterly false it is.† The letters are as follows :—

"8th September, 1651.—Sir Rowland Berkeley to his father-in-law, Sir "Thomas Cave.

"I thank you for sending to inquire as to our condition at this place, which "has been of late very troublesome and hazardous. The storm has fallen "very heavily on the town of Worcester and 4 or 5 miles around, to the ruin of "very many families. You cannot hear too bad an account of the inhabitants "of Worcester, all houses being ransacked from top to bottom, the very "persons of men and women not excepted. That the business succeeded so "ill on the King of Scots' side is much attributed to the cowardice of the "Scottish horse, who hardly stood one charge, and to the unreadiness of their "army in general. The officers, not attending their duty, could not be found "to bring up their men and to send relief where it was necessary. The Par- "liamentary army plied their business with reserve upon reserve until they "had routed all the Scottish forces on both sides of the river and driven them "into the town, and then fell to storming without any reserve. The fight "began at Powick Bridge and in Weike [Wick] fields, the main of it between

* II. Sup., p. 89.   † Hist. MSS. Com., X. Rep., App. 6.

" Perry Wood and the town, and all those grounds between that and the
" Diglesses [Diglis]. We hear that the Duke of Hamilton is taken, being
" wounded in the body with a bullet, and also Sir James Hamilton, who lies
" wounded at the Crown. Your kinsman, Lord Grandison, is a prisoner.
" Being in great want he sent to my wife to inform her of his condition, and
" she supplied him with £5 and some provisions, the town then yielding none.
" The number of the slain is certainly great. On Thursday morning the dead
" bodies lay in the way from Powick bridge to the town, and on the ground
" on either side of it, and in almost every street of the town. Many lie killed
" in the houses, in the College and Church, on the Green, and in the cloisters,
" and quite through Sidbury and about a mile that way. When the King
" charged in person the slaughter was very great, and the Parliamentary force
" gave back, but fresh reserves coming in did the work. The King of Scots
" fled northward with about 4000 horse and Highlanders with him. The Par-
" liament followed him with a greater number, and were about three hours
" behind him. I shall for the present forbear to trouble you with the relation
" of the chances which have befallen me in this hurly-burly. As a man
" that cavilled not on either side, I have had very great deliverances, in my
" person especially. I have given the bearer 2s."

The second letter is :—

" 12th September, 1651.—Cotheridge. Same to same.
" I hope that you have, before this, received a letter from my wife, and
" another from me, by one College, who promised to be with you at Stamford
" by 10 o'clock yesterday. In those letters you were informed of our late
" trouble and present quiet. I now thank you for your kind writing by Major
" Smith's servant, and for your fatherly affection. Your invitation to myself,
" my wife, and my children to come over to you is most comfortable, but I
" cannot be away from home, as you will perceive anon. In my last I only
" intimated to you some difficulties I passed through in the late bustle; I will
" now acquaint you more fully of them. On the 3rd of the month, the very
" day and time of the fight, I was taken from hence by a major with a party of
" horse, who had orders to bring me to the King. I had received several
" private messages from Worcester, while the King was there, urging me to
" come to him, but resolving not to meddle I had remained at home. Before
" I came to the town the fight was begun at Powick, and I, being dismissed
" from the major and his party to await the King's leisure, enquired the
" occasion of my being sent for. I was told that Major-General Massey was
" made Governor of Worcester, and that there was a commission to certain
" gentlemen of the County, whereof I was one, for the aiding and assisting of
" him; which employment I not liking, went presently to my horse, intending
" to get home again with what speed I could, the battle being this time hot
" on both sides of the town. By the time I came to the bridge the King's
" forces were retreating from Wicke [Wick], and the Parliament pursuing, and
" no man was suffered to pass I presently made to the Foregate, where I
" was likewise stopped, and thence to St. Martin's Gate, and getting out there
" endeavoured in vain to go into the Wich [Droitwich] road. I then took the
" footpath that goes to Perry Wood, and made up towards the battle, where
" there was hot service, and, being within musket shot, turned over hedge and
" ditch on the left hand and got into Wich [Droitwich] way at Barbourne Bridge,
" not meeting a man to trouble me, and thence to Ombersley and so to Holt
" Fleet as fast as I could. Having well passed through the army, I rode through
" fields and closes for about a mile, and then, being to cross Worcester Road,
" I was taken by a party of Scots, I having neither sword nor pistol. They would
" not let me pass, and at last began to quarrel as to whose prisoner I should
" be. At last they told me they would carry me to their party of about 120
" horse that were before. When we came to the party they brought the news
" of the forces at Wick, and finding them in disorder with it I lagged by
" degrees until I was in the rear, and taking the opportunity of a blind lane
" clapped spur over hedge and ditch and was presently out of sight. About

"9 at night 1 came home, having been five hours about it. The next morn-
"ing, by sunrise, came a party of the Parliament horse and took me from
"hence, telling me I must go to the general, and took my dun colt with them,
"but by the time I came to St. John's I found that they had no orders for
"what they did. At last they were all gone excepting him that had the colt,
"and for about half-an-hour we rode about the fields among the dead bodies,
"and I persuaded him to deliver the colt to my man again, and gave him all
"the silver I had in my pocket, about 15s. or 16s. Since then I have been
"informed that my name has been given in, amongst many others, for coming
"with the King of Scots, and that there are orders issued for inventorying the
"goods and stopping the rents of all named in the list. If there be any
"justice left upon earth, I hope they cannot touch me."

In the face of these two letters—most interesting letters—it
is somewhat bold to assert that Sir Rowland Berkeley was at
the Pitchcroft meeting, or did much fighting for Charles II. at
Worcester, or to believe the legend about the horse.

The other observation is that although Worcestershire took
so large a part in the Civil War her present attitude rather
tends to shew that she now not only takes no pride in the
"deeds that her children have done," but that, in fact, is
rather ashamed of them than otherwise. Not only has she no
monument to record her part in the Civil War, but the
relics of that war which remain to her are treated as if they
were of no account. The house in the Corn Market at Worcester, where Charles lodged during his stay at the time of the
battle, is not kept in such a condition as befits an historic
monument. Modern hands have practically effaced the Fort
Royal. The bullet marks on the church at Powick are over-
grown with creepers. The remains of Cromwell's bridge over
the Teme were, within recent years, pulled up and sold for
firewood. The pits on Powick Ham, where the slain are
buried, remain "unmarked and unholy." Other Counties act
otherwise. In Warwickshire, Edgehill has its monument.
In Berkshire, Newbury has its battle-fields marked by plantations of trees to shew the positions of the belligerents. In
Northamptonshire, Naseby has its obelisk. But the site of
the last, the greatest, the fiercest fight of all is unmarked,
unhonoured, and unknown. This the story of the English
lady historian (Miss Agnes Strickland), who, having read
up the Battle of Worcester, came to study the details of
the fight on the spot, amply proves. She came to Worcester,
went to an hotel, and asked for a guide to conduct her over
the battle-field. There was some difficulty in finding a
qualified person. At last a loafer in the stable yard of the
hotel offered his services. A cab was called, the guide
directed the driver to go to Pitchcroft. He conducted
Miss Strickland to a spot in front of the Grand Stand,
and told her "this was the place." The lady, consulting her
notes, could not make the spot agree with what she had read
and learnt as to the battle, and expressed her doubts as to its

identity. Where was the Fort Royal, the guns in Perry Wood, the bridge of boats, and the other details of which she had read ? The guide did not know, but stuck to it that the spot was the precise one. On her still doubting his statement, he told her that there was no room for doubt; he was confident he was right, and, on being asked why, astonished the lady by saying: " I was present and saw it myself." Her amazement increased, but the guide, to prove the accuracy of the statement, added, alluding to a celebrated prize fight that took place on Pitchcroft the first half of the nineteenth century, and which was the only battle of Worcester he had ever heard of, " It was here that Spring hit Langham the blow that finished him; " proving the truth of the remark of a modern historian: " The grass soon grows over the graves of those who die in battle." But is it not our duty to see that those who lie in those graves are not forgotten ? It may be said that the best monument of Worcester is Canova's cenotaph in St. Peter's, at Rome, to James III., Charles III., and Henry IX., " Kings of England," as but for Worcester, such a monument in such a place would have been impossible. This may be so; but, still, in these days of local commemorations is it not practicable for us to have " some frail memorial still erected nigh," even if it is " with uncouth rhymes and shapeless sculpture decked," to mark the spot where England's " sorrows began and where they were happily ended " (?).

INDEX.